IDA
TARBELL

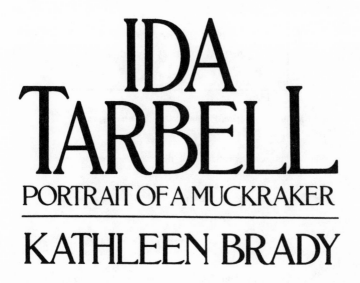

IDA TARBELL

PORTRAIT OF A MUCKRAKER

KATHLEEN BRADY

UNIVERSITY OF PITTSBURGH PRESS

For my mother,
Frances Sellmeyer Brady

Published 1989 by the University of Pittsburgh Press, Pittsburgh, Pa. 15260
Originally published 1984 by Seaview/Putnam
Copyright © 1984, 1989 by Kathleen Brady
Baker & Taylor International, London
Manufactured in the United States of America

The author gratefully acknowledges permission from the following sources to reprint excerpts in this book:

Charles Cather for material from *Uncle Valentine and Other Stories* by Willa Cather, copyright © 1973 by Charles Cather.

Charles Scribner's Sons for material from *Success Story: The Life and Times of S. S. McClure* by Peter Lyon, copyright © 1963 by Peter Lyon; and for material from *Madame Roland* by Ida M. Tarbell, copyright © 1895 by Charles Scribner's Sons.

All photographs in the text courtesy of the Ida M. Tarbell Collection, Pelletier Library, Allegheny College

Designed by Dorothy Wachtenheim

Library of Congress Cataloging-in-Publication Data

Brady, Kathleen.
   Ida Tarbell: portrait of a muckraker / Kathleen Brady.
      p.   cm.
   Reprint. Originally published: New York: Seaview/Putnam. c1984.
   Bibliography: p.
   Includes index.
   ISBN 0-8229-5807-4.
   1. Tarbell, Ida M. (Ida Minerva), 1857-1944. 2. Journalists—United States—Biography.
I. Title.
PN4874.T23B7   1989
070'.92—dc20
[B]   89-40207
                                                                      CIP

CONTENTS

Foreword

Ida Tarbell is the first woman I ever encountered in my history books. I was nine years old and my female consciousness embryonic indeed, but the discovery of a woman in the masculine preserve of American greatness captivated and encouraged me. I had just discovered the delights of writing and of being published in our own mimeographed school newspaper and when I saw her listed as a crusader and reformer, I understood for the first time that words had the power not only to capture life, but to change it.

When I decided to write this book, in 1979, women of achievement were no longer rare, and it was poignant to recall that she had been my only touchstone. Ida Tarbell now interested me more as an investigative journalist than as a woman, yet as I worked I found that Tarbell's femininity was a crucially important aspect of her, albeit one she tried to deny. It was like a strange piece of a jigsaw puzzle, which she could neither fit into the rest of her nor totally ignore.

In her youth she had often wondered what it meant to be a woman and how a woman could create a fruitful life for herself. She looked in history books, statistical records, and among inventors listed in the U.S. Patent Office, but she never dared look within herself.

Instead, she focused on the world outside her, taking on such formidable subjects as the Standard Oil Company, the injustices of the tariff system, and the sufferings of the factory worker. Her political ideals were progressive, but her ideas on women were hackneyed. In terms of woman's advancement, she was a weather vane, not an engine of change.

She seemed to satisfy no one, least of all herself, but satisfaction was not what she asked of life. What she sought was accomplishment. Hers is the story of how one person handled the human dilemma of daring great things, despite galling limitations, and succeeded admirably.

PART I

BEGINNINGS

One

An Unaccommodating Child

In May 1873, a tall, silk-hatted businessman walked through the streets of Titusville, Pennsylvania, extending to a distrustful local populace the olive branch of a fresh deal. Thwarted the year before in his attempt to take over the entire oil business, John D. Rockefeller, onetime purveyor of groceries, was trying again. In his early middle age, a Clevelander dissatisfied with control of only one-third of the market, he took the precaution of visiting the oil region in a party of colleagues. Through his associates, he asked independent petroleum producers to join with him in limiting output and maintaining price. Most declined, spurning him and his Standard Oil Company. *"Sic semper tyrannis,"* gloated a feisty newspaper editor when Rockefeller decamped. Rockefeller himself felt not defeated, merely set back.

On Titusville's Main Street, in a tower room reached by a steep stair, Ida Tarbell squinted into her microscope. Upset to have been deceived by the matter of the Six Days of Creation, fretful over where she fit in a chaotic cosmic scheme, the girl had decided to trust only what she could discover for herself.

With her savings, Ida had purchased a microscope and submitted to its powers such diverse objects as rock salt and hangnails, fly wings and petals; if the minister could not tell her what created the buttercup, she would ask the buttercup itself. At fifteen, she was tall for her age—nearly six feet—and possessed of one other striking feature—a widow's peak from which flowed her long dark hair. God, Nature, or some Darwinian process had also granted her ambition—a trait she hardly recognized or admitted to.

If the young girl and the astute entrepreneur seemed unrelated—if Rockefeller's sway over oil and wealth seemed to have little to do with the plain girl's diligent investigations in the tower room—they would have everything to do with the woman young Ida Tarbell would become.

Fate, in the peregrinations of her ancestors, had given her life in a most unpromising spot. Northwestern Pennsylvania is a place of bitter winters, muddy springs, and scraggy acreage. Pioneers flowed around it in waves seeking more prosperous pastures, and Ida's own father was inclined to follow them. When she was born on November 5, 1857, in a Hatch Hollow log cabin, he was working land in Iowa, where he planned to bring his wife and baby.

Franklin Sumner Tarbell's family had cleared America's land and fought its wars. The earliest Tarbell recorded in America was Thomas, who in 1632 purchased land in Watertown, Massachusetts, near Boston. The Tarbells pushed up to Salem where John, who fought the Indians in King Philip's War, married Mary, whose mother Rebecca Nurse had been hanged for witchcraft in 1692. The family lived in New Hampshire and Massachusetts until William, a veteran of the War of 1812, settled briefly in Oxford, New York, where his son Franklin was born in 1827.

Franklin Tarbell was tall and spare, traits he passed on to Ida. Always fast on his feet, he was like a wire that could coil and spring, and was given to outbursts of frantic activity. His penetrating blue eyes sometimes twinkled but usually peered from deep sockets, which gave him the intense gaze of an evangelist. Children loved him and teased him about his whistling and his endless hunger for casaba seeds.

He loved learning but was the family's least accomplished speller. Franklin's favorite books, besides religious ones, told of travel. He delighted in the adventures of Henry Morton Stanley and eagerly attended the circus, which brought to Pennsylvania animals from India and Africa.

On the maternal side, Ida Tarbell was a McCullough. Alexander M'Cullough, a wheelwright of Scotch ancestry, came to Boston from the north of Ireland in about 1730 and helped to settle Pelham, Massachusetts. In 1785 his son James married Hannah Raleigh, said to be the nearest living kin to the famous Sir Walter. Their grandson married Sarah Seabury, descendant of the first Episcopal bishop and, through him, was related to John Alden of the *Mayflower*. To this couple was born Esther Ann McCullough, Ida's mother.

Ida Minerva Tarbell was the firstborn and the only one of her siblings who would not be given a forebear's name. Her twenty-seven-year-old mother, far from her husband and still under her parents' roof, perhaps found this the only rebellion possible.

At Ida's birth in 1857 a financial panic raged. Land speculation had bubbled until the collapse of the Ohio Life Insurance and Trust Company had the impact of a sharp pin on an overinflated balloon. In Iowa, construction of railway lines stopped abruptly, leaving half-laid tracks in the middle of vast empty fields. Buildings went roofless, and Franklin Tarbell was forced to walk back to his family. He crossed Illinois, Indiana, and Ohio on foot, earning what little money he could by teaching along the way. When at last he arrived home, his eighteen-month-old daughter, indignant to see him take her mother in his arms, cried, "Go away, bad man!"

An amazing discovery allowed him to stay with his family. Edwin Drake, Moses searching for the promised land of oil, had struck at the earth and brought forth wealth. He was the agent of hopeful investors who had commissioned him, a vagrant and onetime railway conductor, to drill for oil. Until then oil for patent medicines, wheel lubrication, and lamps could be gathered only by skimming what oozed from the ground. Drake tapped a supply that could be refined into what mankind urgently needed—cheap illumination.

Men greedily tried to collect the supply before it disappeared. The precious fluid could be anywhere, and there were theories on the best places to look. One held that a subterranean river of oil ran under natural waterways, so drills needled streams and riverbanks. Then it was hypothesized that hills were but sacs of petroleum, so derricks were shifted to higher ground. Finally, when oil was discovered in every pasture, the earth's bounty was fully confirmed.

Franklin Tarbell, by turns teacher, farmer, river pilot, and joiner, saw in this new enterprise the chance to get ahead. He perfected a wooden tank that would hold a hundred or more barrels of oil and thus managed to earn more money than he had thought he could make in a lifetime.

When Ida was three years old and her brother Will three months, Franklin loaded the family into a wagon and for two days and three nights drove them over mud, rocks, and short stretches of corduroy road until they reached their new home in the encampment of Cherry Run, Pennsylvania.

Cherry Run, like the rest of the petroleum regions, was squalid. The teeming population was ragged, muddy, and greasy, but the appearance of poverty was deceptive, for they bathed in oil. An observer noted: "No one lives amid this sea of oil but those who are making money, and all know that the oldest tatters are good enough for the filth amid which they dwell. Men think of oil, talk of oil, dream of oil; the smell and taste of oil predominate in all they eat and drink; they breathe an atmosphere of oil-gas, and the clamor of 'ile, ile—ile' rings in one's ears from day-light until midnight."

The pervasive smell of gas nauseated visitors, but exhilarated oilmen liked even petroleum's taste. Many drank two or three glasses daily to prevent chills and colds.[1]

Women and children had to adjust to the satanic landscape of hiss-ing steam, thrusting pumps, bellowing ungreased wheels, and the treacherous mire that devoured planks carefully laid out as sidewalks.

From all indications, Esther Tarbell did not adapt willingly. She had been raised to remember always that the blood of Sir Walter Raleigh, Massachusetts patriots, and Episcopal hierarchy flowed in her veins. Though the McCulloughs lived in a log house in western Pennsylvania, the rule of a proper New England upbringing obtained. Esther and her sisters had been sent to live with an aunt near Albany to attend normal school and qualify as teachers. For a dozen years before her marriage, Esther had taught school. She would have continued, she told her chil-dren, had her mother not said working was improper for a wife.

The early days of married life were not auspicious. Instead of large acreage in Iowa and continuation of the family tradition of settling the country, Esther Tarbell was living in a place of filth where there were as many prostitutes as decent women. She was forty miles and an era away from her parents' pastoral farm, and she would never forget the indig-nity. Thirty years later she wrote to Ida, "I indured [sic] enough at Rouseville for all the rest of my life."[2]

The transition was as difficult for the child as the parent. Ida had played with lambs and colts at her grandfather's farm. Now a creek raced by the house and open pits of oil gaped not far from their door. She suffered most from a loss of freedom to explore. Warned not to walk on one side of the house nor to climb on the derricks in the front yard, the rebellious Ida was often scolded and once switched for disobe-dience.

"My first reaction to my new surroundings was one of acute dislike. It aroused me to a revolt which is the first thing I am sure I remember about my life—the birth in me of conscious experience. This revolt did not come from natural depravity; on the contrary it was a natural and righteous protest against having the life and home I had known, and which I loved, taken away without explanation and a new scene, a new set of rules which I did not like, suddenly imposed," she later wrote.

In defiance, shortly after her third birthday, she tried to run away. She followed a path as far as she could but was finally overwhelmed by an embankment too high to climb. In adult life she recalled it as a dra-matic scene in a play: "Never in all these years since have I faced defeat, known that I must retreat, that I have not been again that little figure with the black mountain in front of it."

Her baby brother Will intruded on her world and Ida rebelled again. To see if he could float, she led him onto a footbridge and tossed him into the creek. His billowing skirts buoyed him until a workman heard his screams and fished him out. She never recalled her spanking, only the joy of satisfied curiosity. She and the world were too young to term this sibling rivalry.

Despite little Will's brush with drowning, the threat of Ida's childhood was fire, not water. A terrible derrick explosion occurred soon after Lincoln's election and the attack on Fort Sumter. Taking in one victim who had managed to crawl to the Tarbell door, Esther turned her alcove "parlor" into a sick room for three months and allowed her best quilts and comforters to be stained with soothing linseed oil.

Futile attempts were made to shield Ida from witnessing other such horrors. When three women died in a house fire in the early 1860s, Esther tried to ban Ida from the wake; but the curious child stole into the place where the bodies were laid out and lifted the sheets that covered them. The sight of flesh singed red and charred black returned to her in nightmares for weeks and must have lodged permanently in her psyche. When she was elderly, a filling station attendant accidentally spilled some gasoline on her. She surprised her companion by turning in an instant from a calm pleasant woman into a shrew hysterically screaming about fire.[3]

If the town was a tinderbox in physical terms, its citizens also risked eternal fire in the usual ways. Good fought evil, sanctimony battled unruly passions, decency met hedonism. The first step was taken toward forming a community when some, the Tarbells among them, erected a white frame church with a steeple that poked heavenward beside the derricks. When the congregation voted to become Methodist, the Presbyterian Tarbells democratically converted. To regulate boomtown emotions, the group built a school and attempted to drive out prostitution by setting adrift Ben Hogan's Floating Palace which literally floated twenty miles down the Allegheny River before the exhausted revelers awoke.

Though each man was still his own policeman by dint of his gun, fireman by virtue of his bucket, and banker by means of his money belt, a town named Rouseville began to coalesce. Those with a preference for order left the mud flats where individual pine shanties abutted derricks and regrouped along the bluff. Franklin Tarbell moved his family to a house on a hillside that had never been drilled nor stripped of trees and shrubs. In the spring, leafy branches obscured the derricks below and all around them flourished white shadflowers and red maples, laurel, and azaleas. In autumn, the foliage gleamed not with petroleum but crimsons and russets, and the air was crisp and clean in Ida's nostrils. She loved the high-up places where she would take her pony. She loved climbing trees where she would perch in what her grandmother called "the loon's nest." When life was not sufficiently adventurous, she imagined herself as Miss Muffet, a pirate, a fairy godmother, or she marveled over the Civil War.

Ida and Will followed it through a series of engravings in *Harper's Weekly.* They lay on their stomachs, heels in the air, absorbing every detail of the Army of the Potomac encamped, under review, or charging into battle. Franklin Tarbell, now in his mid-thirties, did not go to the front, but was an ardent Republican who saw nobility in the cause. When Lincoln died he and Esther were both so grieved that Ida was astonished that something outside their own world could matter so much.

Iron tanks soon superseded the wooden ones Franklin Tarbell produced, and he began to drill for oil and to sell lumber from the land his drills cleared. Those who stayed in the fast-changing oil business were those who could adapt. Others "went back to the States" as returning to the more civilized parts of America was known. Franklin Tarbell stayed.

He was among the first to exploit the discovery of Pithole. It was the most legendary of oil rush cities where petroleum was so plentiful that pumps fighting fires struck oil instead of water and literally added fuel to flames. Firemen developed catapults to pelt out blazes with mud.

Capitalists with greenbacks thronged to the site, wages and board were exorbitant, land brought fantastic sums. Western Pennsylvania of the 1860s seemed even more promising than California of '49. Many fortune seekers subleased fractions of wells for hundreds of dollars. Others just skimmed oil that ran off hillsides and floated on the surface of streams and sold this runoff to get their start in the oil business.

When the Civil War ended, the idle, the needy, and the avaricious were all lured by the promise of wealth to be made in "Oil Dorado." In September 1865, when Ida was nearly eight, Pithole's population was estimated at between twelve and sixteen thousand and the post office required seven clerks. Hotels, theaters, saloons, and public halls popped up like cutouts in a children's book. Derricks rose to heights of forty-eight feet, and guards stayed on duty lest whole structures be spirited off to other sites in the night.

To spare his wife and children the vulgarity of Pithole, Franklin Tarbell rode his horse the few miles each way. Ida, eyes round with excitement, stayed up at night with her worried mother to await his return, envisioning her father as a sort of Paul Revere figure, pistol in one hand, reins in the other, his pockets bulging with thick, tempting rolls of dollars.

But the frenzy passed. Pithole's reserves were drained in five hundred days and its denizens departed. Meanwhile, the small world of Ida Tarbell was occupied by events more central to herself. When she was six her sister Sarah Asenath, named for her grandmothers, was born, and Ida had her first responsibility—she was told by the midwife to take tea to her mother and see the new baby. As an old lady, Ida remembered holding the cup tightly and carefully, fearful that a drop might spill, thinking that this duty was the most important, the most wonderful thing that had ever happened to her.

Two years later another brother was added to the household, but just before Frankie Junior's second birthday he and Sarah were stricken with scarlet fever. Sturdy Sarah fought it off but little Frankie's screams continued to grow worse. Helpless, eleven-year-old Ida stood outside the closed bedroom door, clamping tight fists over her ears to keep out the sounds of her baby brother's pain, but afraid to leave him. She clenched her knuckles so hard that they were still white days after he died. She was seventy-eight years old before she could bring herself to dredge up this fearsome incident and begged to be allowed to omit it from her autobiography.[4] Ever after the loss of that little brother, Ida panicked when her siblings were sick.

Those days of childhood also brought the pleasure of friendship with Laura Seaver, the daughter of her father's business partner.[5] Laura was a few years older, but the girls visited each other often, playing with dolls and practicing tying back their hair. Then they would look at the *Police Gazette* that Ida Tarbell found lying near the workmen's bunkhouse. These pictures in the *Gazette* portrayed the things her parents alluded to with disapproval and which her mother could hardly bear to explain, and the two girls studied them with fascination. "If they were obscene we certainly never knew it. There was a wanton gaiety about the women, a violent rakishness about the men—wicked, we supposed, but not the less interesting for that." Ida wrote this years later, but to an adult looking at the illustrations a hundred years later, the dance-hall girls looked remarkably anxious.

The Seavers lived in Petroleum Center, which grew rowdier and more raucous as oil strikes grew greater and the population boomed. When Ida rode there she looked up in the night sky to study the constellations, but walking through the streets she pretended to ignore its saloons and dance halls. At night she tiptoed from her bed to look across the way to a brothel where the laughter and curses were loud and the songs were never those she had learned to play on her parents' Bradbury square piano. Esther had told her nothing about sex, but Ida knew that in this forbidden place occurred the too-shocking-to-be-told things which men and women did to each other in the dark.

As a grown woman past menopause, Ida would draw on her own sheltered experience to complain that a child was steered from the facts of life as if they were something evil. She noted that a girl breathed from babyhood the atmosphere of unnatural prejudice and misunderstanding that surrounded procreation and that this miasma grew thicker until in a "mischievous and sometimes snide" way she learned about sex.

To keep her mind on higher things, there was the church. The Tarbells attended services on Sunday mornings and weekday nights, participated in "class meetings" where small groups of Methodists met for spiritual discussion, and took part in the annual revival.

In the Tarbells' day, these conferences were more sedate than the early backwoods camp meetings which engendered them, but a fervid atmosphere remained. When Ida was ten or eleven, she decided to "go forward" and declare herself a Christian as everybody else was doing. She left her pew to kneel before the preacher at the "mourner's bench." This bench, or "anxious seat," where the repentant engaged in varying degrees of emotional display from tears and shouting to choked silence, was the center of attention for the congregation, which joined in earnest prayer for the converted. For Ida, it was a chance to show off the crimson ribbons that cascaded from her hat onto her cream-colored coat. But that night, tucked in bed and praised for her pure white soul, she knew herself to be a sinner. "The realization of that hypocrisy cut me to the heart . . . and the relief I sought in prayer was genuine," she remembered.

In the days that followed the revival, the girl observed that often when she said the polite and proper thing, her attitude was sharp and without charity. "For a long time it made me secretly unhappy thinking that in me alone ran an underground river of thought. Later I began to suspect that other people were like this, that always there flowed a stream of unspoken thought under the spoken thought. It made me wary of strangers."

Although she was beginning to value independent thinking and to question the ironclad assumptions that had governed her upbringing, she took seriously the disciplines of her religion where right doing was toted up against too much backsliding and favors were not to be accepted unless they could quickly be repaid.

With Laura Seaver alone Ida shared her thoughts. Ida described her as "probably the most intimate friend I ever had." As reticent as her descriptions of them were, Ida's friendships were for life. Most of her early companions remained in Pennsylvania where she attended their weddings and funerals and they read her books and articles.

Much as she valued these relationships, the time she spent alone was especially rich. She loved to go on solitary picnics and to bring home from her rambles flowers to press in books, insects to house in bottles, and stones to add to a growing collection of interesting things. She would often lose herself in stories by William Makepeace Thackeray and Mary Ann Evans who later called herself George Eliot. Sometimes Ida would be so engrossed in Dickens's *Our Mutual Friend* that she would be horrified to discover she had spilled lemon pie on the family's *Harper's Monthly* where these serialized works appeared. Such afternoons gave Ida a very different impression about Rouseville than the one her mother had. She felt such fondness for it that whenever she passed through it on the train, even in her old age, she would peer through the window and look up the hillside for a glimpse of the first house her father had built for them. She was not happy when, in her twelfth year, Franklin Tarbell moved his family to Titusville, the area's cultural capital. An incorporated city of ten thousand, it had a police force, and its citizens encouraged the mayor to suppress the kind of vice and ungodliness the boomtowns fostered. The only public boisterousness permitted was harness racing on Main Street, the dust-raising feature of Sunday afternoons.

Titusville was a bustling city. Drains defeated the mud, plank walks stretched in all directions, and at night the streets were lit by gas. There were six large churches, two banks, three newspapers, two public houses, four hotels, a paper mill, a high school, and even organ grinders on the sidewalks. With the completion of the Titusville Oil Exchange, buying and selling moved indoors.

Everywhere the scent of new lumber mingled with the smell of oil. In the summer of 1870, three hundred houses were erected. Of these the Tarbells' was one of the most interesting—it was made from the lumber and ornamentation of a Pithole hotel. Franklin Tarbell, who had admired the long French windows and broad verandas of Bonta House, offered to buy it for six hundred dollars when the Pithole oil run played out in 1869. The owners, who had built it for sixty thousand dollars, were glad to accept. And so it was reincarnated among other commodious dwellings on East Main Street, a two-story, three-sectioned house topped by a tower.

One can easily imagine that Esther, given her sense of self and family, must have felt they were finally taking their rightful place among genteel society. Having shielded her children as best she could from the roughness of an oil town, she was relieved to think they would at last have a law-abiding community and a decent education.

Ida did not perceive Titusville's advantages in this light. She thought of her school only as a crowded room. At the small Rouseville school with the dirt floor, Mrs. Rice had been Ida's friend. Here the teacher, whom she secretly admired, did not seem to know who she was. Ida's response to feeling lost and overlooked was to skip class and go for long walks in the hills of Titusville, wondering to herself how she could have changed from the once so well-mannered child to the currently naughty one. "I must have discovered what fun it was to have a good time. I pursued it with absorption, played truant when I felt like it, never knew my lessons and didn't care," she said.

Thirteen-year-olds often lash out at themselves and the world with a force and tactics that astound even themselves. Being the "new girl" was exceptionally difficult for a proud, shy child. Her rebellious truancy ceased one day in class when the teacher, Mary French, told her it was a disgrace that a bright student like Ida never knew her lessons and was too wild to go to school. Ida was startled that anybody could say those things about her and particularly shamed that they could be true. After that she became a model pupil.

She soon entered high school and found a friend in Annette Farwell, a girl in her senior year. Ida felt uneasy over finding someone to take Laura's place until she learned that Laura had also made a new life. A few years older than Ida, Laura had gotten married. Relieved of guilt, Ida still felt abandoned.

Annette Farwell, whose father was a driller and contractor, shared Ida's love of learning. Annette recalled their pastimes as "the things girls naturally do," but they also spent summer vacations reading Shakespeare and French together. Annette would imagine Ida as Rosalind, the forthright heroine of *As You Like It* who disguised herself as a boy. Ida was regarded as musical and at recitals was probably better at solo performances than duets. Once when she was performing with Phoebe Katz, who tied with Ida as first in her class, one made a mistake. Hearing the false notes, they stopped and treated their audience to a discussion about who was to blame before starting all over at the beginning.

Esther insisted on religious songs to entertain company, but Ida would have preferred livelier rhythms. Now a teenager, she reclined on the couch feigning sleep to hear conversations not meant for her ears, read books intended for adults, and lay awake nights planning elopement with a bank clerk whose name she did not know. Throughout her life, men and boys she did know were less capable of inspiring flights of fancy than those males she could create in her mind.

Besides the anonymous bank clerk, Ida's girlhood crushes were mainly on her father's friends, and she later recalled that she had no thought of actually conversing with them. Annette Farwell remembers Ida as having been popular and high-spirited, but never interested in one particular boy. One can only wonder how a beau would have been received in the Tarbell home, for Franklin had a strict code that ruled out such things as cards, square dances, and cotillions. Instead, Ida played the piano so her little sister could dance with her playmates.

Friends said Ida got on well with her siblings. Her personality was such that she would have savored the role of elder sister instructing the others in how to behave. Sarah, two years younger than Will, was an unruly child who romped and capered and played with her dolls. Little enough to be the family pet, delicate enough to miss school often, she had been strong enough to have survived the scarlet fever which killed Frankie, and for this favor was allowed to go undisciplined.

While Ida dutifully applied herself to her lessons, Will was off hunting or fishing for the area's oily-tasting trout. Will was a brilliant student who seemed to grasp instinctively the lessons his elder sister needed to study. It was Will's place to go to the oil fields with his father while Ida participated in the family business only by asking questions.

Ida was rewarded for her academic diligence. In her first year of high school she was one of three with a grade average over ninety-nine. She was amazed that simply by doing what was expected of her, she had made it to the top of the class. She knew that she would have to be there consistently, for she had proven that she was capable of doing such work.

Of her school books, Colton's *Common School Geography* gave her the most pleasure with its many woodcuts of islands and deserts, waterfalls and tropics. She promised herself that before she died she would see Vesuvius and the natural bridge in Virginia. History seemed to her unnecessary, except for Smith's *History of Rome*, which she read over and over, and her father's books, which he began to acquire as soon as he could afford them. A favorite was John Clark Ridpath's *A Popular History of the United States From Aboriginal Times to The Present Day.* "Aboriginal Times" was the most imposing phrase she had ever heard.

Grammar, rhetoric and composition yielded the pleasure of uncovering the underlying form. "Outlines which held together, I had discovered, cleared my mind, gave it something to follow. I outlined all my plans as I had diagrammed sentences. It was not a poor beginning for one who eventually, and by accident rather than by intention, was to earn her living by writing—the core of which must be sound structure."[6]

But above all, science opened the world to her. Frogs, beads of water on a tabletop, and budding twigs had always intrigued her. In high school she learned she could study them as zoology, chemistry and botany. She became preoccupied by pebbles and plants, collected leaves, minerals, and insects. Now she had an excuse when her mother asked why she wandered off by herself before breakfast or buried her head in books when she should have been sweeping the stairs. The birds' eggs and nests she kept in boxes in her room weren't littering up the house—they were useful in school.

When she learned of Darwin's data showing that the horse had started out as a fish and that the human was cousin to the monkey, she was torn between the demands of her two worlds—the questions raised by science and the solid faith of her religion. Never again would she regard anything as absolutely final until she had tested it herself. "The quest of the truth had been born in me—the most tragic and incomplete, as well as the most essential, of man's quests," she recalled. She knew at last what she wanted to be—not a mother and a wife like all women, but a scientist who would uncover the beginnings of life.

Secret passions and scientific ardors filled her, but she still went to Thursday-night prayer meetings where the smell of wool drying by the furnace mingled with figurative whiffs of brimstone. Ida began teaching the infant class of Sunday school to repent for her doubts but held to those doubts just the same and set about to prove evolution with a fervor that rivaled a saint's quest of God.

She could not bring herself to reject totally the Bible her parents believed in so much. She recalled taking from Scripture the notion of goodness as a practical approach to life. Not to say or do what would hurt others was a principle at home where people did not articulate their feelings. When injured, one was silent until the household made a determined but unspoken effort to soothe the pain. Each felt he knew what was in the other's heart and responded to what he considered the other's reaction.

Of them all, Esther was the most outspoken and the one who first gave way to her feelings. She expressed her discontent in physical ways. When the church, one of her societies, or the household displeased her (as once the coarseness of Rouseville had done), she would be flushed and irritated until she worked out her grudge in rows of knitting. She would repair to her rocking chair and her needles after complaining of the amount of time her husband devoted to his Sunday-school class of girls, or after Esther and Franklin's loud discussions about money.

Domestic economy was an idiosyncratic business generally. Husbands did not discuss their financial situation with their wives—it would not be seemly or appropriate—yet the wives were to manage household operations that naturally depended on finances they knew nothing about. No one applied the notion of budgets to housekeeping; women either asked their husbands for money or charged items to monthly accounts.

Esther was conscientiously, perhaps compulsively, economical. Her prudence was often unnecessary in fact, but since Franklin did not inform her of financial details, Esther never knew how little or how much money they actually had or how much she could spend or buy on credit.

Ida herself tested the limits of this practice when her parents were out of town. They had arranged for Ida to attend the opening of the local opera house and the girl, feeling a special outfit was called for, charged a wide pink sash and yellow kid gloves at the local dry-goods store. It was less comic when Esther made an expenditure for herself or the household only to discover that Franklin was in the midst of a financial squeeze.

Ida often saw her parents at such cross purposes, especially when it came to keeping up appearances versus the cost of doing so. Twice a year a dressmaker took up privileged residence at the Tarbell home. The Grover and Baker sewing machine was overhauled, shears and buttonhole scissors sharpened, and numerous bobbins wound. The Tarbell women spent days at the store comparing fabrics as Esther insisted on pure wools and silks and *fine* cottons.

These semiannual expenditures were followed by the money-saving ritual of sorting scraps for quilts and the immolation of remnants whose ashes would fertilize the garden. As the red tongues of the bonfire lapped in the twilight Ida's father would affirm, "Nothing lost but the smoke." Nearby, she gazed at the flickering colors dreaming of fashions and laces in the comfort of her less demanding second-best dress, which she gathered under her to sit on the steps.

Learning early the importance of money, Ida decided to earn her own. The opportunity came when oil stocks began to climb and even the teachers were tempted to abandon the high school in their avidity to trade. Ida asked her father for a hundred dollars so she could get into the market. "His eyes were steely at first, but they gradually twinkled. He inveighed: 'No daughter of his, no child of his, would demean herself by gambling.'" He warned her that some grew so addicted to the market that after they lost everything, they would bet pennies simply on which way the market would fluctuate. She had to accept his decision, but when she grew up and made her own money, she was good at making investments in the market and in choosing men to advise her.

Despite her father's caution, in early 1872 the oil market promised to spiral ever upward, but abruptly, profits were choked off when railroads raised shipping rates one hundred percent. Independent oil producers learned that railroad companies were making them pay astronomical charges while an outfit called the South Improvement Company, based in Cleveland, was given rebates in direct violation of federal law.

In Titusville, angry oilmen swore they would not be eradicated by an outside alliance. Franklin attended antimonopoly meetings in halls where overhead banners proclaimed proud American mottoes—"Don't Give Up the Ship!" "No Surrender!" "United We Stand!"

The speeches were sufficiently inflammatory that the usually moderate Franklin joined processions of vigilantes who raided oil cars owned by South Improvement and burned out fellow independents who broke ranks.

Franklin Tarbell's personality changed. His old forms of relaxation—playing his jew's harp or telling his family about his day—were no more. He did not sing to Sarah nor take pleasure in his after-dinner cigar. What rankled him was not business frustration alone but a sense of injustice.

He was probably not a very good businessman. He could spot an oil field, build superior equipment, work hard, but his philosophy was too quaint for the times in which he lived. He believed that individualism was good, debt was bad, hidden deals carried a stigma, and fights must be fair. The exemplar of the day was Benjamin Franklin who would never stoop so low as to steal business from a competitor.[7] That the South Improvement Company could prosper through dishonorable tactics outraged him.

Behind the scenes, John D. Rockefeller of the Standard Oil Company was the master of the South Improvement Scheme. Aware of everything in the oil business, he may even have known Franklin Tarbell's name, but he would not have respected it. The oil magnate was calculating about opponents. Those who were bold and resourceful he wanted at his side. In time he plucked the best of those who fought him, such as John D. Archbold (later president of Standard Oil of New Jersey), Henry Rogers, and Charles Pratt, and made them officers of his company. Someone like Franklin Tarbell would not have interested him at all.

But Franklin's interpretations of the oil war were burned into Ida's mind. For her the hullabaloo took on the significance of the fall of the Bastille, which she was reading about in school. She absorbed her father's indignation and made it her own: "There was born in me a hatred of privilege—privilege of any sort. It was all pretty hazy to be sure, but it still was well, at fifteen, to have one definite plan based on things seen and heard, ready for a future platform of social and economic justice if I should ever awake to my need of one."

Public outrage and the law eventually defeated the South Improvement Company. The fact that railroads were chartered as public utilities open to all customers at equal rates meant that the South Improvement Company could not operate under favored conditions. The independents' victory was short. They soon found themselves squeezed in another fashion. John D. Rockefeller agreed to buy all of the Pennsylvanians' oil, but then, claiming they had produced more than was good for the industry, he reneged on the contracts. Rockefeller succeeded not only in depriving the oil producers of customers, but in humiliating them as well.

Ida deeply felt her father's sorrows. However she may have sided with her mother in the matter of household finances, Ida adored Franklin and was protective of him. In general, the Tarbell children all spoke reverently of both their parents, but they were more sentimental about their father. Ida never forgave a neighbor who convinced Franklin to give up his cigar and send the money to the missions; even as old women she and Sarah could work themselves into a dudgeon about it. He was sensitive, even about his appearance, and went so far as to cover his baldness with a brown wig, a vanity that shocked Methodist elders. What can be reconstructed of his personality comes mostly from a memoir by his granddaughter which Ida treasured.[8] If there was a similar work about Ida's mother, it has not survived.

Franklin was fundamentalist in relation to his Heavenly Father, but his posture as an earthly son is unclear. His clan was not numerous or particularly close. There is only one mention of a paternal cousin in Ida's papers. Franklin's father outlived him and died in his eighty-eighth year in 1917, but her maternal grandparents were the only ones she ever mentioned.

William Tarbell, for whom Ida's brother was named, had served in the important battles along the Canadian frontier in the War of 1812; but Franklin had been too young for the dispute with Mexico and too engrossed by business for the Civil War. If he was estranged from his father, Franklin's appreciation of independence is all the more understandable. Ida described how he disdained anyone who would work for wages: "I am sure my father would rather have grubbed corn meal and bacon from a piece of stony land which was his own than have had all the luxuries on a salary . . . to his way of thinking taking orders . . . was failure for an American."

During her teens, Ida saw two significant battles—the independents' against Rockefeller and woman's struggle for the vote. "My mother was facing a little reluctantly a readjustment of her status in the home and in society. She had grown up with the Woman's Rights movement. Had she never married, I feel sure she would have sought to 'vindicate her sex' by seeking a higher education, possibly a profession. The fight would have delighted her," Ida wrote.

The Tarbell home was always open to visitors, especially those with a crusade. Her father particularly welcomed Prohibitionists, her mother those working for Woman's Rights. In Ida's mind, Elizabeth Cady Stanton and Susan B. Anthony took their places beside abolitionists, civil service reformers, and Abraham Lincoln.

Esther Tarbell and her visitors endlessly debated such issues as woman's true nature and what she could attain, but to the representative of future womanhood, the young girl sitting among them, they paid no attention at all.

Ida was too shy to ask questions, to point out inconsistencies in their statements, or to say what these subjects meant to her. Unlike visiting male lecturers, the women did not notice her and she resented it.

"I remember best Mary Livermore and Frances Willard—not that either touched me, saw me, of this neglect I was acutely conscious. I noted too that the men we entertained did notice me, talked to me as a person and not merely as a possible member of a society they were promoting," Ida recalled.

One incident was especially painful. The family spent part of its summers on Chautauqua Lake where there was a celebrated Methodist summer camp that brought in distinguished lecturers. Ida Tarbell, once she grew too old to play tag on the relief model of Palestine, was enthralled by the presentations on science. When two women, the Misses Lattimore, demonstrated a microscope, she longed to look through the lens they handled so deftly and watch the life that swam and quivered in its field. Ida rehearsed a little speech about wanting to be a microscopist herself and asking them to help and advise her. She delivered it as best she could and was rebuffed.

"The two ladies smiled down from their height, so plainly showing they thought me a country child with a queer behavior complex. 'Quite impossible,' they said and turned back to their conference . . . abashed, humiliated, but luckily too angry to cry, I made my way back to my flat-bottomed boat. I would show them, I resolved, clencing my fists!"[9]

Her skepticism about woman's superiority grew as she followed the *New York Herald*'s accounts of how in a fit of pique, Victoria Woodhull, spiritualist and feminist, revealed the adulterous affair of Henry Ward Beecher, the famous preacher and proponent of woman suffrage: "What I picked up about the Beecher trial (I read the testimony word by word in our newspapers) did not increase my regard for my sex. [It] did not seem to substantiate what I heard about the subjection of women, nor did what I observed nearer home convince me. Subjection seemed to me fairly divided. That is all: I saw there were 'henpecked men' as well as 'downtrodden women.' The chief unfairness I recognized was in the handling of household expenses."

Crusade was in the air of the Tarbell home. As the father chafed under John D. Rockefeller's encroachments and the mother churned with the injustice of woman's lot, the daughter struggled with the complexities of evolution and her place in the world. She thought at the time that her interests lay with suffragists, and was so vehement that she later mocked herself. She wrote of young girls confused by the militancy of the 1870s and of course she meant the young Ida: "What it was really about they never knew until it was too late. The young American woman of militant cast finds it easy to believe that the business of being a Woman is slavery. She had her uneasy mother's pains and sacrifices and tears before her and she resents them. She meets the militant theory on every hand that the distress she loathes is of man's doing, that it is for her to revolt, to seize his business, and so doing escape his tyranny, find a worth-while life for herself and at the same time help 'liberate her sex.' "[10]

But in the 1870s, as a girl who loved learning and her own dignity and whose mother felt cringingly dependent, Ida decided two causes were worth working for—the right to education and the right to control her own money. At night she sank to her knees and prayed to God to spare her from marriage and send her to college instead.

Two

Pantheistic Evolutionist

When Ida Tarbell entered Allegheny College in Meadville, Pennsylvania, just before her nineteenth birthday, she felt she had reached her spiritual home. The cornerstone of Bentley Hall, a three-story brick building topped by a cupola, had been laid fifty-six years before, which seemed an aeon to one used to the oil regions. She revered Bentley as the first tangible sign that anything could be permanent.

The campus embraced paths and drives and a ravine through which flowed a rocky stream. It was the Forest of Arden and she was Rosalind taking on a boy's ways for her own ends. Her mother, who had been vexed when Ida classified leaves instead of sweeping the stairs, supported the idea of college for Ida. Franklin consented after the president of Allegheny appeared at the Sunday dinner table. Ida's first choice was Cornell, another "man's college" newly opened to women, but her father decided that the Methodist-affiliated institution which was only thirty miles away in Meadville would be better. He had the money for this frivolous experiment and for a year-long college preparatory course in Titusville, because his heavy investments in the Bradford oil fields promised steady, plentiful return.

To Ida's dismay, she was the only girl in the freshman class. As boarding facilities for the seven girls were not yet ready, faculty wives opened their doors to her. "I went fearfully," she later admitted, "thinking the president of a college on a par with a bishop." Especially intimidating was the home of the classics and English professor, Ammi

B. Hyde, whom she described as "so queer we were inclined to laugh at him, so full of knowledge we revered him."[1]

Her preliminary weeks among the "great ones" were a trial until the promised girls' house opened. Behind a dormitory where a hundred boys lived, "The Snow Flake" boasted seven warrenlike rooms. "Had we not been so well brought up and the housekeeper not been a dragon, we might have made mischief,"[2] she said. They ached to communicate with the boys' hall, but conscious of being on trial, vowed to be good. In this they were unlike the two girls who boarded downtown and were known to smoke in their rooms. Ida always remembered them: "They were rich and beautiful and did not stay at the school long, but created a stir which lasted for years."[3]

Ida's housemates, for the most part well-brought-up girls from Methodist households, were "nice," but they could not have been strictly conventional. For a girl to go to college was a daring thing. Parents who spent money this way would have been at best ambitious for their daughters and at worst eager to display their wealth in a frivolous manner.

The notion seemed to catch on, however. Two of Ida's closest friends from Titusville, Josephine Henderson and Iris Barr, joined her at Allegheny. There is so little record of the Henderson family that it is possible she lived in a stepfather's home. Iris Barr, on the other hand, was a doctor's daughter.

In the group, Ida was adventurous and outgoing. On her own she dreaded places like chapel, the campus, and the classroom where she would come in personal contact with males. Women were subjected to all the discomfort of being a social experiment, but they were still expected to follow the same curriculum as the men—English literature, philology, art history, the sciences, French, and German. While males played baseball and football, the women followed the Delsarte system of calisthenics, dressed in high-necked waists and bloomers and lifted Indian clubs and dumbbells. Ida was as athletic as girls were allowed to be, but she delighted more in the long dark library. There she climbed to the top of the ladder and crouched reading book after book.

Her encounters with people were unlike those she had experienced before. She felt for the first time the thrill of shared interests and the excitement of new ones when Jeremiah Tingley, head of the department of natural science, and his wife invited his students to their rooms in Bentley Hall. "They had no children, and in the years of their study and travel they had gathered around them things of beauty and interest. The atmosphere of those rooms was something quite new and wonderful to me. It was my first look into the intimate social life possible to people interested above all in ideas, beauty, music and glad to work hard and live simply to devote themselves to their cultivation."

Discussions ranged from philosophy to politics and ideas like socialism which radiated from German universities and to bold new ideas like Bell's telephone. Discovering her passion for the microscope, Tingley urged Ida to use the binocular belonging to the college. To her, the thought of it was like a violin to an artist, not only because it was more powerful than her own instrument, but because its two eyepieces meant she no longer had to squint.

As she dared to profess her belief in evolution, Tingley guided her to study a missing link which they called the *Monopomo Alleghaniensis*, a foot-long creature with gills and a lung which adapted itself to mud or water as circumstances required. Others saw it as the repulsive "mud puppy," but she dissected it with awe and grew skillful with the scalpel. This species is not in reference books today. The closest creature is the *crytobranchus alleganiensis* or hellbender which has no external gills.

Tingley encouraged Ida Tarbell to discover things for herself. "That was where I had already found my joy; but I suspected it was the willful way, that the true way was to know first what was in the books."

He allowed her to experiment with the lab's electrical apparatus and induction coil. She warmed to his understanding and attention. "This revelation of enthusiasm, its power to warm and illuminate, was one of the finest and most lasting of my college experiences. The people I had known [in Titusville], teachers, preachers, doctors, businessmen, all went through their day's work either with a stubborn, often sullen, determination to do their whole duty, or with an undercurrent of uneasiness, if they found pleasure in duty. They seemed to me to feel that they were not really working if they were not demonstrating the Puritan teaching that labor is a curse. It had never seemed so to me, but I did not dare gloat over it. And here was a teacher who did gloat over his job in all its ramifications. Moreover, he did his best to stir you to his job." Ida blossomed under his encouragement, both socially and scholastically.

"Ida Tarbell was a fine student," recalled Iris Barr. "She would arise at four A.M. and get to work studying. She was never satisfied with any thing less than perfection. She was really fine in Latin, but she was no grind. She was too interested in people." Barr said this interest prompted Ida to urge Will, who followed her to Allegheny, not to join a fraternity. She preferred that he know people in all walks of life. Ida's sister Sarah attended Allegheny's preparatory courses. Little is known of her academic career except that she experimented with leaving the *h* off her name and Ida used alternate spellings ever after. Sarah left Allegheny when Ida graduated, possibly because she didn't want to stay on alone or because of family finances. Ida never mentioned how her little sister's presence affected her college life. With six years' difference in their ages, they could not have shared many friends.

Ida's social activities with her peers included coeducational parties where students would lock the chapel door and dance on the platform, but Ida, who now called herself a "pantheistic evolutionist," retained enough Methodism not to dance.[4] Throughout the course of the year, she and her friends sledded to neighboring Cambridge Springs and dined at the hotel. They went canoeing on the canal where Ida once fell in. She joined in the class project of rolling a boulder down the ravine and then, discovered by administrators, helped to roll it up again.

She was not a girl one noticed for her looks. Her college photographs show a prominent nose and frizzy hair pulled back behind large ears, yet the luminous eyes balanced other features that were frozen by the shutter.

She could alter herself little physically, but she did what she could with her clothing. Her classroom gown was a tightly fitted black redingote with a tiny train trimmed with forty-eight white quarter-sized buttons. She laid aside hoop skirts and corsets in the interests of female dress reform, and shocked her classmates by wearing a skirt above her ankles. The poor condition of the sidewalks sometimes forced her to lift her hem and thus daintily reveal a scarlet petticoat which her mother had assumed no one else would ever see.

Outside class, Ida was an editor of the college publication, secretary of the junior class, and an active member of Ossoli, the lady's literary society, which doubtlessly was named after Margaret Fuller Ossoli, the nineteenth century's outstanding American woman of letters. Ossoli girls addressed the day's topics and added philosophy and history to their poetry and literature shelves. The Philo-Franklin and The Allegheny societies for men enjoyed far more elegant quarters, as if to punish female sensibility for having the temerity to step from pedestal and onto podium. While men's clubs "debated," Ossoli "discussed," but it also sponsored five of eight public lectures given in one year.

The Campus of July 1878 commended one of Ida's speeches: "She showed that our present results had been brought about by toil and perseverance. That to every age had been entrusted something to develop whose light has been the peculiar work of that period. She spoke of the great interest manifested in women's education and how variously this subject has been viewed in the ages. She touched a chord in every true man or woman's heart when she said: 'Teach woman that she must be educated, not for man, but for her Creator.' "

She did not say that woman had as much need or right to education as a man, nor could she bring herself to state that ambition and glory were worthy of a woman. In a talk on Elizabeth Barrett Browning, Ida balanced the achievement of womankind's outstanding poet by stating that Browning never sought the fame that came to her.

Something extraordinary happened in the class of 1880—half its officers were female and it elected a woman president. Along the way, men and women developed a companionship that lasted through the years and made it one of the most cohesive alumni groups at Allegheny.

When a cornerstone for a permanent women's dormitory was laid in June 1879, Ida Tarbell was selected to speak for the student body: "The movement for the Ladies' Hall shows much of pure pluck. The girls have appreciated its necessity and made the best of their surroundings in the past. They said, 'We were allowed to come to Allegheny College and shall remain, then by and by they will have to prepare a place for us.' As to our classmates, never were women in college halls treated more royally than we are, never was truer chivalry manifested than in the respect and kindness with which Allegheny women are received by Allegheny men. We are deeply debtors to very many for the new surroundings to come in our college life and we purpose by improving these means for better culture, to show you the gratitude of true women."

In her studies and her social life, she involved herself not only with public speaking and the mud puppy, but with "the boy." "I was not long in discovering him when I reached Allegheny, for the taboos I encountered at the start soon yielded under the increased number of women, women in college, in special courses, in the Preparatory Department . . . I was learning, learning fast, but the learning carried with it pains. I still had a stiff-necked determination to be free. To avoid entangling alliances of all kinds had become an obsession with me."

She did not wish to be labeled a Delta girl or a Phi Psi girl, feeling that she could have friends in all fraternities. Thus, in what she described as "a disastrous morning," she wore four pins to chapel. Each boy had presented his as a token that Ida was his girl. No one expected her to amass a collection. Having "non-Frat" friends saved her from being a social outcast during the several months it took bruised feelings to mend.

Some one boy did get closer than the others. In the Allegheny College collection of class pictures there is a photo of a Warren Shilling of Sharon, Pennsylvania. Its identification, accurate or not, reads: "Was engaged to Ida M. Tarbell—neither married." Another clue to a strong attachment is in a poem she wrote a decade after graduation. In fifty lines more wistful than lyrical she writes in the person of a "literary woman" with "views on woman's duty and what by laws her due." The object of the poem is a lawyer named Jack and she would ". . . give my positions/To know, Jack, you have a weak spot/And that the moonlight

on the campus/Makes you remember you have not forgot." Jack may
not have been her beau's name, but there was a John D. Martin in her
class, whose graduation picture shows him to have been a handsome
mustachioed man. He became a Methodist minister.

By the time she had her diploma, marriage no longer seemed so odious nor spinsterhood so necessary, according to her memoirs; but since
she had no particular husband in mind, she felt free to spend her leisure
time with her microscope, save money toward further study abroad, and
earn her own way, somewhat over her father's objections.

College women in the nineteenth century could not readily fit prow-
ess in dissection, a working knowledge of French, and oratorical skill
into the working world. Two possibilities were open to the female grad-
uating without prospect of marriage—teaching and missionary work.
"At home we were entertaining preachers and elders and bishops. They
were very much in evidence at Allegheny too. And they were constantly
urging me to follow a 'call' which somehow I myself couldn't hear."
When two clergymen were particularly insistent, she panicked. Weeping, Ida begged off, protesting she would have known if there had been
a call, though they insisted it was sounding through them. What she
did not add, lest she incur greater trouble, was that her study of com-
parative religions made her think heathens as righteous as her Sunday
school. Instead of Africa or the Orient, she traveled to Poland, Ohio.

The existence of the Poland Union Seminary was the community's
proudest accomplishment, but every church in town had taken a turn as
its sponsor, with scant financial success. Now the Presbyterians inherited the task and had inadvertently forced the departure of a much-
beloved teacher by cutting her annual salary from seven hundred dollars
to six hundred.

After many letters and a personal interview, the board of trustees decided Miss Tarbell's enthusiasm, eagerness, and youth outweighed the
other candidate's twenty years of experience.[5] Ida was appointed preceptress of the school for the year beginning August 23, 1880, at a salary of five hundred dollars per year. "If I had been going on my
honeymoon, I should scarcely have been more expectant or more curious," she said of her first job.

She admired Poland's air of stability, its almost New England atmosphere, its roomy houses with pleasant yards, and its farmland with its
timeless cycle of sowing and harvesting. Yet she never felt welcome
there. "People used to stop me on the street, tell me that they, and their
parents before them, had gone to school to Miss Blakesleys and lament
that their children were now denied that privilege. I felt as guilty as if I
were personally responsible." Trying to be both high school and college, the seminary required Tarbell to teach two classes in each of four
languages—Greek, Latin, French, and German—plus geology, botany,

geometry, and trigonometry. She managed to stay one chapter ahead of her language classes, but she was confounded by the necessity of teaching grammar and math refresher courses to district schoolteachers whose tuition kept the school afloat. Some of the problems were ridiculously arcane and tripped her up. She could not match her students' grasp of the tricky material and they smirked when she faltered in her explanations.

Her discomfort continued for two months until she realized that while she labored to uncover and explain the general principles, her students simply memorized, in yearly ritual, the same solutions to the same puzzles. With a sweet sense of revenge, she procured outside texts. Nonchalantly, she wrote on the blackboard new equations and unfamiliar sentences with multiple clauses. Happy to trick them, she ignored their protests that her examples were not in the books. In this lay the most pleasant recollection of her teaching years.

Ida's friendship with one of the town's most unconventional girls was the antidote to thankless weary days. The first week of school, Clara Walker, whose father was on the school board, presented herself at the seminary and insisted that Ida go for a ride in her buggy. Fifty years later Tarbell would write, "Indeed, it was due to her understanding and affection that my two years in Poland, quite apart from the professional disappointment in them, were the gayest, most interesting, and in many ways the happiest of my life up to that time."

Clara, or Dot as she was known, indicated in her dress and open manner the rebellion Ida expressed by calling herself a socialist. She eschewed corsets and high heels and wore the costume of the free-spirited girl of the 1880s—the high shirtwaist with four-in-hand tie, flat shoes, and a tailor-made coat and skirt.

Their friendship was a revelation to Ida, opening her eyes to social injustice on a far greater scale than she had imagined possible in the opportunity-laden oil regions. With Clara she visited communities of Welsh miners who worked on farms where ore was but another crop. Ida found exploring a coal shaft horrifying, despite the clusters of cottages and cured meat provided for the workers.[6] On drives to Youngstown, ten miles away, she saw the industrial world aborning. One night after the theater she and Dot were stopped by a cortege of carts laden with corpses—the remains of men killed by an exploding furnace. The lamplight showed that the bodies were as charred as those she had seen as a child in Rouseville.

After another trip they were caught up in a crowd of strapping, frenzied women protesting their husbands' layoffs. That night she saw another side of women's dependence and the passions hungry children could inspire. Thus in Poland, as in Titusville all those years before, impersonal industry became highly personal in its effects.

Dot revealed what polite society spurned. She told Ida scandalous tales of how certain fortunes had been made, shared strange tales of depravity that emerged from the less cultivated parts of town. Seldom having heard of incest and lust, Ida professed to think these people had a very jolly time.

Ida was now of an age where interest in "the boy" led naturally to marriage and physical intimacy. She doubtlessly had the curiosity and apprehensions of any eligible girl, but she did not have a desire to wed. Ida righteously disagreed when anyone indicated sex was perverse. "I have never been able to see why nature's method of continuing the race was not as clean as any other of her processes," she wrote a male friend in later years, but on a typed copy for her files she scribbled a note to herself: "Though it does seem to me rather grotesque."[7]

As preceptress of the Poland Union Seminary she was too busy and too exalted to leave time for suitors, but the work was unrewarding. Begun with high hopes, teaching proved a disappointment. She not only failed to save money toward study in Europe, but she was forced to borrow from her father. Her microscope stood unused as she spent week nights parsing sentences and calculating square roots. When her contract ended in June 1882, she gave up teaching forever.

Dot and she remained friends until death, but life was never as good to Dot Walker as it had been in the days of her rides with Tarbell. Her father was ruined and disgraced by association with his boyhood chum William McKinley. McKinley, who proposed a duty on tin plate during his first term in Congress, persuaded the prosperous Walker to establish a stamping plant with McKinley's brother-in-law. When the business failed, Walker was portrayed as having deluded the innocent politician. After she became a journalist, Ida wanted to present his side, but Walker would not allow Tarbell to write of it during his lifetime. She published his story in her autobiography when she was past eighty.

Ida returned home after her first attempt at a career, thinking herself a failure. Students who would not learn and subjects she could not teach had not been part of her plan—nor had insufficient payment. The cold water of the working world doused, temporarily, the flame of her determination. At twenty-four she pronounced her career over and the dream of botany beyond her reach. Disheartened, she returned home facing two possibilities—spinsterhood or marriage.

Her mood of gloom matched her family's—the Bradford oil fields in which Franklin had so heavily invested were producing so generously that supply undercut price. The Standard Oil Company, knowing the only hope of profit lay in storing and withholding production from the market, gained control of companies which transported oil to market in pipelines, and embarked on nonstop tank construction. As the only buyer for Franklin Tarbell's oil, Standard Oil offered little return on his investment.

Thwarted by other independents' increasing capitulation to the "octopus," as Standard Oil was nicknamed, Franklin Tarbell, now in his mid-fifties, again looked to the West for his fortune. In the early spring of 1882, as Ida was completing her term in Poland, he and Will went to Huron in the Dakota Territories.

Instead of traveling by horse and wagon as earlier pioneers had done, they took the train. The railroads were in fact promoting the "Dakota boom" and the Northern Pacific put on a demonstration of how to make a hundred percent profit in wheat growing. Will interrupted his law studies to take advantage of the opportunity. In a letter to a friend in Titusville, Will wrote that nearly every seat on the train had been filled with people bound for Dakota. He marveled over the land: "It's limitless, like looking over the ocean . . . and so much beautiful black soil." Will encouraged his friend to come—"Faro, poker, etc. are in Huron, but if you want a maid [young lady] a carload would pay well,"[8] he advised, but he soon found one of his own. A nice girl, Ella Scott, whose family had left Illinois in hopes of wealth, proved more interesting than bachelorhood and so he married her.

The family legend is that Franklin Tarbell decided against life in the Dakotas when a breeze lifted the toupee from his head as he paced on a railroad platform. At fifty-five, he had had enough of new beginnings. He returned home while Will lingered out West.

Ida, living the life of elder unmarried daughter, looked after her mother and maternal grandfather who lost his wife while Ida was in Poland. When Allegheny College offered her the post of French and German teacher she declined. Instead, she sat in the tower room with her microscope and tested for amnifera, amoebalike creatures whose presence was a geological test for oil.

Three

A Young Lady of Fine Literary Mind

The *Chautauqua Assembly Herald* noted in the summer of 1883: "This unique little paper will be enriched by the pen of Miss Ida M. Tarbell, a young lady of fine literary mind, endowed with the peculiar gift of a clear and forcible expression. . . . Her wide reading and versatile brain, together with her love for children and lively sympathies for Christianity, will make her services of rare value to young people as an editor of this paper."[1]

The camp on Lake Chautauqua where the Tarbells spent their summers had grown into a permanent village of white cottages with high pointed eaves and gingerbread trim. Initially begun to furnish Bible instruction, the Chautauqua Assembly expanded to include lectures on science, history, and literature for those hungry for knowledge and the status it imparted. So that education could continue throughout the year, the magnetic cofounder and director, Dr. John H. Vincent, developed a four-year course of home reading complete with certificates of achievement. He called it the Chautauqua Literary and Scientific Circle.

This inspired the Reverend T. L. Flood, a Methodist minister with a keen business sense, to persuade Vincent of the merits both educational and financial in the establishment of a magazine to accompany the lesson plans.

Flood preached at Ida's church during her first winter back in Titusville and offered her the job of annotating articles. Having little else to occupy her beyond her own studies, she agreed: "To me it was only a temporary thing. I had no inclination toward writing or toward editorial work. This was a stop-gap—nothing more,"[2] she said.

It meant she would stay in Meadville, the magazine's headquarters, for two weeks a month, leaving the rest of the time free for her microscope. If the job had significance to her, it was that the salary meant she would not have to ask her father for an allowance. Gradually, the two weeks stretched out to three, then every few months she would make time to go home, and finally her life centered in Meadville, where she worked fourteen to sixteen hours a day.

The possibility of putting the accent over the wrong syllable terrified her. When she did err, it was brought to her attention not by Flood but by readers so intent that they cross-checked her notations with their own reference works. She plowed through a history of Greece and "Early Lessons in Vegetable Biology," forcing herself to stay alert and to pluck from interminable paragraphs the salient concepts. Annotation wearied her, but the sight of her work in type was like magic which dispelled forever dreams of botany. Plans and calculations, the orderly progress she expected for her life, yielded to a coup of fate.

Flood ran his publication as a cottage industry, using his study and dining room as offices. While she waited for the printer to deliver her proofs, Tarbell began to help out wherever she saw a need, especially in the small and crucial details of putting a magazine together. *The Campus* had been her only experience with editorial work, but she could see that the college effort had been managed more professionally than Flood's. She tried her hand at preparing copy by pasting together the "News From Local Circles" column and following deadline schedules.

The printer, who for two years had been harried by Flood's nonchalance, taught her the basic terms like "galley," which she had thought meant an ancient war vessel, and showed her how to fill in a dummy or lay out the page. She learned to read type upside down and backward when it was in the forms, and to rearrange lines when a much-needed ad was called in at the last minute. He taught her everything except how to set type. They became tacit partners in turning out *The Chautauquan* despite the vagaries of its editor in chief.

Soon Flood began putting what he considered pesky correspondence on her desk. Often these letters were cries for help, confessions of troubles and needs. Ida, wanting desperately to help, poured out her counsel in reply and signed her letters T. L. Flood.

Her advice was so empathetic and heartfelt that an erudite foreigner turned up in Meadville to see the one man in America who had understood his ideas. Confronted by the misrepresented editor, the visitor, and her letters, Tarbell confessed and forswore writing letters of advice.

After mastering routine chores, Ida began to contribute to "The Editor's Notebook," a compendium of news items and comments ranging from the death of Sojourner Truth, the advocate of abolition and woman suffrage, to the doings of President Chester Arthur and the news that Mark Twain was going into the printing business.

She further proved her usefulness by translating articles from the *Revue des Deux Mondes*, a French literary magazine. The United States did not at that time feel the need of a copyright law to protect foreign authors and so American editors, Tarbell included, freely helped themselves to the Continent's literature.

The Meadville office atmosphere is evoked in an article she later wrote on women in journalism: "The editor-in-chief knows what he wants and does not want, and all work must be done in accordance with his views; often in direct opposition to personal tastes." Speaking of women in the field, she reflected implicitly on her own role, seeming to feel that she kept things running smoothly: "Being refined, she will add fineness; being compassionate, she will add compassion; being conscientious, she will add conscience in a larger measure . . ."[3]

Ida advised that, in order to succeed, a woman must be enthusiastic, have wide-ranging knowledge and self-control, especially over tears when a editor criticized a story: "She must not put forward her femininity to such an extent as to demand that the habits of an office be changed on her account; nor can she presume on her womanhood." Tarbell's test of success in the profession was whether one could thrive under drudgery, but the hard work paid off.

From an initial circulation of fifteen thousand in October 1880, *The Chautauquan* grew to fifty thousand by the mid-eighties, when it moved into a two-story fortress with a crenellated roof. The building's unusual features included natural gas heat, steam-powered machinery, and pneumatic tubes through which Miss Tarbell spoke to the printers one floor below.

The Chautauquan was feminist in its concerns and basically benign. Its underlying tone implied that this was the best of all possible worlds, and improvements, should they appear necessary, would soon be made.

Tarbell herself watched events with a different perspective. From her daily reading of the liberal Republican *New York Tribune*, she gathered a sense that outside the scope of *The Chautauquan* the 1880s dripped with blood. Throughout 1886, glove makers, stove molders, meat packers, and other working brethren struck for better wages and the eight-hour day. In Chicago that May, a mass protest in Haymarket Square against the killing of strikers turned into a riot when a bomb killed several policemen, and other officers fired into the crowd. She and others on the magazine supported the eight-hour day, contracts for labor and capital, temperance, if not the politically hot issue of prohibition, and the Knights of Labor, workers who sought to unite in one great union.

At her suggestion, Flood ran articles on social and economic problems and what was being done to rectify them.

She was, in short, the perfect Mugwump: an independent Republican whose first political hero would be Grover Cleveland, the corruption-hating Democrat who fought the protective tariff. She already had her first antihero, a New York politician named Theodore Roosevelt, who broke ranks with independents in 1884 to support the Republican party's nominee, incumbent James G. Blaine, whom Cleveland defeated.

In annexing more and more responsibility, Tarbell discovered she had not only a job, but a career. She worked long hours and assumed the duties, if not the title, of managing editor. She approved articles, saw them through the publishing process, and headed the staff of women that Flood began to gather about him.

The two most important colleagues—and friends—in her life were Josephine Henderson and Mary Henry. Jo had been a year behind Ida in high school and college and had a way of countering Ida's more fanciful dreams with deflating common sense. Her letters indicate that she would have liked suitors, but somehow they failed to appear. Ida wrote of her: "Jo . . . was a handsome woman with a humorous outlook on life—healthy for me. I never had a friend who judged my balloons more shrewdly or pricked them so painlessly."[4]

Mary Henry was the youngest and prettiest of the group. Daughter of a militant in the Women's Christian Temperance Union, Mary came from a family of five children in Silver Lake, New York. There was apparently never enough money but Mary was a bit of a spendthrift, which amazed Ida who grew quite practical when the money she spent was her own. Mary, like many of the women who attended the Chautauqua Assembly, was nearly in thrall to the charismatic Bishop Vincent. Ida wrote with amusement to a mutual friend about Mary's attachment: "Bishop V has been to see her and she told me of the long visit with him which always does her so much good. He took her to lunch, etc. and now she'll run on a few months."[5]

If she teased Mary Henry, she was not malicious. Judging from the affection her co-workers evidenced in letters over the years, she was thoughtful of others' feelings and dignity. She seems to have administered by knowing others' jobs as well as they did—after all, she had done most of them when she was Flood's only assistant. She was willing to set aside a manuscript she was editing if some human need seemed more pressing, even if she had to keep the printers waiting in the process. A school friend recalled, "Some farmer would come into the office and start to tell her about his crops and she would pay him as much attention [as if he were] a brilliant doctor."[6]

As Tarbell's life centered more and more in Meadville, she tired of boarding with the Floods and declared independence by renting a room elsewhere. Finding that impersonal, unhomely, and therefore unsatisfactory, she looked for another solution. In time, she and three friends from the office—Jo Henderson, Harriet Carter, and Elda Long, the office manager—decided to live together "co-operatively." Some of the male students at Allegheny had boarded through such a plan and the magazine ran an article by feminist Mary Livermore proposing that different families should share food preparation and eat together so that woman's work would not needlessly be duplicated. Whatever inspired them, the arrangement probably worked along the lines Carter described in an article: "We had already cared for ourselves so long that each one had grown to be quite a business woman and had acquired that self-reliance and independence which are necessary to make work a pleasure. We proved to be a congenial company and very soon became fast friends. Being members of the same church and entering the same social circle, it seemed as if everything conspired to unite our interests. In private life alone we were entirely separated, four of us boarding—scattered about in different places—and one keeping house with her mother."[7]

The mother of one became "the mother of all" and managed the accounts. Two girls rented separate suites in her house, the others boarded nearby. For twenty-five dollars monthly, they shared kitchen and dining room and hired a maid and a washingwoman. Other women petitioned to join, but the four friends refused to expand their circle; they liked to be able to discuss the office over dinner.

Living in such a manner was innovative and daring, suggesting a commitment to the single state of life. These were not girls awaiting marriage, but women wanting homes of their own, privacy for their own pursuits, and a place where they could initiate and repay social invitations. As for domestic duties, these were farmed out for pay.

Cooking interested Ida only because her family did it well. She learned to make waffles, pie crusts, and Scotch woodcock only to show she could do it. She regarded domestic skills as "parlor tricks," and when finally called to cook for relations in her sixties, she termed the results "so tragic the family didn't speak of them."[8]

Domesticity was not for Ida or her closest girlfriends who were still unmarried in their late twenties, but she had to have noticed that she was missing out another kind of life—marriage, woman's "natural state." About this time Will, who had practiced law in the Dakotas for four years, returned to Titusville with his wife, bought a home near his parents, and joined the movement to rally independents against the Standard Oil Company. His wife gave birth to two daughters and a son. Ida adored the children, but showed no inclination to have her own. She was set on using her abilities in the world.

This state of mind is suggested by two unfinished pieces of fiction she began to write. In one, Margaret Sydney, "determined-looking" in the fashion of Tarbell heroines, had decided on a risky course. "She was not a young girl, was, as her family pointed out, beginning to be an old maid—nearly thirty with no idea of marrying—with the determination she'd had as a high school girl of good family of moderate means to make something of herself."[9]

Ida did not seriously entertain thoughts of any man, least of all a Mr. Kellogg who wanted to marry her. When they were old ladies, one of her co-workers reminded her about it in a letter. "Among the various things I told my young friend about you was the time Mr. Kellogg visited the Floods, how he took us all to the horse farm on an all-day trip and in the evening came to call at the Co-ops intending to propose to you. He had talked it over with Dr. Flood and you were warned. You begged Jo and me to stay in the parlor as long as he did so he couldn't have a private word with you."[10]

One cannot be sure of the identity of this gentleman, but a James H. Kellogg was active in Sunday-school activities and a frequent visitor to the assembly. Most works on Chautauqua cite him as a wealthy merchant and lifelong bachelor of Troy, New York, who in 1889 built Kellogg Hall, an administration building on the Chautauqua community grounds, as a memorial to his mother.[11]

Whether or not this was the fellow, *someone* offered marriage at some point. In late middle age she scribbled a note on a manuscript titled "Disillusion of Women" which read: "I never met a man I would want always at my side night and day and I am sure I will not. A man who even dreamed he would [want] me always by his side—he had his escape."

She did catch the eye of Meadville's most intriguing bachelor, a Judge John I. Henderson some fifteen years Ida's senior, who had been elected presiding judge of Meadville after fifteen years as district attorney. Apparently, he made overtures to Ida but was rebuffed. After she left Meadville, he wrote to her, but she reported to her parents: "Don't be alarmed. It is as informal as he is about as non-committal. He gives me a good deal of gossip . . ."

Both her family and Jo insisted he was interested in Ida, but Ida wrote: "I have a suspicion that you people think perhaps I am inclined to join in the countless victims that mark His Honor's path through life. I hope you'll dissuade yourself of the notion. If there is any victim at this picnic it isn't *I*."[12]

Perhaps the judge had encouraged many young women and Ida felt herself too smart to be fooled, but her letters show she seemed to think it shameful to be admired. She reported to her parents a man's attentions and then dismissed them with hauteur. "Don't worry, I'm not debasing myself," she seemed to tell them.

Up to this point, man was a creature she preferred in the abstract. As a shy adolescent, Ida had feared or shunned boys her own age and fantasized about males she could not even talk to. As a young woman who found work she loved, Ida had little time for men. Her mother's life and the family story of how she was forced to give up teaching after her wedding day were ample illustration that one did not combine marriage with any work outside the home. Even if one found a remarkable man who would allow his wife a career, the realities of pregnancy and child-rearing precluded life in an office. Only in the realm of fantasy was she safe. Ida was transported, or at least quite touched, when a man seemed heroic, his achievement outstanding, and his mind pure. One such male was a dashing rogue who convinced Meadville he was an army captain and sold Flood a story he had copied from a government report. Ida had the distinction of being taken driving by him—before he fled town in a borrowed military cape.

In the summers the Chautauqua Institute, a place of almost postcard Americana prettiness, drew distinguished lecturers who were also unavailable men attractive to Ida. John Pentland Mahaffy, an Anglo-Irish classics scholar at the University of Dublin, was eighteen years her senior and a special friend. He presented her with white poppy seeds from the Nile which she planted first in her mother's garden and later transplanted to her Connecticut farm.

Most visitors were touched by the Chautauquans' desire for knowledge; at the same time they were put off by their ignorant righteousness. Rudyard Kipling, boggled by the preponderance of book-reading girls overflowing the verandas, told one of them he was from India and was mistaken for a missionary. He was struck by the way the very people who said they would rather see their children dead than defile the Sabbath were the same ones who would try to sneak onto the grounds for free.

William James said of the community: "The moment one treads that sacred enclosure, one feels one's self in an atmosphere of success. Sobriety and industry, intelligence and goodness, orderliness and ideality, prosperity and cheerfulness, pervade the air . . . And yet what was my own astonishment, on emerging into the dark and wicked world again, to catch myself quite unexpectedly and involuntarily saying: 'Ouf, what a relief! Now for something primordial and savage, even though it were as bad as an Armenia massacre, to set the balance straight again. This order is too tame, this culture too second-rate, this goodness too uninspiring.' "[13]

Ida shared this view, while also feeling that fine work was being done there. The institute did not shy away from debate, even if it was over the heads of most Chautauquans. James was asked to speak on psychiatry. Controversial educators were also invited, including some innovators from Johns Hopkins University who were prominent in introducing social sciences like economics and local American history into college curriculums. One of these was Herbert B. Adams who later became a close friend. She wrote him asking him to show someone the institute and implored: "I don't want her to see only the surface Chautauqua. It would displease her as it always did me and if I don't mistake, does you."[14]

In her own life, writing was now the most important thing. Ida discovered she loved creating stories or at least beginning them, for they trailed off without conclusion. At night, fiction flowed from her pen and onto paper torn from old ledgers at *The Chautauquan*. Judging from surviving fragments, her creativity ebbed as quickly as it flowed. Once inspiration ran out, she laid the work aside, thus making the critical error of many unsure beginners.

Throughout her life she would protest that she never had "the writer's call," that she happened upon the profession and labored painfully until she could produce acceptable work, but the stories indicate she was passionately committed to writing.

In common with most writers, she wrote out of her own experience and obsessions. One heroine with literary ambitions was a source of fun to the author and to the mother Tarbell endowed her with: Jane considered her austere room an atelier and littered it with a writer's appurtenances. She had "twenty-nine varieties of pens, pen holders of twelve sizes, ink of all colors and spectrums, wood pulp blotters, mucilage and devices for ungluing postage stamps." One can imagine the adolescent Tarbell's microscope and scientific paraphernalia taking the place of the welter of stationery the character Jane acquired.

Ida also played with the concept of an "anti-utopia" based on the panoply of trusts which sprang up patterned after Standard Oil's organization. These included the American Cotton Seed Trust, the National Linseed Oil Trust and the Whiskey Trust. These symptoms of rampant industry had already been the butt of satire. In 1888, Edward Bellamy published *Looking Backward*, criticizing nineteenth-century capitalism from the vantage point of the year 2000 when, as he portrayed it, all would have been perfected through socialism and the higher instincts of man. Tarbell, like most of the reading public, was riveted.

More sarcastic than satirical, her own effort took the form of a letter suggesting that those who controlled trusts could become America's aristocrats: "There will come to exist a set of families with common interests—we'll have an Order of the Oyster, an Order of the Olive, the Order of the Poultry, according to the article which it controls. The wealth policy and privileges of order will descend from father to son. We will have at last a heraldry worthy of the nation of everlasting accumulation. In the [here she wrote and crossed out the word "Standard"] Order of Zinc, for instance, we shall have Smith I, Smith II, Smith III and so on from generation to generation."

From social comments on upward mobility she returned to fiction. Again incorporating her own experiences into her writing, she attempted a novel that would show how the oil business changed and divided those she knew. The plot revolved around the growing shadow that a sinister firm called M & M Vacuum cast over the boomtown of Pithole. A young man named Tom grew fascinated with oil and began to fall under the sway of an agent of M & M as he fell in love with Norah, daughter of a farmer who stood in the way of the firm's land grabs. Ida abandoned the work after about six thousand words, dissatisfied with her effort and convinced she lacked the ability to turn the story into art. Frustrated by fiction, she decided journalism might be more in her line.

Unlike botany, journalism was a field where women had made a place for themselves and Ida Tarbell could try to do the same. She could become the best on Dr. Flood's publication, but what if she tried herself outside the Allegheny foothills? In the fortnightly *Revue des Deux Mondes* she read the work of Ferdinand Brunetière, who wrote of French writers in terms of their evolution from predecessors and their contributions to the literary generations which followed. Above all, Brunetière insisted art should serve a moral purpose. With great constancy, she set about to follow his example. Her first major attempt, thorough but dauntingly ponderous, was "The Arts and Industries of Cincinnati," published in *The Chautauquan* of December 1886. She then took up a topic which concerned her more personally.

She purported to be interested in woman suffrage as a social issue rather than as a question of her own rights as a citizen. Jo Henderson and Harriet Carter were firmly against woman's franchisement; but before deciding, Ida wanted to know if women would accomplish more with the vote than men had, if woman's nature fit her for a public role, and how she could make a fruitful life for herself.

She was like a scientist considering what this gender, this subspecies of which she was a member, could accomplish. Could it invent? Could it contribute? She doubted woman would reform the world with the vote, but she was insulted by suffragists who said women had secondary status and inferior minds.

When *The Chautauquan* ran an article by Mary Lowe Dickenson saying that only ninety of twenty-two thousand patents issued one year went to women and that these were "merely" for household inventions, Ida was provoked. She traveled to the United States Patent Office in

Washington, D.C., and did her first investigative reporting. "I had been disturbed for some time by what seemed to me the calculated belittling of the past achievements of women by many active in the campaign for suffrage," she wrote fifty years later. "They agreed with their opponents that women had shown little or no creative power. That, they argued, was because man had purposely and jealously excluded her from his field of action. The argument was intended, of course, to arouse women's indignation, stir them to action. It seemed to me rather to throw doubt on [their] creative capacity ... I had seen so much of women's ingenuity on the farm and in the kitchen that I questioned the figures; and so I went to see, feeling very important if scared at my rashness in daring to penetrate a Government department and interview its head. I was able to put my finger at once on over two thousand patents, enough to convince me that, man-made or not, if a woman had a good idea and the gumption to seek a patent she had the same chance as a man to get one."[15]

She discovered that, although the article had said that women had won 334 patents in the history of the United States, the number was actually 935. In a four-thousand-word article, Tarbell claimed that it was no disparagement if women patented household devices—invention was invention: "Many of the patents suggest pictures at once pathetic and comical. Who cannot fancy the desperation into which the woman was driven who patented a preparation for kindling fires?" She cited contrivances for driving barrel hoops and improving train wheels and predicted women would innovate still more as industrial education increased.

Although she tried to vindicate her American sisters, Ida aspired to the achievements attributed to France and Frenchwomen. She was transported by the notion of a Parisian salon where worthy people gathered and matched wits, but writing for *The Chautauquan* did not allow her to give an unqualified endorsement to anything but Scripture.

Tarbell concluded that although Mme de Staël wrote novels and political observations, her life was unsatisfactory because she neither savored solitude nor learned contemplation of higher things. In Mme Manon Phlipon de Roland, however, she found her ideal. It appeared that this woman had influenced leading Republican and Girondist men to throw off the yoke of the king. An intellectual architect of the revolution, when she herself went to the guillotine her last words were "O Liberty! What crimes are committed in thy name!" Wife, mother, foe of the status quo and prominent personage, Mme Roland was the most powerful woman Ida had encountered and embodied all the traits Tarbell thought most admirable but would never admit she aspired to.

Had this legendary figure been alive—a lecturer at Chautauqua or a visitor to Meadville—Ida would have found her as vulnerable to scrutiny as leading feminists. As ever, idealizations appealed to her more directly than actual people.

In an article titled "The Queen of the Gironde,"[16] Tarbell portrayed Mme Roland as a studious girl, intellectually without sham. Manon Phlipon de Roland was, like Tarbell herself, a dutiful and studious woman of keen intellect. When finally obliged to marry, Manon Phlipon chose a man who gave her access to national power, but Tarbell described this as a fortuitous accident, not an inspired choice. Ida seemed unable to treat ambition—Mme Roland emerged as a force without personal assertiveness whose merit won her a role in events. Just as Ida lacked insight into how women traditionally got on in the world, she also lacked research material and was rankled by it. "Soon I became heartily ashamed of my sketches, written as they were from so meager an equipment. I felt this particularly about Madame Roland."[17] Indeed, the vision of Mme Roland was the spark that exploded the frustration within her.

Writing had become too important to be fitted in at the end of the day or early mornings. It required a concentration that could only be given in the best working hours. Her time and energy were owned by *The Chautauquan*, so she wrote what would be of use to it. T. L. Flood insisted her job was to edit. He told her she was no writer. Still, she kept on writing.

She was increasingly offended by the pseudoacademia of Chautauquan education, with its mock graduations complete with girls strewing flowers. Those around her were intellectually half asleep but seemed wholly satisfied with their limited forays into the world of ideas. Now an old maid of thirty-three, rooted in a secure world where she held a respected place, Ida felt established to the point of being trapped. She once wrote: "I had always a vision of myself settled somewhere in a secure corner, simple, not too large. I never had wanted things; I always had a dislike of impedimenta, but I wanted something cheerful and warm and enduring." Now that she had it, she knew it wasn't enough. She desired to do one thing well. Her job required that she do many things adequately. "The work I was doing demanded a scattering of mind which I began to fear would unfit me for ever thinking anything through."[18]

Visits home only aggravated her claustrophobia. Aside from Will's three young children, her family had remained exactly as they had been for decades. Her father's interests were still his Sunday-school class and the oil wells that remained to him. Her mother was concerned with escapes to the parental farm she had inherited and with unwelcome baby-sitting. Sarah alternated neurasthenia with a spinster's social life, and Will was consumed by the Elks Club and the independents' futile attempts to unite against the Standard.

Beckoned by the work of Brunetière and the shade of Mme Roland, Ida Tarbell began to think of revolt, of escape, of studying in Paris and writing Roland's biography. Visions of Paris, its medieval stones and the succulent sounds of French which she had taught herself to read fluently, made her believe something better was waiting for her and that she could seize it.

Now that she was on the brink of giving up security, she saw corroboration for the idea everywhere. She sensed a message the day an elderly visiting minister leaned over his lectern to shout to the congregation, "You're dying of respectability!" She saw an omen in the defeat of a gubernatorial candidate who had seemed a shoo-in. She grew increasingly confident of her decision to leave Meadville and all it had come to represent.

In her mind her plans worked beautifully and carried her forward to a new and happier, more profitable world; but when she broached the idea at "The Co-ops," she was assaulted by "good sense." "There were friends who said none too politely: 'Remember you are past thirty. Women don't make new places for themselves after thirty.' There were friends who resented my decision as a reflection on themselves. A woman whose friendship I valued said bluntly: 'You are one of us. Aren't we good enough for you?' "[19]

Ida deliberated and wavered, but at last the decision was made. She left her job precipitously, taking with her Josephine Henderson and Mary Henry. In effect, it was a walkout.

Flood's parting letter commended her as a "high-minded Christian woman whose strength and force of character he had learned to admire" and said he hoped her health would soon improve. However, it is too much to believe that three vigorous young women had been forced to resign simultaneously.

The Methodist community of western Pennsylvania and New York shared scanty bits of information about it for months. Half a year after her departure, Tarbell reported to her family: "Mr. Nichols put a note into his wife's letter in which he said he met Mr. Duncan of Chautauqua fame at Duluth in the summer, that they talked about me and that Mr. Duncan told him that Prof. Cumnock told *him* (Mr. D) 'how brutally' Flood acted about me." Ida also heard that Frances Willard told Flood: "I think that Miss Henry and Miss Tarbell probably had sufficient reasons for leaving as they did,"[20] but apparently, no one was so indecorous as to put the whole story in print and gladden the heart of a future biographer.

What could have caused them to leave? It is possible there was some impropriety, but more likely, Ida made some request, was denied it, and left. Flood never allowed any name but his on the masthead of *The Chautauquan.* Ida's title, one shared by others on the staff, was assistant editor. In 1889, Flood named his scrapegrace nineteen-year-old son Ned editor of the *Daily Assembly* summer paper. The following year Ned became associate editor of *The Chautauquan*. It is likely that Ida threatened to resign unless she received a promotion and in response Flood either fired her directly or forced her to resign.

Whatever happened, Ida was so uncomfortable about it that she mentioned it only in family letters. She loved a good joke even at her own expense and often mocked herself, but she was never casual about the Reverend T. L. Flood. In family letters she referred to having left *The Chautauquan* beaten. She felt she was a failure and a disgrace, rejected by the Lord, and was haunted by Flood's prediction that she would starve. The closest she ever came to saying she was fired was demurring that someone who had complimented her "must have been trying to comfort Mother for my beheading at Meadville when he made that pretty speech."[21]

Ida Tarbell had always derived a certain strength from being forced into a corner. Unceremoniously returned to Titusville, she was pressured into doing the bold and unexpected. She saw nowhere to go but Paris where she could study at the Sorbonne and write the story of Mme Roland. Since she had not been able to save much money, she would somehow have to earn some in France. What better way than by writing?

"I had heard of newspaper syndicates, and it occurred to me that I might write articles in Paris and syndicate them. I hadn't the faintest idea of how to go about it, and I took the hardest possible way. I went to Pittsburgh, Cincinnati and several other cities, saw the editors of the leading newspaper in each town, and explained my scheme. How I ever managed to sell them the idea I can't understand! But in some way I did persuade half a dozen editors to take articles from me, at six dollars an article."[22]

She now read French so well that she could translate articles for *The Chautauquan*, but doubted that she spoke fluently enough to get herself a room. She asked Titusville's Frenchman, a dyer named Séraphin Claude, to tutor her. Three times a week she went to his shop for conversation and lessons until he pronounced her sufficiently facile in common phrases.

She was an inspiration to Jo Henderson and Mary Henry who decided they too would come along to Paris, study French, and write syndicate letters of their own. She rejoiced at the news, partly because she wanted their company and partly because she wanted to share expenses.

She had broken free and was moving to a larger sphere. "It was not to be 'See Paris and die,' as more than one friend had jeered. I knew with certainty it was to be 'See Paris and live.' "[23]

PART II

EXALTATION

Four

Une Femme Travailleuse

"There is nothing more curious than the state of dilation of the American when he first sets foot in Europe. Reserve is broken, discretion is forgotten, sentiment glows. He returns for a period to the naive expansiveness of his childhood. Sometimes weeks pass before he recovers his normal attitude of mind, or he is shocked into a realization of his condition."[1]

Thus Ida Tarbell described her situation in August 1891. She had never known that a place could enfold her and captivate so completely. Strangers were responsive. Boys on the stairs tipped their hats, patrons greeted her in restaurants, and people on the street cared if she found her way. Everything seemed in harmony from the scale of the buildings to the gray facades coloring like a Monet painting in the play of sunlight.

Paris in the 1890s was a city renewed. Sacré Coeur was under construction, the Eiffel Tower and Gare Saint Lazare were spanking new, and electric lights had just begun to twinkle on the boulevards. The Paris of modern imagination had debuted, bringing with it the Impressionists, Marcel Proust, and anarchism. Above all, to Ida Tarbell, the city offered beauty and infinite possibility.

The cost of spiritual fulfillment was poverty, a bohemian poverty of twenty-cent bouillon dinners and penny tours of Paris atop a horse-drawn omnibus. If the diet was unvaried, the open-air rides seemed ever-new—traveling inside would have been twice as expensive and she would have seen only half as much.

With her were Jo Henderson, Mary Henry, and Annie Towle, a friend of Mary's from Evanston, Illinois, who was welcomed in part because she would pay a share of the rent.

Ida, a scant year older than Jo, announced that since she was the eldest, she was the chaperone and would look after all of them. She was so serious about her responsibility—despite the fact that she led them to the wrong pier before they boarded their steamer—that men they met on the boat nicknamed Ida "Mammy."

As leader, she focused their quest for rooms in the area of the Musée de Cluny because she liked its particularly French sound. After three days of inspecting bug- and odor-infested lodgings while trying to make themselves understood in French, Ida toted up the cost of their Right Bank hotel, plus fees for candles, soap, and fire, and convinced her companions of the merits of boarding in the house of Mme Bonnet which offered two tiny bedrooms, a salon, and a kitchenette commodious enough to hold a sink. They had dreamed of a French balcony, but settled for a window seat and learned to crane their necks to see the sky. By August 21, 1891, seventeen days after leaving Titusville, Ida was at work writing descriptions of Paris in her bedroom at 5 Rue du Sommerard.

Only on Sundays did she relax. Men they had met crossing the Atlantic drove Ida and her companions through the Bois de Boulogne in elegant barouches and took them to dinner at the Hippodrome. Ida sipped wine and quaffed beer with her gentlemen friends and dutifully wrote home about it: "You mustn't think I am getting Frenchy in my morals because I do things here on Sunday which I don't do at home. I only do these things to see what the French life really is."[2]

When the gentlemen expressed concern over whether they would be safe living in the Latin Quarter, Ida airily assured them that their nearest neighbor was a prince. Indeed, the Bonnet establishment was an improbable household of the kind possible only in student districts. Besides the quartet of Methodist maidens, it included members of the royal Tewfik family of Egypt. Mme Bonnet had told them that her only other boarder was a prince studying at Saint-Cyr Military Academy who only used his lodgings on weekends, but the Americans came home one night to discover they were living with eleven Mohammedans. They reacted as if they were confronting Ali Baba's band: "They wanted us to *dance*. Think of it! On Sunday night! We thanked them and explained in broken French that we did not do that in America on Sunday," Ida told her family. "They took it politely and whispered among themselves that we were *très religieuse*."[3]

The Egyptians wished to know about life in America, particularly marital customs, as they were interested in reforming the Muslim practice of not looking on their brides until after their weddings. One of the

Tewfiks was quite taken with Annie and she responded by going alone with him to the zoo. Ida was aghast and took great care to convince Annie not to do such a thing again, but the Egyptians' good-heartedness soon won Ida over.

Prince Said Toussoum was exceedingly handsome at age twenty, but Ida was taken by his boyishness. "I am growing very fond of the Prince," she wrote home. "He is such a simple-hearted fellow and it is a splendid lesson in politeness to see the way in which he makes everybody love him. I didn't suppose I would ever be willing to call anybody 'My Lord' but I do it with the greatest ease." She added that she had invited him to visit Titusville.[4]

One Sunday, Prince Said served Egyptian gumbo and personally prepared for them powdered coffee—a substance quite finer than the ground variety of Titusville. That night Ida joined in the dancing and when she left she took with her Prince Said's gift of a fez.

So close did they all become that the death of the khedive hit her as if it had been President Benjamin Harrison. The Egyptians mournfully passed around his picture, dwelt at length on the beauty of his wife, and speculated that one of their uncles would be elected president of the council. In their lamentations, they began to fear for their own health and talked of their hatred of English occupation. In sympathy, Ida herself grew irate. She raised her glass of *l'eau sucrée* [sugar and water] and drank repeatedly to roars of *"À bas l'Angleterre!"*

Prince Said Toussoum was more open-minded toward the British. He married an Englishwoman and died in Alexandria in his twenty-sixth year.

Although Ida persisted in thinking them childlike, the Egyptians were multilingual, having been schooled in Europe, and quite cosmopolitan. They were sensitive to slights, and Ida thought it was for that reason that they declined to visit on Thursday nights when the girls "received" acquaintances. In the beginning, the Americans' social life revolved around the McCall Mission, a community of American Protestants doing evangelical and social work in Paris, and occasional visitors from Meadville and Titusville.

Their weekly entertainment budget was twelve cents, but callers seemed not to mind. Ida described the evenings in a letter home: "Our salon is about as big as the west bedroom so you can imagine that *receiving* more than one is hard. We had seven last week. We borrow two cups and saucers of Madame and have three of our own and manage to give everyone a thimbleful of tea."

Eventually, the Tewfiks were persuaded to join in: "We delighted the Egyptians by telling them they are more like Americans than the French are. And they are! These French!! but I cannot describe them. You'd call me home by cable."[5]

Her disapproval of men amazed the Frenchwomen she met. After she complained that a man had interrupted her work in the Bibliothèque Nationale to flirt with her, her French teacher laughed and said that Ida was very modest and might have enjoyed being admired. "Isn't that Frenchy!"[6] Ida commented.

Inspired by everything around her, Ida let fanciful ideas about her Titusville French tutor Séraphin Claude and his wife play in her mind and filled the backs of steamer announcements with a story about them. Ida called it "France Adorée" and in it she revealed much of herself by creating characters who hid their feelings under feigned aloofness. The story, set in Paris, traces two couples: a devoted older married pair named Bonnet, after her landlady, and a young American man and woman who talk constantly about dedication to their work. Before leaving America for France, the heroine, named Bertha, has arranged for the Bonnets to see France one last time with her. But M. Bonnet dies on the boat just in sight of land, and Bertha promises the wife she will visit his Paris grave. In Paris she meets Scott (whom the author named after her nephew) and strikes up a friendship with him that centers around their studies and work. When she is ready to return home, she reveals this sentimental duty and asks Scott to tend Bonnet's grave so she can leave with a good conscience. After seeing this new side of Bertha, Scott responds with unexpected tenderness. The tale concludes: "Could it be that Scott had a vein of sentiment, too?" The reader is left to think they may meet again in America, but it is important to note that Tarbell leaves Scott not with a girl but a corpse.

Feeling that anything was possible now that she had come to France, Ida decided to submit her story to *Scribner's Magazine*. She balanced the fact that her manuscript was unsolicited against the fact that it had the cachet of a Paris postmark. After mailing it, she forced herself to forget about it. She returned to work on Mme Roland and to her one-woman newspaper syndicate.

She was eager to tell her readers how fine the French were. She had been warned that they were vicious, but she found them decent, polite, and enterprising, especially the women who had resolved the dilemma of work versus home by being partners with their husbands in family businesses. Their knowledge impressed her. Her landlady Mme Bonnet scoffed at the idea of education for women; at the same time she herself was well-read and sufficiently fluent in English to compose letters in that language at night when she couldn't sleep.

"To my surprise I found these people, working so busily and constantly, were not restless like the Americans; nor were they generally envious. I had a feeling that my concierge, who never had been across the Seine to the Right Bank, who lived in a room almost filled by her huge bed and its great feather puffs, who must have looked long at a sou before she spent it, would not have changed places with anybody in Paris."[7] If Balzac found the bourgeoisie scheming, and Zola portrayed them as hypocrites, Tarbell idealized them as respecting themselves and their tasks.

In turn, she noted that they regarded her single state "with a mixture of horror and commiseration which to a genuine American old maid is one of the most delicious things in the world to see."[8] They called her *"une femme travailleuse,"* a hard-working woman. "I was treated with respect because of my working quality. It was not saying that I should not have gone farther and faster if I had been a beauty, if I had had what they call charm and the fine secret of using it, but they were willing to take me for what I had."[9]

Starting out, Ida paced herself to the rhythm of the industrious bourgeoisie. She would arise at six and buy breakfast rolls and *café au lait*; write from eight to noon; then clear up for lunch, dress, and explore the city, returning at last for supper and an evening of reading. She read *Le Figaro* in particular as it gave her story leads.

She sent as many topics to as many newspapers as she could. The month she arrived the *Chicago Union Signal* published her report on Paris safety: "The woman who sees nothing while seeing everything and who preserves her countenance . . . can go to restaurants and find she is not by any means the only woman who is dining alone." She added the startling news that girls in cafés took out their compacts to check their appearances in public, but did not feel it advisable to add that these same mademoiselles openly nuzzled their escorts' shoulders.

In September 1891, the *Pittsburgh Dispatch* published her report that *Lohengrin* had been presented under police protection because anti-German sentiment still festered twenty-five years after the Prussian War; hunters were requesting to use the government's smokeless gunpowder; and that there was talk of reducing the number of hours Frenchwomen might work daily to ten.

The *Dispatch* introduced her work with the announcement that Miss Tarbell had a syndicate of prominent journals which she would furnish with a series on Parisian municipal affairs: "From what we know of Miss Tarbell, she is bound to make a place for herself in American literature," it said. As autumn gave way to winter, all her editors seemed pleased, but not one was inclined to pay.

She told herself that poverty was picturesque. At the Bibliothèque Nationale, where she worked almost daily, the poor came in to warm their toes and groom themselves with broken combs. Those snapping the frayed threads of their clothes were often too old to work, were victims of the bankruptcy of the Panama Company, or they were deposed aristocracy. From her bedroom window, Tarbell often watched "The Countess," a tall white-haired woman who lived in a garret across the street. Wearing a gown and cape of faded and patched silk, she turned over the contents of the garbage cans scavenging for food. Tarbell saw the poor as gallant and convinced herself that if they could survive so could she.

On November 12, 1891, her first payment arrived—six dollars from the *Cincinnati Times-Star*. When her calculations revealed that her fee amounted to four words per penny, she realized that she had never worked harder for so little. Still, at least now she could buy shoes. Focusing her next article on the poor, she volunteered to work at a soup kitchen in Faubourg Saint Antoine where people had once gathered to storm the Bastille. While researching how the city licensed its beggars, she bought a preprinted fortune from a blind man. It read: "You are going to have an uncomfortable affair with a young person, but two of your friends will console you and introduce you into better society. You will spend many happy days in a great city, but at last your interests will force you to leave. Afterward surrounded by friends and all the pleasures of life, you will see your days pass happily by."

The mendicant's prediction proved nearly correct, if the affair with the young person and the consoling friends are interpreted as referring to a group of people Ida met when her Sorbonne classes opened after traditional postvacation delays in November.

Americans found each other quickly in the Latin Quarter and Ida soon grew close to a group of young scholars connected with Johns Hopkins University: John and Ada Vincent, Fred and Mary Emery, and Charles Downer Hazen, a young historian whose specialty was the French Revolution. Hazen was eleven years Ida's junior and so short he came only to her chin. Although he was well aware of the need to carve out a career, he was easily distracted by simple desultory loafing. After she mentioned him in several letters, her family began to tease her. She replied that he was "the dearest little fellow in the world and Mary Henry's particular friend (you see I am careful to explain that he isn't mine. And don't any more misunderstand about my relation to *boys*)."[10]

Ida's desire to do literary work, which her family found so alien, was a matter of course to the Johns Hopkins men. Now the social life of Ida and her roommates moved beyond the McCall Mission. In this new group their animation could be unbridled and Ida, who ordinarily had a shy primness in the presence of strangers, soon forgot herself and entered in. Once, en route to Saint-Germain-en-Laye and the tombs of French kings, a hapless Frenchman entered their train compartment. They took out their guidebooks and simultaneously read aloud until they drove him from their midst. Later, Ida showed off by plucking a yellow posy from the tomb of England's exiled James II.

In couples they went to see the cancan. In the Moulin Rouge, a vast dance hall glowing with rosy-orange gaslights, the air was full of the scent of rice powder and tobacco. Toots from a powerful brass band heralded the arrival of high-kicking risqué dancers in long skirts which they tossed above their heads. The garden outside offered roving monkeys, a mammoth wooden elephant which opened like a Trojan horse to reveal an orchestra, and a comic who "sang" opera through his derriere. One can only guess Ida's reaction to all this and speculate as to whether she ever noticed a man about twenty-seven years old, pince-nez on his nose, swaying his small body forward with the aid of a cherry wood cane and answering to the name of Toulouse-Lautrec.

Ida reported her experience in a comparatively short paragraph placed between news of the Sorbonne and an excursion to Saint-Germain. "I'm not going to do anything I daren't tell—if I can help it," she wrote as if she were a woman teetering between childhood and adolescence, "but here goes—I have been to see the *can-can* ... It was intensely interesting you may be sure. We went to a place called the Moulin Rouge (Red Mill). The outside is built like a mill and painted red. The huge blades of the wheel, which revolves, are filled with red lights. There was a stage performance which wasn't at all bad and a great deal of good music. There was no noise, drunkenness or disorder."

Perhaps evil is as evil thinks—perhaps she really did not know why groups of girls sat around at little tables soliciting for their gentlemen friends, but clearly she did sense something vaguely disturbing: "When I get home I'll tell you what I saw. Someway I don't like to write it. *Strange*, isn't it?"[11] Titillation wasn't something Ida knew how to describe.

Ida and her Americans made a particular point to go to all the art exhibitions and to note what was new: "What is called the Impressionist School have several pictures and they are very interesting though not always particularly beautiful. It is surprising to see the way some of these French men handle color. The blues and greens fairly *howl* they are so bright and intense."[12]

In her own life there were sharp contrasts of tone and intensity. Ida had lost a sale to the *Dispatch* because overseas mails were slow; she was worried about her sister's health and the suicide of her father's partner, which left Franklin liable for debts. All at once a bonanza of communications arrived. First, Bishop Vincent wanted her to teach in Calcutta, suggesting that literary work might open up there. This she ignored. *Harper's Bazaar* bought her story on blue-and-white Copenhagen china and encouraged her to submit more. The McClure Syndicate asked her to write on "Marrying Day in Paris" for a munificent ten dollars. And finally, *Scribner's Magazine* sent a check for one hundred dollars—almost as much as she had brought with her from America. Ida read the letter in one amazed glance—the editors said they would accept "France Adorée," her story about her French tutor, provided they could make some changes.

As Mary Henry announced triumphantly that they could now move to the Champs Elysées, Ida sat down weeping with joy. Here was vindication for all she had endured at the hands of T. L. Flood. Success at *Scribner's* canceled out failure at *The Chautauquan*. Here was the first proof that there was a place for her outside Meadville.

Scribner's editors asked her permission to condense the beginning of her story and improve the Bonnets' broken English. In the first thrill of acceptance, Ida sat down and wrote a gushing letter saying how right they were to ask for these changes and how foolish she had been not to have done that in the first place. Rereading it, she realized her gratitude was making her grovel. She destroyed her first letter and wrote a simple reply thanking them for accepting the manuscript and inquiring if they would be interested in a short biographical series on Mme Roland written from the standpoint of newly released material. It was the first formal step toward publication of her projected book.

Far more than her syndicate's success, the sale allowed Ida more freedom to plan what she wanted to do with her time in Paris. She had been toying with the notion of taking a degree but decided to enroll only in those classes which would further the biography.

She decided to extend her stay to two years, hoping at the end of that time to have a manuscript to submit to a publisher, possibly even the august Charles Scribner and Sons. Knowing she would not go back to Titusville for years made choosing her first Christmas decorations especially poignant. Fashionable jewelry stores displayed cakes of diamonds and bouquets of rubies and pearls. She lingered before the windows of religious supply houses gazing at the life-sized Nativity scenes until she settled at last on a little ceramic dog, a model of the ruffled canines owned by rich Parisians, to send to Titusville as a Christmas present to her entire family.

Ida and her roommates were homesick at Christmas, but they made a family of themselves and gave each other five-cent presents. Ida's gifts reflected the long hours she worked and the items she had to borrow. She received a candlestick, a pen so she would no longer have to use Annie's, a paper knife, French flags, and a pipe to curl her hair with. "Nobody in Paris had more fun, I'm sure, than we. It isn't money after all that makes the best of things,"[13] she wrote home.

The Tarbells had no cause to complain that Ida never wrote them. She was as faithful in her letters to her family as some are to their diaries, and she had the strange habit, which her father shared, of signing her full name: "Lovingly, Ida M. Tarbell" or "Ida M.T." Judging from her missives, Ida missed her family, worried about being so far away from them, and felt guilty about being in Paris when she could have been helping them at home. She did not write of those moments when she was nearly mad with love of Paris or when she thought she could not bear to again live in the United States, but she insisted on knowing every detail of their lives. If a week passed without a letter from Titusville, she was furious. She once lashed out: "This is a rather large piece of paper, but I think I can fill two sides of it in scolding you. I am in a very bad state of mind to be candid. I have had no letter from you this week and I am cross in consequence."[14]

Esther did her best to fill her absent daughter's request and sent ten-page letters whose bulk never failed to amaze Ida's landlady. Under orders to tell everything, Esther wrote letters that were streams of discontent. She said she found peace only in Hatch Hollow and complained about her daughter-in-law Ella: she was always ill when company came and either lay abed with nameless vapors or returned to her parents in Illinois, leaving Esther to cook for Will. "When I was sick no one took care of my children—they were left to run wild while I struggled back on my feet,"[15] she once wrote. But of Ida, Esther never complained. She expressed her love and joy over Ida's progress: "It is all so much more than you could have expected when you left America."

Esther was the family correspondent, but Sarah and Ida sometimes exchanged private letters. In these, Ida was much jauntier. Letters from Sarah, who was now almost thirty, were not so full of fun and often brought Ida pain. News that Franklin's partner had committed suicide, leaving him responsible for debts, came from Sarah. So did word that Sarah had told a Mrs. Chamberlain the full story of Ida's troubles with Flood. She wrote that the woman was on Ida's side and that her family had never liked Flood: "They all thought Dr. Flood could do the meanest little things of any man they knew and shan't tell our folks I said anything."[16]

The sisters' relationship is not entirely clear. The six years' difference in age which had made Ida an occasional baby-sitter in her youth was insignificant in their adulthood. Sarah had lent Ida money to help her finance her stay in Paris, something which haunted Ida when she learned that Sarah's surgery (the exact nature of which is unknown) incurred medical expenses. She had implored her family to sell some of her own household possessions—particularly a treasured rug—but that had not proved necessary.

As Sarah recuperated, she occupied her time with the craze for spiritualism until she and Will's wife suspected they had contacted Ella's late grandfather and gave up in fright. Sarah's more serious pursuit was painting.

Franklin Tarbell built a studio for Sarah in an upstairs room with a window so large it was like a wall of glass. Unfortunately, Titusville had an inordinate number of cloudy days when Sarah had to contemplate the exhibitions Ida wrote about from Paris instead of painting her own works.

Sarah Asenath Tarbell was a feisty woman with as much spirit as her mother and elder sister, but less stamina to support it. Her health was a worry until her late twenties, and she seemed also to have allowed herself to be tied to home. Will once wrote Ida unsympathetically of the relationship between Sarah and Esther—"the old series of making each other sick" is the way he described it—but they were also overcome by tears whenever they left each other for long.

However much Ida worried about her family, her own poverty was a greater problem. As winter began to make its chill presence felt, Ida burned coal in her grate. She would sit with knit slippers pulled over her shoes and her shawl about her knees and would don her mackintosh before slipping under the covers. The romance of the garret gave way to its squalor. She learned the first lesson of bohemian living: appearances matter less than keeping warm. She now wore the skirt Sarah had given her three years before over her flannel underwear and used some precious savings to buy thick shoes to withstand the rain and cold. Always susceptible to colds, she had four in the first three months in Paris and worried that she was coming down with the influenza which had half the city bedridden. After a bout of intense work or prolonged celebrations with her friends, she would spend the next day prostrate with fatigue, treating herself with what the French called St. Raphael, a solution of quinine and water. She blamed the milk for upsetting her stomach and began a lifelong habit of drinking her coffee black.

When "France Adorée" appeared in May 1892, she became a minor celebrity in the American community. After services at the American Church on Rue de Berri, acquaintances, including Theodore Stanton, head of The Associated Press in Paris, and Mrs. Whitelaw Reid, whose husband was the minister to France, sought her out.

Her projected biography of Mme Roland began to interest them and she was asked to lecture on the subject. A few months in Paris had made Manon Roland more real to her, more intelligible. Ida could now imagine her as a child on the Pont Neuf and as a condemned woman in the Conciergerie. By now the biographer herself had stood there and realized what a moral and spiritual triumph it must have been for Mme Roland to read at appointed hours each day, then write of her life as outside the mob cried for her head. In Sorbonne classes on political economy, French revolutionary history, and sixteenth-century literature, the age which made Manon Roland possible became clearer. Ida conveyed this so well that she was asked to repeat her addresses, and she began to think of lecturing as a way to support herself during her visits home.

But interrupting her work on Madame Roland or her Sorbonne studies to prepare speeches and write five- and ten-dollar articles—for which she might not ever receive the checks—was excruciating and reduced her to tears she was too proud to shed before roommates.

During the week she would restore herself by sitting in the cavernous hush of the Cathedral of Notre Dame, staring at the rose windows with their circles on circles of violet-tinged light. The motif drew her mind into order and silenced the clatter of fears and promises, obligations and possibilities, the endless discord that filled her head.

Attending Catholic Mass also soothed her. In an ancient unknown tongue (despite Latin studies at Allegheny College), the words could not be filtered or evaluated by her mind. They were simply there to be felt. The rhythm of the chanting calmed her brain, the incense and the colors beguiled her senses. Her need to feel overcame her need to know, and she felt a oneness with these French whom she believed must be affected in the same way.

Financial uncertainties and cramped living conditions sometimes made her think she should turn back. After a troubled American woman of her acquaintance was arrested for shoplifting and the consul told Ida he could not help because he was busy intervening in a compatriot's paternity suit, Ida cynically questioned whether women were wise to go out on their own.

What woman had ever succeeded on her own terms? she wondered. She thought Frances Willard and her colleagues in the temperance and suffrage movements too strident to be held up as positive examples.

The loneliness, hard work, and poverty she experienced seemed to be signs that she was somehow inadequate. She assumed that men managed more easily. Fred Emery and John Vincent had the comfort and support of their wives. Downer Hazen had natural ability. Ida Tarbell had only her will. Mary Emery was content in the role of wife, was in fact jealous when she thought Ida and other women were too friendly with her husband. Ada Vincent, for all her work copying paintings each day in the Louvre, did not drive herself as Ida did because she had the responsibility and security of John. For Jo and Mary and Annie, Paris was an adventure. They would soon return home and take up their lives. Ida alone wanted something else, but she was without a model.

Contributor to *Scribner's*, assorted American newspapers, and the McClure's Syndicate, Ida felt she was not so much succeeding as being unnatural. Ambition was a quality that she thought woman should never dare to name or avow. Standing outside, Ida looked into the warm little circle of what women were supposed to be and conjured up the image of domestic bliss they were supposed to enjoy. She had never seen it in the lives of women closest to her, in her mother, her aunt, her sister, or sister-in-law, but she believed that other women had that domestic security, even if she could not.

In late spring of 1892, her roommates left for home. Ida felt the pang of abandonment, but her spirit grew freer now that she did not live among the hubbub of missing curling papers and girlish pranks. The Johns Hopkins crowd were a decade younger than she, but Ida Tarbell was one of them. Most women of thirty-four would have had children and husbands to tend. Not so with Ida Tarbell, who in her mid-thirties was enjoying the self-absorption of student days.

Her lack of service to others created in Ida's mind a debt to fate, and she awaited calamity to balance the luck. It came one spring night. She had picked up the evening papers outside her door and, as usual, scanned the news from America. "Cloud burst—awful fires—Titusville all wiped out save the depot—150 killed." Envisioning her entire family clad in their nightshirts clinging to the cupola on the roof, she wondered in horror if she would ever see them or her home again.

Additional papers provided more harrowing details. Titusville had been hit by both fire and flood. Oil Creek had overflowed its banks and the high waters had dislodged large tanks of flammable materials which ignited. Sixty lives were lost and property damage had been great. After a long sleepless night, she received a telegram. She braced herself against the wall, then let out a shriek as she read its one word—"Safe!"

Purged of her worst fears and superstitious guilt, she worked with renewed enthusiasm. Having faced the prospect of leaving France to nurse her family, she set about the business of staying and enjoying it with her friends and especially with Downer Hazen. The man she described in letters home as "Mary Henry's little friend" was growing closer to her, drawn probably by her air of self-sufficiency and her earnest industriousness.

For her part, the better Ida knew Downer, the more she liked him. He was safe—so much younger, and so inexperienced in the practical world. He had no inkling of the kind of pragmatism she had had to develop during her years at *The Chautauquan*. She could feel she still had the upper hand. He was too young and naive to try to dominate her or inspire her to confusing emotions. Yet he looked after her when they went sight-seeing, and she always enjoyed his conversation which ranged from gossip to the French Revolution. He agreed that marriage was confining, that one must be free to pursue one's own path. Twenty-four-year-old Hazen may have inspired her to make this observation about Mme Roland: "A woman who preserves her illusions, her enthusiasms, her sentiments as Madame Roland had up to thirty-eight, rarely finds in a man much older than herself the faith, the disinterestedness, the devotion to ideals, the purity of life and thought which she demands. She is continually shocked by his cynicism, his experience, his impersonal attitude, his indifference. Life with him becomes practical and commonplace. It lacks in hours of self-revelation, in an intimacy of all that she feels deep and inspiring; there is no mystery in it—nothing of the unseen. But with a young man of character and nature like [Roland's lover] Buzot, she finds a response to her noblest moods, her most elevated thoughts."[17] Now in her thirties, Ida enjoyed youthfulness in a man as much as she enjoyed the mature experience of older men.

She and Downer Hazen would sit for hours in cafés, she describing Mme Roland's essays, he talking out his theories on the French Revolution and insisting on uncomplicated enjoyment of being where they were. They would linger until she insisted that she had to go home, that she had to get up early. But he would gladly have stayed for hours and slept late the next day. They once grew so engrossed in the moonlight on the broken wall of Pierrefonds Castle and tarried so long behind the others that even John Vincent called their behavior improper.

They spoke of subjects closest to them, of their families and the confinement of small-town life. She could talk to him as she had never spoken to anyone else, because he was from outside her world. For each, Paris had been an escape from their families, however much they loved them. To each other they could speak of the deficiencies and mediocrities of Titusville, Pennsylvania, and Saint Johnsbury, Vermont, places which had permanently molded them, but of which they were never wholeheartedly a part.[18]

There was no pretense with Hazen, no keeping up of appearances. He had not come into her mother's parlor after school nor was he ever likely to appear on the streets of Meadville, and he was intellectually keen and educated. He had her passion for French culture, her avidity to know and understand and transmit knowledge.

But for Tarbell, tenderness did not kindle into love. She was able to savor a man's company to the point of giddiness, yet not dream of him when he was out of her sight. She did not worry about his opinion of her, or whether she would see him again. She took what was there for the taking and never fretted about the rest. Peace of mind was perhaps offset by loss of passion, but whether this was a deficiency or an advantage is impossible to tell.

Thus she was able to console herself when Hazen and the Hopkins crowd left France. Ida planned to get even more work done, but she described herself in a letter as feeling like a tree without limbs, so much of her life was being lopped off. She now lived in the smallest room in Mme Bonnet's new house at 17 Rue Malebranche. She had lace curtains at her windows, a huge desk, a little closet, and a big velvet chair to hide her garbage pail. She stored provisions on the balcony and only when she craved a beefsteak did she go out for meals.

To pay for French lessons—for she had redoubled her determination to become fluent now that she had no Americans to talk to—she tutored a young Hungarian baron in English. In letters home she wistfully described a deliberately lonely life—she had cut out larking, she now spent time only with people involved with her work.

Loss, however, encouraged metamorphosis. The cosmopolitan phase of her Paris adventure began. It arrived in the form of a hatless man in her doorway, breathless from bounding up four flights of steps. He was towheaded and pale, with eyes that caught the color around them and seemed to change from blue to hazel. As he talked, his voice was like scissors, clipping sentences and words and giving urgency to everything he said.

This was the editor Samuel Sidney McClure. He brought to her serious quarters the scent of action which interested her as library research never could. If he did not change the course of her life, he accelerated it, demanded the best of her, and so energized her that she became not merely competent but a force in journalism.

They would both always remember this meeting, retell the tale to others such as Guglielmo Marconi, Robert Louis Stevenson, and H. G. Wells over lunch when their magazine was the most prominent forum in America. Years later, when they were both old curiosities of Americana, when they had said and done painful, unforgettable things to each other, they would regale a class of Columbia University history students with the story of that afternoon when they had been young and everything had been before them.

Samuel McClure, a man meant for the jet age, was imprisoned in a time of steamships. He had things to do, ground to cover, and work to accomplish, all in an instant. His joys were intense, his confidence intense, and his fears, when he allowed himself to have them, were intense too. His nonstop vigor captivated Ida until the day she came to think of it as mania.

Irish by birth, Sam McClure had come to America as a penniless, fatherless boy of nine with his widowed mother and three younger brothers. Even then his hallmarks were curiosity and restless energy. A friend once told him: "Be idle once in a while! You will be all worn out before you are thirty-five."[19] But he was thirty-five when Tarbell met him, and he felt he was just beginning.

He had worked his way through Knox College in Illinois where he made friends who helped him seize control of the student newspaper. One of these boys was John Phillips in whose home he encountered something which awed him—a whole stack of magazines. As he was an insatiable reader and quite poor, the Phillips' ability to stock thirty-five-cent magazines seemed the height of affluence. McClure became almost a part of the Phillips family.

After graduation, McClure worked his way East selling pots and pans and asking people what they liked to read. He reached Boston, landed a job editing a magazine for cyclists, and hired Phillips to assist him. A year later, McClure moved to *The Century* magazine and Phillips went to study literature at Harvard and Leipzig. Then McClure started a newspaper syndicate with his wife Hattie as his chief assistant, but once children started coming along—there were four by the time Ida met him—Hattie concentrated on motherhood. When Phillips returned from abroad, McClure met him at the dock with the announcement that they were going to syndicate features to newspapers around the country. They started their service, but McClure had dreams of starting his own magazine. In the early 1890s, *Scribner's*, *The Century*, and *Harper's Magazine* presided over the publishing scene. They were highly literate and, for those times, lavishly illustrated. McClure wanted to match their quality while treating his readers to lively journalistic style.

Breakthroughs in the technology of printing made it possible for McClure to realize his dream. The new process of photoengraving and the development of cheap glazed paper allowed publishers to make illustrations from photographs instead of costly drawings and wood engravings. Whereas the august trio of *Scribner's*, *The Century*, and *Harper's* charged thirty-five cents an issue, McClure figured he could sweep in and grab readership by asking only fifteen.

But to Samuel McClure, good writers were essential to a magazine, and in Ida Tarbell's work he saw the clarity and reportage he had in mind. One day in New York, McClure had seen her article "The Paving of Paris by Monsieur Alphand." McClure perused it and said, "This girl can write. I want to get her to do some work for the magazine."[20]

When McClure was in Europe, he made a special detour to talk to her in Paris. Confident of her writing skill, he wanted to test her editorial judgment so he asked her to evaluate an article he was planning to publish on the newly discovered, almost otherworldly family legends of the Brontë family. Whatever she said, he approved of both her assessment and the lady herself. He asked her to return to America immediately to help him with *McClure's Magazine*.

He allowed her time to think it over, but he made a final request— could he borrow forty dollars? They had talked past the hour when the banks closed. She quickly gave him the money. Then, after McClure left and the effects of his personality wore off, she told herself she was a fool: he'd never remember to repay her and she would never dare remind him of the loan. But the next day, to her surprise, his London office wired the funds.

His job offer tempted her. In exactly the time she had allowed herself, she had secured an opening on a magazine, but now Ida wanted more. She was halfway into her book on Mme Roland and refused to give up her long-cherished dream for one more immediate. She wrote her family of McClure's offer: "It would be a good joke on the Mogul (Flood), wouldn't it? To go back into an editorial position as good as the one with McClure will be within a year of my scalping? But I shall not do it if I'm going to make this literary business go—if there is anything in me."[21]

She declined his offer of a job in New York, but agreed to work for him as a free-lancer in Paris. *Scribner's* editor had also mentioned to Ida the possibility of a future position, but McClure set her to work immediately. *Scribner's* represented the scholarly pursuits she thought she wanted, but the McClure enterprise promised action and excitement. It would not, alas, deliver the income he promised. Common wisdom said one needed two hundred thousand dollars to found a magazine; McClure and his partner had seventy-three hundred between them. McClure would later say that if they had had fifteen thousand they would not have known an anxious moment, but as it was they knew many, and their inability to pay writers—including Arthur Conan Doyle and Stephen Crane—caused Ida Tarbell many unhappy days in Paris. In the heady first months, however, McClure raised her spirits. Her first assignment was to interview the literary women of France, a task which perfectly suited her inclinations.

Ida had been seeking proof that a woman was capable of doing serious and well-informed writing and in these writers she found it. More remarkably, they demonstrated something she had never seen—women helping each other professionally. Ida wrote home enthusiastically about Thérèse Bentzon: "She gave me all the points for my sketch of her and told me about her friends. Better than that, she took a lively interest in *me* and asked all about my plans and has promised to introduce me into a lot of places generally sealed to foreigners . . . It's a great strike and if she does half she offers to I'm in an El Dorado of opportunity."[22]

Marie Thérèse de Solmes Blanc, a noblewoman who wrote under the name of Th. Bentzon, had been a close friend of George Sand and a lady-in-waiting at the court of Louis Napoleon and was forced to support herself by her pen after an unfortunate marriage. Now fifty-two, obliged to compete with younger writers and fearing she was growing stale, she was embarking on an eight-month tour of America, but before she left she led Ida to other prominent figures.

One of these was Mlle Séverine, née Caroline Rémy Guebhard, who had created a stir by interviewing the pope. Her specialty was advocacy journalism, and she campaigned for jobs for chosen individuals and funds for the poor. She dismissed criticism of such stunts as the product of envy. Ida quoted her as saying: "Jealousy of a woman's success is, after gallantry, the most difficult thing a French woman trying to support herself has to bear from the men she meets."

Tarbell's account, carried by the *Boston Transcript* on October 20, 1893, expressed surprise that this woman was no suffragist. She cited La Séverine's letter to the Woman Suffrage League of France, declining to be a political candidate: "I do not see the pleasure of universal suffrage, whatever the sex which participates in it, and it isn't when an apple is rotten that it should be bitten. . . . Since I am so far 'behind' as a woman, so proud of the self-denying and maternal role which nature has given me that I do not care to attempt to overthrow masculine ambitions, and so 'advanced' as a blue stocking that I am rather skeptical of the usefulness of a vote, I feel I am ripe only to abstain." Consciously or not, Tarbell closely paraphrased these words in a private letter twenty years later.

Tarbell was more amused than inspired by Jeanne Dieulafoy. Archaeologist and author of a book on Persia, she smoked cigars and wore, with the necessary permission of the French government, men's trousers. She explained she had picked up this strange habit when she went on excavations with her late husband. Ida found her a "pretty man" of immaculate if incongruous appearance who delighted in patting Ida on the knee to make her blush. Dieulafoy encouraged her to write a history of women starting with Eve. The idea did intrigue Ida, but what actually resulted was "The Relation of Woman to the French Institute." In this Ida said that woman's impact on the Académie Française was indirect—Voltaire had attributed his election to Mme de Pompadour and remarked it was more important to be on good terms with the king's mistress than to have written a hundred volumes. Quite dispassionately, perhaps in agreement that women should be forced to meet the highest standards, Tarbell expressed the hope that a woman of exceptional talent would be the first elected so as to make admission to the academy "comparatively simple for women of lesser talent." (That first place was offered in 1981 to Marguerite Yourcenar.)

Had selection been up to Ida, the academy might have admitted Arvède Barine. In private life Mme Cécile Vincens, Barine had translated Tolstoy's "Souvenirs" and written sketches of George Eliot, Mary Wollstonecraft, and Jane Carlyle. Thanks to Ida's efforts she had also appeared in *The Chautauquan* in translation, but Barine may not have been informed of that fact. Barine minimized her achievements although they involved mastery of Russian, Italian, English, German, Swedish, Norwegian, Spanish, and French. In Barine, Ida saw a vision of herself as she wished to be. Her description for the *Boston Transcript* called "A Paris Press Woman," and published December 16, 1893, was close to the highly personal *I*-littered style of 1890s French periodicals.

In that piece, Ida summed up woman's progress in journalism: they had succeeded as editors, journalists, and novelists—in all areas where "pluck, prompt action and racy writing are necessary," yet women had not produced a writer of "sustained, brilliant, virile, authentic biographical, historical or scientific articles." Women advanced by their grace, fancy, and femininity, not by "their grasp of a subject, their largeness of learning, their skill in treatment." She saw a place to be filled: ". . . the woman who has the power and the learning to do scholarly and interesting magazine articles and reviews will win appreciation and position long before she has to go a-begging. However . . . an apprentice as a reporter and editor is not enough. Sincere study with constant writing are the only means by which one can arrive at the goal."

Six years earlier she had written that ambitious women could succeed as journalists provided they had a rare constellation of talents—power to work incessantly, varied knowledge, a good English style, self-control, and the power of growing. Now she saw that these could take a woman only to the second rank. In order to excel in letters, a woman must understand and interpret facts as well as know them. Tarbell proclaimed that the accomplished female must possess "the power to grasp immediately the salient features of a subject, to see its true color and to add to it facts, comparisons, opinions which shall help others to comprehend your exposition of it. It means the power to express all this in easy clear language with enough humor to entertain, enough seriousness to impress without fatiguing. The power to write in this way is not a natural gift, nor is it attained in two or three years of practice. It is the result of a ripened mind and long practice." At the end of this article on Barine she admitted she had written it to provide a model to women in American journalism who wished to do serious and lasting work but did not know how to go about it. "It is not an easy model which I offer, I admit. But it is worth following."

She had written her manifesto.

Five

The French Salon

The French literary world was now open to Ida, good fortune she credited to her ability to get names mentioned in American periodicals. She was judicious about where she went and how often she visited, because she could not easily repay hospitality. Jo, Mary, Annie Towle, and she had had at homes during which they boiled tea on an alcohol lamp, but she could not imagine Mme Blanc enjoying such "a lark" nor could she picture Arvède Barine conversing in Ida's room at Rue Malebranche. But with her serviceable black dress, quick wit, and professional contacts, she did enter French intellectual society.

Through Mme Blanc she met a writer for the *Revue des Deux Mondes* who invited her to join an opera party that evening, adding that she must go décolleté. Agreeing nonchalantly, Ida sped home, cut the sleeves from her light silk dress, removed the collar, and attached a mass of tulle. By the time the writer arrived to fetch her, she had managed to find a feather for her hair. Now she could sit in a box at the Opéra beside two women dripping diamonds, across from the president of the republic, and convince herself, as she smoothed out her long gloves, that she managed to hold her own. No one would guess that she wrote home that night begging her family to send one- two- and three-cent stamps which she could sell at a profit to tide her over while she waited for McClure's checks. She also asked for the names of notables (Franklin, Washington, and Andrew Jackson) commemorated on the stamps in case she was asked. Before sealing the letter, she enclosed a lock of hair. "Observe the color," she demanded. "If you don't think I suffer from being away from my family, look at that."[1]

Work—and going hatless—had dulled it. Paris was experiencing its hottest summer ever recorded. Ida routinely arose at six, thirsty and fighting fleas, reached the Bibliothèque before it opened and spent the day poring over Mme Roland's papers. "I could not afford to hire anyone to copy them for me, so I did it all myself. I wasn't experienced enough to know just what I should need; anyway, I was afraid I might have to go home before the book was finished. So I copied endless pages. When the library closed, I would go down to the Seine and take a ride on one of the little steamers to rest and cool off. I could afford this for it cost only three cents."[2]

Living research material was soon provided. Through the English poet Mary Robinson and her scholarly French husband James Darmesteter, Ida gained an introduction to Léon Marillier, the great-great-grandson of Manon Phlipon Roland, and a professor of the École des Hautes Études at the Sorbonne. Not only did he freely lend her a large number of essays which Roland had prepared at the age of twenty on topics from "Suicide" to "The Good Man" and drafts of letters to her girlhood friend, but he also introduced her to the family circle which included his mother Cécile and her lover, Charles Seignobos, who had been the family tutor and was now crowned by the academy for his scholarship in history.

Ida became a regular at the Marillier salons, meeting there people like Lucien Herr whose protégés in socialism included both Léon Blum, future premier of France, and Jean Jaurès, a future Socialist party leader.

Ida, nicknamed "Mademoiselle Mees" (for "Miss"), was one of the rare women at these gatherings. Polite society had closed to Mme Marillier after she left her husband to live openly with her sons' former tutor. Madame both welcomed the female companionship Ida offered and was sometimes jealous of the acceptance the American woman enjoyed. Irrationally fearing that she would soon die, and possessing the magnanimity of many Frenchwomen toward their young lovers, Mme Marillier wanted Seignobos, fifteen years her junior and a few years older than Tarbell, to marry the younger American. Ida thought he liked her well enough to do it, but wanted no part of the arrangement.[3] Despite Mme Marillier's marital plans for her, it was not for months, until the two women spent a fortnight at Le Clos, the Rolands' ancestral home, that Cécile Marillier and Ida became friendly.

Seignobos and his students did not fail to perceive both Ida's spirit and the reticence she cloaked it with. On one occasion, Mme Marillier was too ill to serve as hostess to the bright male students, so Seignobos rushed at Ida when she arrived and danced about her crying the French equivalent of "You're to be mistress! You're to be mistress of the house!" Ida decided to outwit him and described the results as follows: "They thought it would frighten me for they take a malicious sort of pleasure in seeing me blush[ing] or disconcerted . . . I staid [sic] in that masculine wilderness until 10 o'clock. I then fled. Ever since they have treated me with more respect. 'She didn't get frightened' [they said]. It is very funny. I think they regard me as a sort of specimen, and like to see what I'll do under different conditions. They can't get used to the idea of a woman really working . . ."[4]

Ida had pined for the conversation of the French salon, but once included, she sat wide-eyed and very quiet. Her French was inadequate and women were not expected to contribute anyway, but she noticed the men did not always know their facts, especially when they spoke of America. Her main contribution was Henry Wickham Steed, whom Ida forced on the group despite his Englishness. Steed, some fifteen years younger than Ida, was a fellow student at the Sorbonne and eager to know Seignobos and his favorites better. She and the young Englishman were so fond of each other that some erroneously guessed they were lovers.[5]

Tarbell thought of the salon as "the meeting place of some of the most vigorous spirits of the Latin Quarter . . . a seat of learning and wit unique in its kind."[6] The flaw Steed detected in it was that logic and intellect ruled at the expense of instinct, but he was inestimably grateful to Ida for introducing him to the French intellectual circles. In 1920, he sent her a picture inscribed "To My Fairy Godmother." By that time he was editor of the London *Times*.

Ida's favorite among Seignobos' circle was Charles Borgeaud, a Swiss scholar of constitutional law a few years younger than she. Borgeaud often took her to dinner or cafés after evening lectures, or saw her home after soirées. When an assignment for McClure took her to Geneva where Borgeaud had gone for the summer, he introduced her to his mother, a woman Ida found terrifying. A slip of her pen in a letter home was inarticulate but revealing. In describing the church of Brou which she saw soon after leaving Geneva, she wrote: "This church is the work of a woman and erected in honor of a mother-in-law, so I feel I must take it all in, both for the sake of the sex and my future condition in life."[7]

Whether or not she thought she might one day be a daughter-in-law, she was certainly merry around Borgeaud. Ida wrote John Vincent: "How often do I see your friend B? *Tiens!* You may be sure it is not my fault when I do not see him. He is dining opposite me this minute and sends you *mille amitiés* (He doesn't know what I've written here)."

If she discovered "the boy" at Allegheny College, in Paris she discovered the escort. "Keeping company" in the Latin Quarter was not courting and had no more significance than one wanted to give it. Ida's French tutor, Mme Goinbaut, who had amazed Ida early on by helping a young lover make a profitable marriage, marveled at Ida's luck in never being without a cavalier. Americans also figured on her roster of escorts. There was a Mr. DeFields, an Allegheny College professor who called on her once a week to assail her with his logic, reduce her opinions to formulae, and adduce the contrary of her every statement.

There was also George F. Southard, who had come to head Standard Oil in France. Referred by Laura Seaver Wheeler, her childhood friend, he called on Ida in a crush hat and opera coat. The maid showed him into Ida's tiny box of a room where no fire was lit and the hostess sat in her work clothes. He was taken aback—as any dandy would be in the presence of the genteel poor—yet she put him so at ease that he stayed three hours and took her to dinner the following Sunday. She allowed herself to hobnob with a general director of Standard Oil on the grounds that he was married and safe—and scheduled to return to his wife. She may also have enjoyed doing some informal spy work. Over dinner one evening, he told her that Standard Oil was establishing refineries at Rouen and Marseilles. She promptly sent this intelligence off to her parents and advised, "I suppose these are secrets and I prefer you shouldn't say anything about them as coming from me."[8] In time-honored journalistic tradition, she would allow them to retail the news as they wished, as long as they protected their source.

She was also sought after by editors as well as gentlemen callers. Edward Livermore Burlingame, like McClure, visited her obscure dwelling. Editor of *Scribner's*, he was about forty-five, intimidatingly well-educated, and the son of a famous envoy to China. Burlingame was exacting and reasonable and never promised what he could not produce. He announced to Ida that his magazine would publish her article on Mme Roland and the firm would publish the Roland biography. Excited, she wrote to her family: "I know I can make a good and fresh book if I have leisure. I've a mass of material and the help of the family itself. The bread-and-butter problem is all that prevents my having the book done . . . but I'm going to do it and do it well if it takes five years. You know what that means. I can't go home this year. I dare not think about it but so long as you are all well and happy, I'll stick to my work here."[9]

Typically, the Roland biography was not the only project on which she was hard at work. McClure continued to give her assignments as well. Once her series on French women writers was completed, he asked her to interview the great Louis Pasteur. She was as awed by his achievement in vanquishing hydrophobia and purifying milk as she was appalled by how feeble he had become.

She found Pasteur with his wife in their carpeted library. He who had grappled with mad dogs now sat, elbow on his desk, head resting in his hand, wearing a silken skullcap over iron-gray hair. His left side was paralyzed. He spoke haltingly, moved uneasily, and was so warmly human that she was tempted to feel at home. She met the scientist in the twilight of his life when the family album interested him as much as bacteria once had and he seemed to accept that his work was done. "If I have a regret it is that I did not follow . . . the study of crystals. A sudden turn threw me into the study of fermentation [which had led to sanitary processing of milk, beer, and wine] . . . I am still inconsolable to think that I never had time to go back to my old subject,"[10] he told her. In her article, she summed him up in a way that indicated her own sense of inferiority: "This is a great man, one feels instinctively. A man so great that he despises notoriety and a journalist. It is reassuring." But she also carried away the memory of an old man's trepidations. He was so concerned that she would trip on her way out that he peered out over the railing as she went down the stairs.

Part of her story on Pasteur included an interview with Pierre Émile Roux, the functioning head of the Pasteur Institute, who clearly preferred research to giving interviews. Tarbell kept pressing him on the matter of whether he expected to conquer diphtheria as well as hydrophobia. Roux, a slight, fortyish man who had been devoting his nights to the subject for years, was sensitive on this topic which had consumed his life, but he told her the institute was testing the work of Emil von Behring in Berlin, which seemed very promising. "This is absolutely our last word on diphtheria," he insisted, closing the subject. In fact, Roux and Behring perfected the diphtheria serum in 1894.

Pasteur read Ida's published article with chuckling delight, according to a letter she wrote her family. Later she called on him again, and he asked for a replacement copy—Dr. Élie Metchnikoff, pioneer in immunology, had carried off the first magazine because he liked his own picture so much.

After she submitted her story, McClure assured her she had a secure position at his magazine as soon as she was ready to come home. She was thorough and accurate, could quickly grasp and explain the substance of what scientists were discovering. Others could do human interest pieces, but Ida Tarbell could explain facts.

McClure then commissioned her to write on new methods of criminal identification. Alphonse Bertillon had developed a method of measuring the head, spine, feet, and fingers of malefactors and plotting their moles and scars for cross-reference. His system would later give way to simple fingerprinting, but in its day, anthropometry was an exciting technique. On her way to his office, Ida accidentally locked herself in the prison stairwell with a criminal who was as astonished as she to be in the predicament. Rescued and taken to Bertillon, she and a man who had poached rabbits posed for their criminal identification cards. Hers revealed a serious and somewhat nonplussed Ida Tarbell with a lock of hair falling over the incriminating dimension of her ear. She sent her own card home to Titusville as a souvenir, but for *McClure's* she obtained the card of the murderous Ravachol, Paris's most infamous anarchist.

She also produced "A Chemical Detective Bureau: The Paris Municipal Laboratory and What It Does for Public Health." In this article, laced with humor, she said the lab could uncover cost-cutting "vintners" who tried to dispense with grape juice in wine and inadvertently poisoned their patrons.

Ida observed that the French demanded an explanation when coffee was muddy, milk blue, and wine sour, and she saw who suffered first from adulterated food: "One realizes here, perhaps as never before, what it means to be poor—that you are the first victim, not alone of epidemic and contagion, but of man's violence and fraud; that because you have not great things, the little that you have shall be taken away. [One] realizes too, what such a service may do towards restoring the quality of the poor man's food."[11]

She was becoming more aware of social issues and orders. She knew that governmental and civic systems were the means whereby society took care of its members and they aroused her interest. While she was writing these articles, she was piecing together material on the maintenance of Paris streets for *New England Magazine*, detailing how the city was paved, lit, and landscaped. She carefully noted the communal facilities for domestic life—public baths, water, and laundry systems—all of which, she wrote, would be a great blessing to the poor of the United States. Hers was the zeal and sensibility of the reformer. In lauding French civic virtues, she was tacitly holding up for censure America's neglects in these areas.

Now she was truly independent with only letters to tie her to her past. She was Ida Tarbell and no one else: she was an achieving woman, accepted by French intellectuals, sought out and encouraged by *Scribner's*, the magazine she most respected, and being wooed by a new publication, *McClure's*, which she thought would surpass it. The earnest, naive Ida Tarbell who had been so demoralized by T. L. Flood was gone.

No one could snicker at the enthusiasm or the bohemianism in which she indulged. When the student revolt of 1893 exploded below her windows, Ida climbed on her balcony clad only in her nightgown to observe it merrily with the quaking Egyptian at the next window. She continued to go about the city at night until she was caught in a charge of soldiers and had to throw herself against a doorway to avoid the whizzing bullets.

After the czar's sailors entered Paris that fall to celebrate the Russian-Franco Alliance, she at first dismissed the gesture as a cheap attempt to get a loan. She watched their parade indifferently until the rousing French enthusiasm captured her; she jumped onto a chair, waving her handkerchief and cried, *"Vive la Russie! Vive la Russie!"*

Still, she was sometimes so homesick that when a long-sought picture of her father arrived, she hugged it to her breast and lovingly examined each line and shadow. Two and a half years had produced wrinkles she had not noticed before. She wrote home insisting there must be a mistake in the proof: lines could not exist in the original and they must make the photographer erase them.

She cheered herself up by going to the Jardin des Plantes. "The kangaroos and red-legged flamingos are what I go to see. There is nothing in Paris which will cure me of the blues so quick as seeing a kangaroo hop."[12]

And she often needed cheering. Her problem was money and her need so dire—especially after a night of pain convinced her she needed seventy-five dollars' worth of dentistry—that she humbled herself and sought an assignment from Dr. T. L. Flood. McClure's promised payments—which now totaled one hundred dollars—were not forthcoming. He, like nearly everyone else in America, was the victim of the stock market crash and financial depression known as the Panic of 1893. In the United States, over eight thousand businesses failed, banks included. McClure held on by selling shares of his magazine to anyone he could cajole. Doing his share, Phillips mortgaged his parents' home. Ida forgave her debtors, but had to pay her own debts.

She knew that Dr. Flood was one editor who would be honor-bound to pay her promptly. Her family was horrified when she told them what she planned. Esther offered to sell one of her prized cows from Hatch Hollow to provide her with money, but Ida was adamant. She also suspected that Flood might be in a fence-mending mood; he had run for Congress and voters, particularly those in Meadville, had soundly rejected him. Flood was indeed conciliatory. He commissioned two 2500-word articles on "The Salons of Paris" for which he would pay one hundred dollars.

She well remembered the instructive tone of *The Chautauquan* and came up with the moral to be gained from these social gatherings. She conceded that the salons of the eighteenth century were often scandalous, but said that those of the 1890s were, for the most part, models of propriety which fostered good manners and offered people a chance to form social networks. She recommended that American women adopt the custom.

Meanwhile, Ida had been putting off Mme Bonnet about her rent and her pride would allow her to do it no longer. She took her courage and her sealskin coat to a pawnshop. But the pawnbroker was suspicious of her when Ida admitted that she had never registered as an alien. He said he would not return her coat until she provided proof of her identity or a person to vouch for her. She wanted no one to know of her predicament, so she hurried back to Rue Malbranche, scooped up letters from editors, her exhausted checkbook, and all her papers. She presented them all to the skeptical pawnbroker, but only when she unrolled her diploma from Allegheny College with its Latin and seals and engravings did he give her enough money to pay pressing stationery bills.

In a few weeks, quick by the standards of the day, a check for twenty-five dollars arrived from her family. She thanked them in a fervent letter which ended, "I feel like a genuine 'black sheep—prodigal son' and all that."[13]

After money, her greatest woe was that she no longer liked the woman she was writing about. Ida had slept in Mme Roland's provincial bed, handled her jewels, touched her clothes. She had read the journals of the day and had come to understand the motives of her heroine's antagonists. Mme Roland had fortitude, but instead of a model woman, a disillusioned Ida had found a multidimensional human being with a "Providence complex," who observed "that eternal and necessary natural law that the woman backs up her man."[14]

Roland's evolution from Royalist to Republican and Revolutionary followed the trail of the man she loved, not ideological conviction. She fomented bloodshed and toyed with lives to achieve power. She was not wise and idealistic, but ambitious and theatrical. The French Revolution itself no longer seemed to Ida a glorious purge but a human folly that merely redistributed abuse.

Studying Mme Roland's private papers and interviewing her descendants convinced Ida that her subject had been a glory seeker. Had she judged prominent men as severely as she examined women, she might well have found self-love and personal ambition buried under the myths. In a woman, however, Ida thought these qualities base.

Ida was as unsettled by Mme Roland's imperfections as she had been by evolution. Darwin had cracked her trust in religion. Mme Roland shattered her faith in woman. Now Ida knew her heroine to be more instrumental in her own fate. Mme Roland had pursued her future husband, then manipulated him.

The biography Ida eventually produced went against several literary conventions. Victorian biography tended to reproduce the full context of an era, which made for massive life-and-times works in which detail often eclipsed the person's story. Most contemporary biographers eulogized their subjects, but Tarbell was critical of Mme Roland and came closer to the "debunking" school of later years which dismantled heroes.

In letters at the Bibliothèque Nationale, Ida discovered the story of Mme Roland's having sought a title before the revolution. "Those biographers who had access to these letters have been too ardent republicans or admirers of their heroine to dwell on an episode of her career which seemed inconstant with her later life," Tarbell announced in her introduction. In fact, she was wrong about this. John S. C. Abbott's *Marie Jeanne Roland de la Platière* related this incident on page 93. Tarbell herself was guilty of deliberate omission. Her scholarly sin was to suppress what she regarded as unsuitable. She ignored what Mme Roland proclaimed in her memoirs—that she had been molested by her father's apprentice and was so traumatized that she decamped to a convent and avoided marriage for years.

Mme Roland's handwritten memoirs told in some detail how the youth had forced her to sit on his lap and caused her to cry out, "What is that thing in my back?"[15] Tarbell was appalled that Roland would repeat such a vulgar thing and attributed this tasteless lapse to the influence of Rousseau's *Confessions*. Today a biographer would examine closely the professed cause of a girl's flying to the convent after her first sexual experience, but Ida obscured the matter by saying simply that the profane atmosphere of Roland's home had interrupted her devotions, so she had asked to leave.

Ida observed of Mme Roland's candor: "When she came to writing her life, she dragged to light unimportant and unpleasant details because Rousseau had had the bad taste to do the same before her. The naiveté with which these things are told will convince anyone that cares to examine the *Memoirs* that they mean nothing but she had taken the foolish engagement to tell everything she could about her life."[16]

Other nineteenth-century Anglo-Saxon chroniclers might have felt likewise. Such an admission as Manon Roland's could not have been published in the America of that day; however, Ida's insistence that these details were merely "unimportant and unpleasant" and her censuring tone are further examples of her own determined avoidance of the sexual life. One can only speculate why this is so. Mme Roland overcame her early trauma well enough to be able to write about it for the world to read, but if Tarbell had a similar experience, she certainly did not allow it to be known. It seems more likely that Ida, who needed a fierce sense of herself to defy conventional modes, feared surrendering herself in any way and was most uncomfortable with the thought of sexual surrender.

Her conclusions on Mme Roland indicate that she thought love made a woman unfit for the public world. She charged that Roland's republicanism sprang solely from jealousy of the king's grandeur: "It was the woman's nature which, stirred to its depths by enthusiasm or passion, becomes narrow, stern, unbending—which can do but one thing, can see but one way; that inexplicable feminine conviction which is superior to experience and indifferent to logic."[17]

Fifteen years later, Ida Tarbell admitted she might have been too harsh. "Mme Roland made a reactionist of me. I think I was pretty hard on her sometimes but it was not on her really. It was rather on myself and my sex. You see I started out thinking I had an impeccable heroine and I found *qu'une pauvre femme* ["only a poor woman"] and I fear I took it out on her rather stiffly."[18]

Ida Tarbell found Manon Phlipon Roland guilty of falling in love and thus making herself liable to error. A short story Ida wrote during this period, together with quotes from the manuscript of *Madame Roland*, show that painful vulnerability quivered under the game and self-deprecating Tarbell facade. Ida Tarbell romanticized love but expressed cynical doubt as to whether or not love was actually possible or enduring. In her view, love, while it lasted, so consumed a woman that it incapacitated her for anything else.

She stressed that Madame Roland's judgment had been clouded by thoughts of her lover and wrote what she would repeat for the rest of her life: "A woman in love is never a good politician. . . . The sentiments, the opinions, the course of action of her lover, become personal matters with her. She is incapable of judging them objectively. She defends them with the instinctive passion of the animal, because they are *hers*. Intelligence has little or nothing to do with this defense. Even if she be a cool-headed woman with a large sense of humor and sees that her championship is illogical, she cannot give it up."

Of the Rolands' marriage, Ida wrote: "Their relation had come to the point to which every intimate human relation must come, where forebearance, charity, a bit of humorous cynicism, courage, self-sacrifice, character and nobility of heart must sustain it instead of dreams, transports, passion."[19] Noble tolerance, not love or physical need, was required once infatuation ended.

One can only wonder what happened to Ida Tarbell that she found love such a sharp and jagged condition. It was true that her parents were not ideally suited, nor was her brother's home ideal: still, her repeated insistence that matrimony inevitably cooled to mere arrangement suggests the subject must have had some personal resonance for her. One could wonder whether the intensity of her statements stems from some early attraction to a married man, perhaps even the Reverend T. L. Flood. Possibly she wrote this thinking of Sam McClure. In any event, an unconsummated attachment to someone who remained loyal to his wife would have given her romantic fervor an outlet and would have ennobled her spinsterhood while not jeopardizing it in any way. Unfortunately, Ida Tarbell, unlike Manon Roland, would never confess to an unhappy love affair or leave traces of any such circumstance in her papers. Tarbell's life shows that she did not dare make the mistake of allowing herself to become preoccupied by anyone. She felt clearly that woman could never achieve both love and a profession. Ida chose the world, but as a working woman and an unmarried one, she felt twice vulnerable, according to a piece of fiction she produced at this time.

Her short story heroine, Helen Walters, who wrote for *Earth* and *Moon* magazines (just as Tarbell herself wrote for anything under the sun) expresses Ida's own sensitivities: "Like many young women who follow the hard path of journalism alone, Helen Walters had grown suspicious and acutely sensitive to slights. She could endure overwork, grumbling editors, loss of position, she could make her way out of tight places with cat-like agility. What she could not support was the critical stare of women of assured position, the questioning regard of a society which felt itself superior to her. A suspicious look stung her like a blow. She might support it with an appearance of indifference; but once alone, she had a feminine crisis of bitterness, of tears, of humiliation. She was mortified when she realized Mrs. Ford's tolerance and the men's half-amused glances. She was furious that she had forgotten her maxim of trusting no one—why should she have believed people were kinder in Paris than New York?"[20]

The plot of the story is simple—and revealing—enough: Helen Walters meets a man named Fullerton who invites her to visit his married friends, but Helen learns the wife, Mrs. Ford, objects to meeting a woman so déclassé as to run around Europe alone doing journalism. Helen becomes ill over all the slights, but refuses Mrs. Ford's help. Imagine the passion of Ida Tarbell when she wrote Helen's retort: "You take care of me! You, who despised me because I was alone! Do you suppose I would accept help from a woman who thinks herself better than me because she is loved and cared for and supported; who scorns me because I earn my bread; who, when I come friendless into the same house with her in a strange land turns her back on me! Take care of me! No! No!"

Mrs. Ford realized the girl's accusation was just: "She had a swift new view of herself: a harsh uncharitable woman, a woman sheltered on every side, wounding a woman exposed on every side." She fled in tears to her husband, who approved of the transformation.

Meanwhile, Helen Walters is taken to the hospital. To save her job, Fullerton and his friends write her articles for her and find this much more challenging than they expected. Among Miss Walters's notes, Mrs. Ford finds Helen's description of a poorly dressed American woman whom she recognizes to be herself, but she helps Helen anyway. A late twentieth-century woman would have been furious that they did her job as well as she—going so far as to win an editor's commendation for their "Stunning Seaside Effects"— but Helen was grateful. She and Mrs. Ford had a good cry and Fullerton at last proposed to her.

The emaciated Miss Walters responds: "Why, I never thought of loving you. Only when I feel as I do today, I want a million dollars and somebody to take care of me. I have no judgment left. I suppose that if it were anybody else who had been kind to me and asked I should say 'yes.' I don't think that it is you in particular. It is simply that you offer to look after me and I should love anybody who should do that."

Impervious, Fullerton is certain she will learn to love him. But as Tarbell points out, Helen does not feel she is submitting to the higher calling of marital partnership; she simply throws in the towel because she is exhausted. Whether Helen Walters lived happily ever after or not we can only surmise. Her story ended when she found a man.

The most powerful dynamic in the story is the relationship between Helen and Mrs. Ford. The two were in competition not, as in many stories, for a man, but for the right to exist. Mrs. Ford was challenged by Miss Walters's independence and Miss Walters was intimidated that Mrs. Ford had the love and protection of a man. Miss Walters is more likable, but Mrs. Ford's way of life triumphs. Certainly Ida never analyzed or explicated her story in this fashion, but when it was accepted she wrote home: "*The New England Magazine* has been idiot enough to take a story. I'm half sorry they did. I believe I could write short stories if I had a little more leisure, but as it is I'm afraid I only murder them."[21]

She did at last attend a series of lectures given by Ferdinand Brunetière, the critic who had so impressed her during her *Chautauquan* days. He was short, thin, and nervous, so puny as to appear almost ill; but when he spoke it seemed his voice thrived at the expense of his body. Ida was enthralled. She found in his talks exactly the methodical laying of idea upon idea that she had come to Paris to learn. But his other students were less admiring. Brunetière's contempt for women, society, literature, and anything less than a hundred years old made him the pet of fashionable society, and his students resented it. One day he entered the *grande salle* of the old Sorbonne preceded as was customary by the janitor carrying a tray with a carafe of water, a glass, spoon, and sugar. As Tarbell made her notes, others began to chant "Brunetière, Brunetière!" He began again. So did they. Tarbell sat shocked and quailing as the lecturer tried to drown out his hecklers, but they advanced on him and inch by inch pushed him from the room.

When not in this lively classroom, she scurried about Paris securing comments and photographs of leading French writers, most of whom

McClure wanted for the first issue of 1894. She returned to Pasteur several times before he was satisfied with his contribution: "In the matter of doing good, obligation ceases only when power fails."[22]

She then ventured to the homes of Alphonse Daudet, Alexandre Dumas *fils*, François Coppée, and Émile Zola. Daudet, a naturalist, was a chronicler of his times whose vivid improbable characters won him comparison with Dickens. Unknown to Ida, an anarchist called on him while she and his wife had tea. Ida was led into his study to find the author displaying his revolver and sputtering that his visitor had asked him for a louis with which to buy a wagonload of dynamite to blow up the hôtel de ville.

Ida wrote home that she was very pleased with her visit: "I was overjoyed for I have never had a sight of the *Master* as they call the big men over here. It was in a very pretty room, not very large, that D. was writing his verse for me. He smiled up at me very good-naturedly. He is a little man with a shock of straight black hair which stands out like the new-fashioned dress shirts. His face is pale and his eyes astonishingly black and bright. I think he's lost two or three teeth and the rest aren't very good."

His contribution to *McClure's* was: "What will the France of tomorrow be? Will she even have a literature? Everything is to be feared in an epoch when the Academy [to which Daudet was never elected] amuses itself deforming the national orthography; when the high priests of the dictionary threaten to become its murderers."

Ida was careful to tell her family what he was wearing—"a common black suit which struck me as a little soiled"—for others she spoke with were more eccentric. François Coppée was a poet and playwright with a great, and somewhat simplistic, sympathy for the underdog. When she first called, he didn't realize she wanted only a quote and tried to get rid of her. She described to her family her tenacity: "I went to see him and he thought I wanted an interview. I hadn't dreamed of such a thing but as he suggested it, I took my chance quick and said I did. He was awfully busy and danced wildly around me trying to get rid of me without hurting my feelings. He's been a journalist and hasn't forgotten what dirty work interviewing is—and I danced around him trying to persuade him that I would love to go away at once—and come back. He gave me a day to return and of course I went."[23]

On that day, all prepared, Coppée received her as he sat before a fire in a scarlet flannel working jacket and skullcap. He said he deplored irreligion in France and the proliferation of Protestant sects (such as Methodism) in America. He wrote out a maxim for *McClure's* feature: "Give without hope of return; give without knowing who receives; the noblest gesture there is, is to open wide the hand." Then he insisted she stay on for the interview. It turned out to be one of her most vivid

newspaper profiles: she said his total sympathy for the poor
sentimentalized poverty and its causes and called him "puerile" for defending a murderer simply because the victim had a miserable life.
Dumas *fils* seemed more comfortable with wealth. He greeted her in
a gray flannel caftan which reminded her of her nieces' nightgowns, but
his home seemed to her exquisite and the paintings on the wall quite
rare. She described his head as "noble," though his eyes were grave and
cold. His solemn quotation was indicative of the man: "It is sometimes
painful to do one's duty. It is never so much so as not to have done it.
When man no longer causes the death of his neighbor, and no longer
fears it for himself, he will be God. Let us begin by admiring what God
shows us; we shall no longer have time to search for what He conceals
from us."

Besides the unquestioned celebrities of her day, Tarbell also called on
Zola, whose literary eminence was then in dispute. Her judgment did
not fail her here. She pronounced him "the greatest of them all in spite
of the bad things they say about him."

He awaited her in his enormous salon filled with armor, Chinese lac-
quer, tables, sedan chairs, tapestries, and old carvings. In his simple gray
jersey suit, he was nearly camouflaged by the clutter, but the force of his
personality impressed her. She described him as "a rather small man,
slight and nervous with exceedingly penetrating eyes and an air of great
intelligence and quick decisions."

Zola held forth on his enemies, his realism, and gave broad hints that
she should define him as the new Balzac. He glorified battle for
McClure's: "War is the very life, the law of the world. Is it not pitiful
man has introduced the ideas of justice and of peace, since impassive
nature is only a continual field of slaughter?"

Ida blamed the clutter of his house on Mme Zola: "He married the
daughter of a street peddlar, I believe, so you cannot expect him to have
much help from his wife in an artistic way. He really is to be admired
for marrying her though. Most of them do not think of such a thing as
marrying the woman they fall in love with. Zola is a good husband too,
they say, and very domestic." It seems Ida was not up on all the gossip.
Zola had installed his young mistress and their two small children a few
doors away, where, it was true, he was quite domestic.

A few months later, in the spring of 1894, McClure dispatched her
to Glasgow to interview Henry Drummond, a Scottish clergyman who
had achieved fame for writings reconciling evolution with faith in God
and who, in the course of a successful lecture trip to America, invested
three thousand much-needed dollars in *McClure's.* McClure promised
to pay her expenses as long as she traveled third-class and stayed in two-
dollar hotels. At the delicious prospect of a free trip to Britain, she
threw over her carefully arranged plans and, in anticipation, had her old

black silk dress restyled with dotted crepe. She ordered big balloon sleeves which she could detach when she wanted to transform her gown into an evening dress, describing this construction as "a bigger scheme than a combination folding bedstead."

After France, and a violent crossing which left her stomach tender for days, Queen Victoria's London in the spring of 1893 seemed discordant and fantastic. Shop windows, women's dress and the restaurants, all lacked the order and taste that had surrounded her in Paris. She was appalled that in London she could not get a cloth napkin in the cheap restaurants she patronized and she found the women's hats tawdry and awkward. She was amazed to see children running home from school unattended and claimed that the English ate all the time.

On McClure's allowance she could afford only "vegetarian stuffs" like oatmeal porridge, and wrote home: "As usual, I'm on the ragged edge of bankruptcy and gay as a cricket about it. The McClures are very taken with my work, so they write me. I suppose they can't find anybody else poor enough to tackle these wretched subjects. I've just received a letter saying the magazine is growing . . . they ask me what I'm going to do the next five or six years and hope I'm not going to get married and thus 'cut short my career' (I wish to goodness I was and then I'd have a notion I had a career). I'm only sure of one thing, I'm going to try to borrow or steal enough money to get back to America and see you this summer, then I'm going to finish my book. There! If McClure wants me and has the money he can have me, but it must be for money this time."[24]

By the time Samuel McClure joined her, hunger and hard work in the British Museum left her in no mood to compromise. If he wanted her to work for him in New York, he would have to pay for it—especially since he owed her money. When McClure took her to lunch, she ordered the best, deciding he would repay her in other currency than compliments. The duel began. McClure told her that her articles had been praised by "high sources" for their accuracy. She retorted that was like being honored for ability to add. He spoke glowingly of her future, of all she could do for *McClure's*, of how they could raise her pay—but this time, however he might charm her, she demanded specific commitments. He was rosy with enthusiasm; she was confident of her moral position and the cut of her restyled dress.

They finally agreed on the following terms: he would pay for her trip to America, providing enough money so that she could replenish her wardrobe and travel decently. She would rest with her family for a few months. Then, in October, she would join his staff as editor of its Youth's Department. It was a $2100 position which he promised to raise quickly to $3000.

McClure promised that Ida would be rich in fifteen years, but she knew the publication was nearly bankrupt and expected little for the present—let alone the future. For now, she was sure only that his offer meant going home. She envisioned returning to Paris to live in a high apartment five or six stories up where she could see the sky and hold salons. "Life would be full and satisfying while I cleared up my mind on woman and revolution and continued my search for God in the great cathedrals."[25]

McClure sent her money for second-class passage, but she traveled third-class instead, spending the difference on a porcelain doll for her nieces which at the pull of its string could say "Mama." The sacrifice was easy for her. Her repayment came when she stood in the doorway of 119 East Main Street in Titusville and the children threw themselves into her open arms. She was home. Paris had given her all she expected and far more than she dared to dream.

PART III

SUCCESS

Six

The Americanization of
Ida Tarbell

Ida Tarbell invited McClure to call upon her if he needed her during her vacation and he did. She went to work for him, not in October as editor of the Youth's Department, but in July as biographer of Napoleon Bonaparte.

After the initial joy of being home, Ida's time in western Pennsylvania had not been a success. She was treated by neighbors with deference for having been abroad, but was expected to do an impossible thing—to confirm that America, especially its women, was superior to Europe in every way.

The Tarbell family fortune, like that of the rest of the country, was at a low ebb. The United States was living in the aftershock of the 1893 "panic" or stock market crash which was compounded by a long agricultural depression. Early financial failures, especially that of the Reading Railroad, had engendered others, until the National Cordage Company, the so-called "rope trust," went into receivership in May 1893, thus precipitating the panic. In a chain reaction, banks, corporations, and mortgage companies failed. This crisis rippled out to Ida personally in Paris. Since McClure's creditors did not pay their debts, he did not pay Ida and thus her funds ran so low that she had to pawn her coat.

Titusville also had unique problems with the oil business. John D. Rockefeller's Standard Oil Company was systematically undermining independents like Franklin Tarbell by undercutting prices. Throughout 1893 and 1894, Rockefeller held the price of refined oil fairly steady while the charge for crude almost doubled. When the cost of business doubled for refiners, they were able to buy less from producers like Franklin, or at least forced to delay payment.

Ida found her father hopelessly looking after his devalued oil leases while her brother Will was active among those who tried to break Standard Oil's stranglehold by selling oil to Germany. The family mood was grim and Ida felt stifled by it. She missed her life in France and her presence at home did not seem to be of use to the family.

McClure's hasty summons enabled her to leave this scene. She was delighted by the opportunity to earn money to assist her family and to prepare for her own eventual return to Paris. Ironically, she could have been just as much help to McClure if she had stayed abroad. He had decided to capitalize on the Napoleon craze of the 1890s which marked the centennial of Bonaparte's victories and had contracted to publish engravings of the French emperor collected by Gardiner Hubbard of Washington, D.C. Originally a Boston lawyer, Cambridge city planner, and chief backer of the Bell Telephone Company, Hubbard was a man used to having things done his way. McClure had commissioned Robert Sherard, grandson of Wordsworth, to tell Napoleon's story, but the Englishman's disdain for "Bony" showed in every line he wrote. Hubbard was furious and threatened to withdraw from the project. In desperation, McClure summoned Ida Tarbell.

Having spent three years in the Bibliothèque Nationale researching the life of the relatively unimportant Mme Roland, Ida was shocked to discover that she was expected to produce the life story of the emperor of the French using only the resources of Washington's Congressional Library.

Hubbard, wanting no further mistakes, installed her under his own roof where each night he might have the opportunity to discuss the progress of her research. His estate, Twin Oaks, near what would become Dupont Circle, was the finest in the area. Its sloping lawns adjoined those of his two daughters—Mabel (Mrs. Alexander Graham Bell) and Roberta, whose banker husband Charles Bell was the inventor's cousin.

Washington's air of comfort and leisure and its stately architecture lent it charm to most eyes: but to Tarbell it seemed raw and unfinished. She found everything distastefully new, sprawling and exposed. Paris had seemed to her like a great sage; Washington was like a man on the make for success, ignorant of his own inadequacies, knowing only where he wants to go.

Sultry as Paris had been the previous summer, Washington was hotter and more humid. Ida worked at a little table surrounded by towers of books and thought of herself as having been placed in the furnace room. Her major satisfaction was convincing the librarian that, though a woman, she was worthy of his help. As the weeks wore on and Ida finished successive installments, McClure appeared and spread galleys and proofs over the floors of the Hubbard study and living room to survey the engravings and decide which should be used. McClure's visit to Washington added to her discomfort. Painfully conscious of her Paris-worn wardrobe and thinking the sunny Hubbard home the most beautiful she had ever seen, Ida was horrified by McClure's antics. But when she tried to restrain him, Hubbard's wife Gertrude replied: "That eagerness of his is beautiful. I am accustomed to geniuses."

Ida had to learn first how to cope with McClure's genius for promotion. He knew that *The Century*, the magazine he regarded as his chief rival because it was the one he most admired, would begin its own series on Napoleon in November, and he wanted Ida's to run concurrently. To meet his deadline, Tarbell put herself on a war footing. She worked Monday through Saturday in the library and rested Sunday, in order to work more efficiently the rest of the time.

Her recreation was the bicycle which was then considered a controversial pastime for women, involving as it did the obvious action of limbs. Ida had taken up "the wheel" on New York's Riverside Drive, encouraged by the magazine staff and Sam McClure. In Washington, she cycled with old friends Ada and John Vincent who had returned to the history department of Johns Hopkins in nearby Baltimore. Since Charles Downer Hazen had gone to teach at Smith College in Northampton, Massachusetts, the Vincents brought along their friend Herbert B. Adams to round out the party.

Ida had known Adams slightly when he lectured at the Chautauqua Assembly. With some diffidence she had asked to use him as a reference in Paris and requested that he show the assembly to her friend Mme Blanc while she was in Paris.

Adams looked every inch the turn-of-the-century scholar, with a serious smooth face, a big mustache, and center-parted hair. He had taught at Johns Hopkins since its founding in 1876 and numbered among his students Frederick Jackson Turner, the celebrated historian who wrote on the significance of the frontier in American imagination.

During spring terms, Adams taught at Smith where he could be near his widowed mother. One Smith girl remembered him as being "natural, easy, spontaneous and sparkling" with female students—and a delightful contrast to other male instructors who were often shy in the all-female environment.

In 1894 when Adams pedaled with Ida, he was forty-four, a longtime bachelor some seven years older than herself. Cofounder of the American Historical Society and its first recording secretary, he was particularly interested in local community history at a time when few Americans regarded their early days as worthy of study. Adams was a

good friend to Ida for five years until 1899 when he was told he had ar-
terial trouble. His own father had died in his forties, so Adams might
well have felt he too was doomed. He curtailed his schedule, passing up
a chance to head Amherst College, and died in 1901 just after his fifty-
first birthday.[1]

Judging from the correspondence between Adams and Tarbell, she
seemed to have spared little time for their friendship, or for many
others, once her career in Washington became more demanding. Always addressing him as Mr. Adams, and called Miss Tarbell in return,
she maintained a nineteenth-century formality, but she would apologize
for neglecting him, regret that it had taken as long as four months to
thank him for a book he had sent, then finish her note with a question
about some McClure contributor or to elicit his own observations on
some point pertaining to her own research.

She was diligent in her research and never more so than in her early
days in Washington. Her hopes of being sent to Paris faded when she
saw that the capital possessed a great deal of material on Bonaparte.
Hubbard's personal library contained the latest books and key memoirs
in English. The State Department provided Napoleonic letters, and libraries throughout the city offered contemporary French newspapers
and pamphlets in German, French, and English detailing Europe's response to the Corsican upstart.

Ida finished the first installment in six weeks and Hubbard approved
it. His trip to California in October complicated but did not curtail his
participation. Hubbard had the proofs sent to him, observing, "The second [installment] is better than the first, but there was still room for improvement." Now that she had more time, he said (but not much more,
she may have thought), she would be able to do still better. He said he
felt so much interest in her that he must make her a success: "You are a
born lady and always will be one whom I will be glad to call a friend."
He promised he would be home in time to make her future articles
"right."[2]

In successive letters, he made further corrections. When the first installment was published, he wrote her that he had compared her work
to *The Century* article and that if she had had the same opportunity to
procure material hers *would have been* the better one. But Hubbard
should have rated Tarbell higher. Her series was distinguished by its
clarity. *The Century* writer set forth the historic movements which
made possible Napoleon's rise, but Tarbell did not allow her hero to be
swamped in background. Her narrative was driven forward by the energy of her subject and her talent for discarding what was not crucial to
an understanding of the man himself. For example, the Battle of Tra-
falgar which ended Napoleon's hopes of invading England got short
shrift because Napoleon himself did not personally take part in it.

It is still a joy to read her series. One understands the French hero from the inside, identifies with the boy and triumphs with the man. Tarbell skillfully captures the young Bonaparte growing up on tales of the Corsican rebellion and criticizing his father for being conquered by the French. The boy was so impassioned that he volunteered in the British navy. Only when Napoleon was sent to a French military school does one see him begin his assault on power.

Tarbell explained that besides being a military genius who made Europe the empire of France, Napoleon was a rare executive who codified and clarified French laws and improved French educational and banking systems. Because he began life in barely civilized Corsica, some thought his achievement divine or diabolic. Tarbell took pains to demythologize him and claimed that along with his formidable gifts such as insight into complex situations and the ability to see what needed to be done, Napoleon succeeded because of his appetite for hard work and his willingness to handle details himself.

The biographer ultimately judged that Napoleon had two cardinal faults—he abused the rights of others and he overreached himself. She moralized: "He was the greatest genius of his time, perhaps of all time, yet he lacked the crown of greatness—that high wisdom born of reflection and introspection which knows its own powers and limitations, and never abuses them; that fine sense of proportion which holds the rights of others in the same solemn reverence which it demands for its own."[3]

Napoleon did not seize her imagination as other biographical subjects later would, but he was an early prototype of the Tarbell hero—entirely self-made, born in squalor and risen to power on the world stage. But she did not have time to let her fancy play over Napoleon, nor to do original research. She called her life of Napoleon "biography on the gallop" and she was amazed by the thunderclap of response. Her series debuted in November 1894, and circulation jumped from 24,500 to 65,000. Even The Century's author, William H. Sloan, wrote her. He said: "I have often wished that I had had, as you did, the prod of necessity behind me, the obligation to get it out at a fixed time . . . no time to idle, to weigh, only to set down. You got something that way—a living sketch."[4]

Critical acclaim was immediately forthcoming. The New York Press called the work "the best short life of Napoleon we have ever seen, and its illustrations are admirable." The Boston Globe noted: "It is familiar with the latest as well as with older data, and is so painstaking in research that it brings out much that is new to most readers. It recognized the scientific spirit of modern historical criticism, and is firsthand and attractive in style." McClure's itself came in for a share of the glory in the Topeka Democrat review: "McClure's Magazine for November [1894] challenges public admiration, both in its illustrations and in its literary contents. No magazine within the past year has come to the front more rapidly in popular favor."

Tarbell would have been the first to say that the illustrations were essential to the series' success. To *McClure's* contemporary readers, they were like first sight to a blind man. Everyone had heard of Napoleon, but few knew what he looked like. Even today those familiar only with stereotypes are struck by pictures of the slim young Bonaparte with lank and flowing hair.

An upstart magazine like *McClure's* could compete with a quality publication like *The Century* only because of technological innovation. The new process of photoengraving and the development of cheap glazed paper allowed McClure to have his pictures reproduced from photographs rather than costly engravings—with notable exceptions such as the Napoleon collection. *The Century* clung to the engraving process longer than any other magazine, but its aesthetic advantage was lost on the general audience.

If Tarbell and her rival Sloan spoke well of each other, McClure and his counterpart at *The Century* knew they were joined in battle. When *The Century* stressed the care that had gone into its Napoleon, McClure sent out promotional material announcing that Ida Tarbell had spent three years of preliminary study in France before beginning her work.

McClure, who had peddled pans in the Midwest and operated a newspaper syndicate, knew what his public liked. It wanted articles about other people, especially those with romantic careers. Shrewdly, he did not assume that his readers knew about opera or the great battles of history; rather, he told them who and what were shaping their world. He gave them a popular magazine of quality, introduced them to important people like Alexander Graham Bell and Thomas Edison, and to such immediate topics as the "national disease of nervousness" (the climate was responsible, he claimed). As British writers were then the rage, he published Rudyard Kipling, Robert Louis Stevenson, and a writer-physician named Arthur Conan Doyle.

Tarbell's Napoleon boosted circulation and other writers kept it going in a whirligig of popularity in which they all shared. The magazine's readership had swelled to 100,000 by the time the series ended. Only once in that time had they been able to print enough copies to meet demand. McClure was emboldened to be the first to set firm advertising rates and it took time for advertisers to realize they could not bargain them down. Even when the magazine had a particularly acute cash flow problem, the business staff refused to discount a $750-dollar contract down to $600; they wanted to convince advertisers they meant what they said. That firmness did not weaken their revenue. From 1895 to 1897, *McClure's* carried the largest amount of advertising of any magazine in the world. Although others like *Munsey's* exceeded them in circulation, *McClure's* received more advertising patronage because of its quality and because of the type of people who subscribed—what is today called demographics. Business manager Albert Brady announced monthly circulation figures whether they increased or decreased. By the late 1890s, the publisher guaranteed a circulation of at least a quarter million and comfortably exceeded that.

Their printing facilities were so modern that *McClure's* could turn out the magazine in an astonishingly short period of ten days which enabled it to publish books as well as print the magazine.[5]

Ida's involvement with the life of Napoleon did not end with the appearance of the last installment of her series. *McClure's* produced a book edition of *The Short Life of Napoleon* which was the first of its many diversifications. McClure printed a second edition in May 1895, which brought total copies printed to thirty-seven thousand. Tarbell profited from it all her life. In 1901, she added *A Sketch of the Life of Josephine*, the first full account to appear in English. Basing her work on the research of Frédéric Masson and others, Tarbell depicted Josephine as profligate but good-hearted and concluded that had Josephine been faithful, Napoleon probably would not have divorced her. Interestingly, Tarbell ignored the primary question of Napoleon's need for an heir.

The Life of Napoleon remained one of Ida's enduring successes. In 1911, after schoolboys who had founded a Napoleon club peppered her with questions, she reread her book and wrote to George Brett of Macmillan, who was then her publisher, that it was a better popular biography than she had realized. She was even more pleased when she was seventy and King Features paid Macmillan $750 to synopsize her work.

But in 1894, Ida Tarbell had expected nothing from her effort but $40 a week in salary and a better understanding of France's revolutionary period. She was pleasantly amazed, just as she had been in school when by merely doing her work she was found to be the smartest person in class, that Bonaparte scholars and even her subject's grandnephew desired to meet with her and that readers wrote in requesting to know more about her. Charles Scribner had been debating whether or not to publish Mme Roland as the subject lacked popular appeal; but when Ida Tarbell became known, he decided to go ahead. She so heavily corrected the proof and sent out so many free copies that her first royalty check amounted to only forty-eight cents. Tarbell did not care about the size of her profits. What concerned her was the book's quality and the critics' approval of her efforts.

Fame beguiled her and she knew it. It upended her former expectations and presented her with a whole new life. She had accepted the job solely as a means of getting home, but now employment no longer seemed like such a bad thing; being footloose no longer seemed so appealing. Return to France could be postponed. She now thought there could be nothing more invigorating than the vitality, adventure, and excitement of being part of *McClure's Magazine*: "What really startled me about that sketch [of Napoleon] was the way it settled things for me, knocked over my former determinations, and went about shaping my outward life in spite of me. It weakened my resolve never again to tie myself to a position, to keep myself entirely footloose; it shoved Paris into the future and substituted Washington. It was certainly not alone a return to the security of a monthly wage, with the possibility that the wage would soon grow, that turned my plans topsy-turvy, though that had its influence. Chiefly, it was the sense of vitality, of adventure, of excitement, that I was getting from being admitted on terms of equality and good comradeship into the *McClure* crowd. . . ."[6]

Now she made her home in Washington as a member of the Hubbard set. In the 1890s, the *nouveaux riches* hobnobbed with titled foreigners. The Hubbards, however, entertained the aristocracy of achievement—diplomats, scientists, and statesmen like Edward Everett Hale, author of *The Man Without a Country*, and Samuel P. Langley, secretary of the Smithsonian Institution.

Tarbell boarded at the establishment of a Mrs. Patterson on I Street. The fashionables had recently decamped toward Dupont Circle, yet among Tarbell's fellow boarders was Senator George Frisbie Hoar of Massachusetts. Now nearly seventy, he had been a leader in Reconstruction legislation and antitrust law. Hoar was a crusty classicist who declaimed Homer at the Sunday breakfast table as well as waxing eloquent on the perfection of his hostess's codfish balls. The senator and his wife, Mrs. Patterson and her daughter, and Ida Tarbell made up a little family, a home Ida described as "one of the most comfortable and delightful living places into which I had ever dropped. Such food! And best of all the Senator!"[7]

To be in Hoar's presence was to take a crash course in American ideals of public service, the rights of the individual, and freedom from foreign entanglements. But an internationalist point of view contrary to Hoar's was gaining ground as Cuba agitated for independence from Spain. Many felt that Washington should intervene since the dispute was so close to American shores. American designs on foreign territory grew as the great foreign powers expanded. As the nineteenth century closed, almost as if trying to meet a deadline, Germany, France, Belgium, and Great Britain had agreed to separate "spheres of influence," whereby they apportioned the seaboard of Africa and then proceeded to do the same in China. Ambitious public servants in America felt the Monroe Doctrine had delineated their own sphere of influence and began to look with some impatience at Spain's continued dominance of an unwilling Cuba.

Just as Ida's father had described for her the injustice of Rockefeller's take-over of the oil business, so Hoar discoursed on the immorality of America's designs on Spain's empire, especially the Philippines. He had a noble concept of America's role as an example to the world, and it was a useful antidote to Ida Tarbell's loyalty to France.

Her work for McClure required Ida to steep herself in a subject in which she had no initial interest—American history. Whether or not great personalities shape history, they do sell magazines. After Napoleon doubled circulation, Sam McClure conjectured Lincoln would do the same and he chose Tarbell to oversee the project. The Lincoln series was to encompass only two or three dramatic articles by those who had known him. Ida Tarbell was not enthusiastic about the project.

Her enthusiasm was for France and for its revolutionary period, not for American icons. She had made herself sit through congressional debates, thinking they were a mandatory sight for visitors, but she had much preferred absorbing the atmosphere of Mme Roland in the museums and libraries of France.

She accepted McClure's assignment to gather and edit the Lincoln material, but to herself she fretted that she was never faithful to what she chose for herself. She had given up her microscope for journalism, then turned from the woman question to the French Revolution. Now she was turning from Napoleon and her success as a writer to edit the reminiscences of others in the uninspiring realm of American history.

She felt the harness of employment pulled firmly around her neck and knew McClure was tugging her away from the play of her own ideas and the freedom to cultivate her own tastes and friends. "More than once I told myself that the sacrifice of my ambitions, of my love for Paris, for my friends there, was too much to ask of myself . . . but I was replacing them and suffering as I realized what was happening . . . . I was beginning to repeat dolefully as well as more and more cynically, 'Tout passe, tout casse, tout lasse' (Everything passes, perishes, palls)."[8]

In giving up the life of an independent writer, she had met a crisis in life. She decided in favor of what was useful; and having once made that decision, she held nothing of herself in reserve. A McClure's staffer recalled her obedience to the demands of McClure and her job: "One little thing that I marvelled at in those days was that she could mobilize just as swiftly as any lad in the place—could accept a decision at noon to start for Chicago that night without turning a hair. I suppose there have been other females like that—I glimpse them in books [on] great travellers but she is the only one I ever saw keep it up right along; thereby in her case wiping out one good ground for paying women less than men."[9]

Tarbell would cover many miles in researching Lincoln, but she began her efforts close to home at the Washington Literary Society where John Nicolay was a member and she an honored guest. Nicolay was a former private secretary to Lincoln and coauthor with John Jay of a ten-volume study of the late president. Southern hospitality, Victorian formality, and some wit flourished at the meeting of the society, but Nicolay gave her a chilly reception when she asked him for any material he might not have included in his own work. He at first assured her there was nothing more to be published, then told her the subject was his and that she should stay away.

She had hoped, with naïveté or calculation, that Nicolay would share his insights with her and possibly an unpublished letter; but his rebuff had the effect all rebuffs had on Ida Tarbell—it inspired her to the exceptional.

Previous biographers had focused on private papers to which they had access or on their own firsthand experiences with Lincoln. Tarbell decided to investigate court records, county histories, and newspapers for traces of Lincoln's life and early cases, and for information about his years of obscurity which had become a field for sometimes unpleasant conjecture. She wanted to come up with something original, something others might have missed.

Finding fresh material about Lincoln thirty years after his death seemed as likely as uncovering a new Washington or an unknown Franklin. The slain president already had several biographers and was fixed in the public mind.

Undaunted, in February 1895 she boarded a train for Knob Creek, Kentucky, to begin her quest around Lincoln's birthplace. She was to be gone a month, journeying through the scrubby fields of Indiana and on to Springfield, Illinois. Seeing her off, McClure showed a sudden pang of concern for the woman he was sending to the boondocks of the South. "Have you warm bed socks?" he asked. "We'll send you some if not. It will be awful in those Kentucky hotels."

That prediction proved entirely correct during her first month of what she called "Lincoln hunting." Small town hostelries varied in their cleanliness and respectability; she was an object of lively curiosity as she traveled alone, asking questions about local inhabitants and taking pictures. Certainly she herself was uncomfortable. Strange hotels so dismayed her that her hand shook every time she signed a register.

One could not lay groundwork in the backwoods by telephoning ahead; the only way to check out leads was to appear in person. Ida gleaned valuable new material because of her thoroughness; she also took time to be kind to those she met. At a farm near Keystone Post Office in Clinton County, Missouri, she found her hostess in need of medical care and urged her to try a new doctor. The woman's daughter later wrote Tarbell that the patient was improving, had gained ten pounds, and that in every letter she spoke of Miss Tarbell's "constant thoughtful kindness."

As Tarbell interviewed people she saw that even thirty years later they could not fathom how one of their own had become president. The elderly Roland W. Diller, in whose Springfield drugstore Lincoln used to relax with friends, was as interested in flirting and calling her "Tarbucket" as in recalling his old friend. His tales of Lincoln—not all of them verifiable—inspired the "Billy Brown" stories she later wrote about Lincoln's younger days. Best of these was "He Knew Lincoln," which appeared in *The American Magazine* in February 1907.

Tarbell had expected every encounter with Lincoln to be burned into people's minds, but she found his own neighbors could recall him only with difficulty. Most had realized Lincoln was special, had looked forward to his visits, but they could not see his great gifts.

To her dismay, some fabricated recollections for her. Senator John M. Palmer of Illinois, who had been a Lincoln manager at the Chicago Convention, gave her a detailed account of the part played by a Judge Hornblower in Lincoln's nomination, but Ida could discover no records that such a person had ever lived or functioned in Lincoln's life.

After heroic travels through the backwoods, her story came together in a society woman's parlor when Lincoln's son Robert presented her with a daguerreotype of a Lincoln no one had seen or imagined: a young, clean-shaven man who had somehow been buried in all the mythologizing that had come afterward. Lincoln had always been vaunted as an uncouth man honed to nobility, but here was a confident man handsome enough to go onstage. Modern medicine has attributed the gnarled appearance and melancholy of Lincoln's later years to Marfan's syndrome, a genetic disorder which can distort the face, but in any event, the daguerreotype Tarbell received shed light on Lincoln's dark past and infused her work with new power.

Robert Lincoln, the late president's only surviving son, had served in the cabinets of James Garfield and Chester Arthur, and was soon to be appointed president of The Pullman Company. He was concerned about what biographers had done to his family's reputation and was wary of them. Abraham Lincoln's bodyguard, Ward Hill Lamon, had stated the president was illegitimate; William Herndon, a law partner, had told of Lincoln's rough manners and Mary Todd's shrewishness. Robert Lincoln had cooperated with Nicolay and Hay at the expense of changing every paragraph in their monumental work.[10]

For whatever reason, either because of her cajoling or the persuasion of their mutual friend Emily Lyon, Robert Lincoln gave Tarbell the earliest daguerreotype he knew of. He withheld everything else; his papers were not opened until 1947 and other caches of material have since been revealed.

But the picture was worth all the papers he could have provided. Readers—even the experts—were dumbstruck by the frontispiece. *McClure's* published a selection of comments in December 1895: Woodrow Wilson, professor of finance and history at Princeton University, wrote that he found it "both striking and singular—a notable picture." He added that he was moved by "the expression of dreaminess, the familiar face without the sadness." Charles Dudley Warner, a literary figure who co-wrote *The Gilded Age* with Mark Twain, said that it "explains Mr. Lincoln far more than the most elaborate engraving which had been produced."

McClure's Magazine was now in the Lincoln business. In November 1895, when the picture appeared, circulation reached 175,000. When the next article ran the following month, it hit 250,000, surpassing *The Century* and *Harper's Monthly* and proving that Tarbell had accomplished a remarkable feat.

Her first article appeared ten months after she set out for Kentucky. Others had portrayed Lincoln's achievement as an act of fate or the miracle of a country lout's becoming leader of his country. In Tarbell's rendering, Lincoln's rise to the presidency was the well-tended flowering of early ambition. As a boy, Lincoln told one woman he would be president, and when her daughters mocked him, he retorted, "Oh, I'll study and get ready, and then the chance will come and I'll be prepared."[11]

Response to this new Lincoln swelled *McClure's* mailbags. It seemed as if the whole country were collaborating in recovering Lincoln. People wrote in with information and invited her to call on them when she was in the area. Even Southerners wrote affectionately of him. From Nebraska came word that a Western newspaper had written of Tarbell as Lincoln's oldest living playmate.

It may have been at this time that William Dean Howells, then America's foremost man of letters, confessed to her the greatest mistake of his literary life. When asked to write a campaign biography of nominee Lincoln, he refused to travel way out to Illinois to see someone he thought "didn't amount to anything," and so he sent someone else to interview Lincoln. Tarbell had done her own research and it made her the star of *McClure's Magazine.*

Hamlin Garland produced a series on U.S. Grant which ran concurrently, and biographies of Washington and Franklin also appeared, but none could boast success like this. *McClure's* also featured stories on a new marvel in photography—the X ray, with pictures of X-rayed hands,

tools, and frogs—and "A Century of Painting" with engraved repro-
ductions, but it was Tarbell's biography people talked about.

After editing three issues comprised mostly of unpublished manuscripts culled in small-town libraries, Tarbell began to write the installments under her own by-line. J. McCan Davis, a young Springfield
attorney who acted as her assistant in his spare time, combed early Illinois newspapers and turned up documents on Lincoln's early life. Tarbell's series stretched to twenty articles over four years, which were later
reprinted in book form and rewritten into a work of two volumes dedicated to her father.

Hers was a scholarly method driven by demands of magazine deadlines. She was tenacious in following leads and cross-checking them.
While gathering data she could dictate as many as twenty letters a day,
inviting contributions, declining others, clarifying points, and correct-
ing dates as she worked through the "To be Answered" pile on her
desk. She would ask one whether Lincoln's hair was black or very dark
brown, whether a phrase was "sown corn" or "sowed corn," and
whether Lincoln used the correct phrase. She had the historian's ped-
antry, the journalist's instinct, and the friendly guile of one seeking
help. Tarbell sent off books and copies of illustrations to those from
whom she was cajoling help. She read and reread proofs, and when
errors did creep in, apologized contritely to McClure and Phillips.

Her Lincoln articles, like her Napoleon series, were submitted to rigorous editing. McClure read each three times. If the third reading no
longer interested him, she rewrote the article. Just as he insisted that
McClure's short stories make the reader feel better, so nonfiction features, whether biographic, scientific, or general, had to present the
nobler side of life. McClure felt that a magazine, to be successful, had
to be edifying, but above all, it had to be lively.

Sensationalism, albeit well-documented sensationalism, was at the
core of her investigation. Her passion for her subject and McClure's
desire to capture readers led her to commit several errors of fact. What,
she thought, could intrigue the public more than finding a lost speech
by the author of the Gettysburg Address? Tarbell was assured by two
sources—an Indiana judge and noted *Chicago Tribune* editor Joseph
Medill—that there was such an address, one so wonderful that reporters
had been so enraptured by Lincoln's words that they forgot to take
notes. Tarbell found this hard to believe, but she uncovered one man's
recollections of the speech and Medill authenticated it. This version
was generally accepted as genuine until 1930 when the actual speech
came to light in *The Alton Courier* of June 5, 1856.

Other biographers had claimed that Lincoln's mother, Nancy Hanks,
had been born out of wedlock. Tarbell could not accept that this was

true. Thus, when a writer named Caroline Hanks Hitchcock brought "proof" of a legitimate ancestor named Nancy Hanks who married Thomas Lincoln, Abraham's father, Tarbell wanted to believe it was so. She soon saw that Mrs. Hitchcock was flighty and tried to double-check her work, but Tarbell finally wrote an enthusiastic introduction to Hitchcock's book. In the 1920s, Mrs. Hitchcock's work was shown to be in error. Nancy's mother did not marry Nancy's presumed father until seven years after her birth. Tarbell gamely urged those biographers who could discredit Nancy Hanks's legitimacy to do so for the sake of truth, but she was privately confident that Lincoln must have come from a more honorable marriage bed.[12]

Tarbell not only wanted Lincoln to be from a knotless family tree, she wanted true love for him as well. William Herndon, biographer and erstwhile Lincoln partner, had hated Lincoln's wife Mary Todd and insisted that the only woman Lincoln had ever loved was a girl from New Salem, Illinois, named Ann Rutledge. According to Herndon, only this girl's death prevented Lincoln from marrying her. Feeling that a lost love was highly romantic and finding Mary Todd Lincoln so unappealing, Tarbell decided to believe and repeat this story. Other biographers said that Lincoln had gone half mad with grief over her death, but for Tarbell this was too morbid. She insisted that he had only been profoundly saddened and never forgot his love for her. Most Lincoln scholars today discount the "romance" because the only testimony for it is the unreliable Herndon.

Possibly because of her indebtedness to Robert Lincoln and the hope of prying more material from him, Tarbell treated Mary Todd Lincoln more gently than she was otherwise inclined to do. She suppressed a story told her by Carl Schurz, a Lincoln confidant and appointee, that Lincoln's wife had been the tragedy of his existence and that she tried to influence the president after accepting a diamond necklace as a bribe. After Robert died in 1926, Tarbell wrote a profile of Mary for the *Ladies' Home Journal* in which she said simply that Mary felt she had a right to some of the gifts favor-seekers offered.[13]

In short, Tarbell accepted hearsay if she liked it, could not disprove it, and if it made for a good story. When the whole truth was disappointing, she glossed over it. Despite her biases, however, Tarbell was considered the preeminent Lincoln biographer of her day because she amplified and clarified his life.

She established that Lincoln's father was not shiftless "white trash," but an orphaned younger son who had overcome significant disadvantages, and that Lincoln's early life, though crude, was honest and upright. She was exceedingly fine on detail and disproved much that had been glibly stated as fact. Herndon had cited John Hanks as the source of Lincoln's vow against slavery at a New Orleans auction, but Tarbell found that Hanks had never been there. She contradicted William Cullen Bryant's belief that he had seen Lincoln during the Black Hawk War by showing that Lincoln had left his command a month before Bryant ever arrived. Despite Nicolay's contention that he had published the complete Lincoln correspondence, Tarbell discovered three hundred more letters of varying importance. "From Miss Tarbell's books," said Lincoln scholar Benjamin Thomas, "came new appreciation of the power of the American West and what it could do in the way of fashioning a man."[14]

Having been born in the backwoods of Pennsylvania on her grandparents' farm, Tarbell had a special feeling for the frontier and for pioneer life. Napoleon, like Lincoln, had risen from rocky soil, but Tarbell did not draw a parallel between the two. To her it seemed that a Lincoln could appear only in America and she appreciated her country the more for it. On her seventy-fourth birthday, after a distinguished career, she said that *The Life of Abraham Lincoln* had given her more pleasure than any other work she ever did. She revered Lincoln because he was totally self-made—he was without educational background, yet his great moral and intellectual qualities, his seriousness of thought and purpose, and the tradition of American individualism had enabled Lincoln to make himself great.

Her work provided a feast of what the public wanted to believe about Lincoln and the great nation he preserved, and reviewers approved of it. *The Nation* said that the aggregate of discoveries "made a story considerably softened from that which had commonly been accepted . . . The book deserves, on the whole, the popular welcome . . . because it satisfies in an honest way the cravings for details of Lincoln's wonderful career."

The *Philadelphia American* observed: "Not only has she written a book of unusual interest throughout, but what is even more to the purpose, she gives her readers a comprehensive insight into the life and characteristics of this man who rose to every occasion and emergency no matter how trying or difficult."[15]

McClure had long seen that additional money could be made from Tarbell's popular biographies, and he dreamed up *McClure's Quarterly* which would be devoted to a subject already covered in the magazine. The entire Napoleon series was reprinted in one quarterly and the Lincoln in the next. Since Tarbell's work was the basis for the publication, he asked her to supervise production. Thus, she became the victim of his gift for turning a peak into a precipice. In a letter to Herbert Adams she described in telegraphic fashion two months of concentrated editorial work: "Since Christmas I have seen one book—a pamphlet—it is a book in size and a whole encyclopaedia in trouble—our Lincoln quarterly—through the press. And I have read all the proofs for another. A biographical study of Madame Roland."[16]

Unable to project demand, McClure overprinted the Napoleon quarterly by sixty thousand copies. However, the Lincoln issue proved so popular that they could not afford to produce enough. "*The Life of Lincoln* saved us from absolute ruin,"[17] he told her much later, attesting to her ability to balance seesawing McClure ledgers. So that he would never again be unable to meet popular demand, McClure proceeded to buy a printing plant on credit. Thus in January 1896 the McClure operation of books, magazines, and quarterlies was the success of the editorial world and over a quarter million nineteenth-century dollars in debt.[18]

Tarbell could not physically cope with the stresses she and McClure had placed on herself. In the summer of 1896, overcome by exhaustion, possibly complicated by neuralgia, she checked into Clifton Springs Sanitarium near Rochester, New York. Two principles guided Clifton Springs—the efficacy of chapel and the water cure. Tarbell was one of the first patients in the new six-story building which was so modern as to be fireproof, well-ventilated, centrally heated in winter, and fanatically clean. In their scrupulousness, her doctors allowed her to sit up only two hours a day. For the next thirty years she regularly repaired to Clifton to restore herself and hide out from the world. "I like it because I can hang a card saying 'No admittance' on my door and see no one but those who wait on me," she told a friend. "When I am low or down I can cut out demands on my time or emotions by coming here."[19]

Hazen, teaching at Smith College, teased her about wearing down her health: "I am so used to your defying laws of God and man that I am shocked to find you aren't as superior as I thought. . . . It's that book of yours and all that editorial work and no golfing and no bicycling that have been your ruin. New York is all well enough if you want to see the opera or have a good dinner, but Northampton is better if you want health. Perhaps, however, you don't care to have me continue in this somewhat highflown strain steadily getting points all the time for my own uses."[20]

Once she was out of bed, Hazen went to Clifton Springs to cheer her up. Together they climbed the rocks and enjoyed the four parks and waterfall. He was her summer tradition for four years—they had joined the Vincents on Cape Cod the year before; in 1897, they met in Loches, Switzerland, with Sarah and saw each other in Boston the next year.

After leaving Clifton Springs that summer of 1896, Ida resumed her schedule, commuting continually between New York and Washington. If hostesses sought her, if people wanted to meet her, she was just out of their grasp. She never took herself seriously enough to appreciate the flattery, and attributed her popularity to her friendship with Mrs. Alexander Graham Bell. She would arrive in New York, check into the Fifth Avenue Hotel, or the St. Denis, or the Hotel Manhattan, and find that McClure, who had summoned her, had just left. Her ceaseless peregrinations and the logistics of transporting personal possessions, letters, and office supplies to or from Washington occupied much of her time and energy. And, adding to the confusion in the process of trying to ease it, she decided to renounce the Patterson establishment and move into an apartment at 919 I Street NW where she could have the solitude she needed to recoup her strength.

She seemed unable to comprehend the success which had come to her with apparent suddenness, but really after many years of work. A reporter from *Leslie's Weekly* was astonished to find her oblivious to her fame. He observed her spending interminable hot summer days reviewing letters from readers from every town and mail station in America. Now and then some ancient visitor would arrive to tell her about Abraham Lincoln and she would give him full attention. She regarded herself simply as a worker, going to her tasks as a mechanic with his lunch pail. *Leslie's* anonymous interviewer observed: "Life is an everyday matter to her, but the most ordinary incidents of its routine are too real and full of significance ever to become common. She has no pride in her success. She plods persistently through any task, meeting every new emergency with a new resource and when finished puts it aside as a cooper does his completed task . . . She is both sensitive and sensible . . . her biographies are vital because they are true . . . it is because she never invests her characters with anything not theirs and because she is never tempted by sentiment to conceal or evade that even Napoleon and Lincoln heretofore rendered impossible or preserved as mummies are now before us, alive and well, raised from the head by the hand of a plodder."[21]

Tarbell was apparently unaware of the effect she had on young writers who were dazzled at meeting her and who lapped up her courtesy with slavish gratitude. She was goddess of the Olympus which was *McClure's Magazine.* She, McClure, John Phillips, and art director August Jaccaci (pronounced "Yakatchy") worked together, lunched together, and dined together, and occasionally a lucky young writer might be allowed to accompany them.

William Allen White, a rotund, rambunctious, and startlingly bright young newspaper editor from Emporia, Kansas, had garnered a national reputation for his editorial, "What's the Matter With Kansas?" which attacked populism. McClure accepted his "Court of Boyville" short stories and invited him to visit New York. White would become the interpreter of Midwestern life, an able political commentator, and biographer of presidents. Ida would come to love him and his wife Sallie enough to profess that Emporia was one of her favorite places on earth, but that was much later. The first night White met her in 1897, he was simply agog: "John Phillips, Jaccaci and Ida Tarbell took me far uptown on a street car amid an unbelievable squirming army of bicycles to Grant's Tomb, where we had a gorgeous dinner and much tall talk about the magazine business and current literature," he wrote in his memoirs. White recalled his awe: "These people knew Rudyard Kipling. They knew Robert Louis Stevenson. They had dealt with Anthony Hope Hawkins, whose novels were quite the vogue. The new English poets [Yeats and Housman were published by *McClure's*] were their friends."

White was relieved to find that these people were like those he knew back home. "They were at heart Mid-Western. They talked Mississippi Valley vernacular . . . They were making a magazine for our kind—the literate middle class,"[22] he said. Unlike editors of established quality publications, McClure and his cohorts had faith in the intelligence of the mass of Americans.

White was not the only new writer swept into the McClure circle in 1897. Ray Stannard Baker was a slim, dark-haired, twenty-seven-year-old newspaper reporter with a serious manner and a cleft chin. He had covered the Pullman Strike, marched with Coxey's Army, and tagged after the British reformer William Stead when he researched *If Christ Came to Chicago*. After Baker read Tarbell's Lincoln series with fascination, he took up his courage and asked if *McClure's* would be interested in an article on his uncle who had helped to capture John Wilkes Booth. *McClure's* happily printed the story, gladly pointing out that Baker's account corrected false information previously provided by *The Century*.

Like White, Baker recalled in his autobiography his first meal with Phillips, Jaccaci, and Ida Tarbell: "I went out with them to the jolly table at the old Ashland House where they lunched together, a spot that still glimmers bright in my memory. . . . I suppose I was in the most stimulating, yes intoxicating, editorial atmosphere then existent in America—or anywhere else!"[23]

Unlike White, Baker was willing to spend time in New York and he became a contributing editor. He took his career seriously, settled his patient wife and children in Wisconsin or Michigan for long stretches so he was free to go off on assignments at the drop of a hat. He was given to introspection and to pondering the importance of what he was doing. Should he write a novel? Would California be more conducive to good work than New York? Thus he bedeviled himself throughout a distinguished career that spanned investigative journalism, essay writing, and handling the American press at the Versailles Conference.

What Tarbell called "the unconventional intimacies of the crowd"—
the camaraderie of men and women, and their talk—were a joy to him.
All the writers, including Tarbell, felt they had something vital to tell
their colleagues and fairly burst with chatter; but Baker, Tarbell observed, was the least talkative and the best listener of them all.
McClure well knew the merits of his talented staff, but Tarbell held a
special place. Whatever he assigned her she did well, as he was fond of
telling Phillips, and he utilized her qualities by having her ghost or edit
memoirs for which she took no public credit. As a result, she channeled
her writing energies into work which required her to understand such
varied topics as the sequence of the Vicksburg campaign and aerody-
namic principles. Her fondness for one of her subjects, Carl Schurz,
made her feel her efforts were especially worthwhile.

Schurz had a staggering record of accomplishment. Driven from his
native Germany because of his libertarian agitations, he emigrated to
the United States. There he became an active abolitionist, friend of
Abraham Lincoln, general in the Union army, American minister to
Spain, senator from Missouri, secretary of the interior under Ruther-
ford B. Hayes, and editor of the *New York Evening Post*. His vast range
of experience had given him the demeanor of a philosophical activist
plus eager common sense and a trove of newsworthy memories.

Tarbell stole from *The Century* the right to publish his memoirs by
offering Schurz a large sum of McClure's money and by promising to
save Schurz embarrassment by breaking the news of Schurz's defection
to *Century* editor Richard Gilder. She may have taken delight in this.
Gilder was reported to have scoffed at her by saying, "McClure's got a
girl trying to write a life of Lincoln."[24]

Ida worked on Schurz's memoirs from August 1898 until his death in
1906. She liked best to see him at his home on Lake George where he
indulged his high spirits. While awaiting breakfast, he sang snatches of
Wagnerian operas in a clear, strong voice. Sometimes, in the middle of
their work, he sprang up to improvise some lively tune on the piano. He
was then a longtime widower of seventy: she was in her early forties and
possibly a little in love with him. As she wrote in her autobiography:
"There never was a more lovable or youthful man of seventy than Carl
Schurz . . . He had come to mean more to me as a human being than
anybody I had studied. I never doubted his motives, and he never bored
me. Still, whenever I have the opportunity I pick up [his books]. The
greatest regret of my professional life is that I shall not live to write another life of him. There is so much of him I never touched."[25]

His special status became explicit in a letter she wrote her brother at
Christmas in 1908, about three years after Schurz's death. She presented Will with Schurz's memoirs and said they represented "the only
piece of editorial negotiation of which I am in any way proud. It can be

fairly said that I secured *The Reminiscences* for *McClure's*. Mr. Schurz told me repeatedly that they would not have gone there if it had not been for me . . . I should like you to keep these volumes beside my own 'Completed Works' in your library."[26]

She was not as susceptible to all her subjects. Her experience with Charles Dana, editor of the *New York Sun* and a War Department insider during the Civil War, was of another sort entirely. She thought him a curmudgeon pure and simple, and when Phillips and McClure told her she was to be his ghost, she uncharacteristically tried to beg off. Dana's biases, writ in acid on his editorial page, were in favor of the protective tariff and the sanctity of business, and against the evils of strikes and Tammany Hall. Schurz once told Ida that Dana's malice proved the existence of a personal devil.

Dana had told McClure that Tarbell's *Life of Lincoln* was one of the ten foremost books for Americans to read because it presented a true picture of the late president, but in his dealings with Ida herself, he conveyed no morsel of respect or warmth. Dana at seventy-eight, with a generous white beard and pince-nez, possessed the vigor of a man of forty, but he was so impersonal he did not even politely inquire "How are you?" The episode would stand in her mind as the only one of her business relations that included nothing but the job at hand.

Reviewers praised the Dana work as a contribution to the history of the Civil War, despite the fact that its style was simply that of a chronological narrative. One critic praised Dana for referring to accounts he had written at the time, but that touch was entirely the work of Ida Tarbell.[27]

Samuel P. Langley, the third man she helped to "write" for *McClure's*, was a scientist. Secretary of the Smithsonian Institution, a pioneer in the mechanics of flight, and the first to show how birds soar on wind fluctuations, he insisted that man too would someday be able to fly. Before the Wright brothers, Langley was the hero of American aviation. He caused a model plane weighing twenty-five pounds to fly for ninety seconds over the Potomac. Ida's account of the flight, complete with explanations of Langley's theories—all under his by-line—so pleased Langley that he arranged a special treat. He invited her to the National Zoological Park in Rock Creek Park one day after the crowds had gone and, with the help of the director, made the kangaroo hop and the hyena laugh in an exclusive performance for Ida Tarbell.[28]

As in Paris, when she wrote about Pasteur and his institute, her enjoyment of science and her ability to understand its fundamentals stood her in good stead. McClure wanted more such serious efforts to present popular science. In that day, the farthest reaches of technology—the electric light, the telephone, the squawking phonograph, cable cars and trolleys—could be grasped by the average human mind, and McClure intended Tarbell to help him in this effort.

Washington, D.C., was at that time a center of science and Ida was at its hub. Each Wednesday evening, Alexander Graham Bell hosted informal receptions for a score of scientists and a few women of the family. As a close friend of Bell's wife and mother-in-law, Tarbell was invited to hear papers and lectures on subjects ranging from the races of man to the life cycles of eels. The group called itself The National Geographic Society and privately published its papers until Tarbell successfully negotiated arrangements whereby McClure, Phillips and Co. published *The National Geographic Magazine*.[29]

Her major disappointment was that Bell refused to allow her to write his biography, saying he wanted nothing published in his lifetime; as consolation, he asked her to undertake the private commission of classifying his materials for a future biography. She declined, but suggested that H. G. Wells, who was writing for the syndicate, might produce something called "Pages from a Scientist's Notebooks" based on the inventor's papers.

Washington was of course about the business of government, as well as being a scientific center. In forging an unusual and rewarding working relationship with General Nelson A. Miles, commander in chief of the U.S. Army, Tarbell developed an opportunity to see how that government functioned in wartime. She was at Miles's elbow the day the U.S.S. *Maine* blew up in Havana Harbor. The coming of war had been in the air, and typically McClure was one of the first to sense it, but he had not known which war it would be. General Miles had been dispatched to observe the Greco-Turkish War and the standing armies of Russia, Germany, and France which threatened to become embroiled in it. McClure wanted Tarbell to write up Miles's conclusions; Miles, however, wanted to present a travelogue and show off his cultural attainments by digressing on the sarcophagus of Alexander the Great. Tarbell at last convinced him that McClure's was interested only in military matters; she accomplished this with so much tact that he still modeled for her the special epaulet he had designed.

On February 16, 1898, when word came that the American ship had been blown up, Washington was taut with quiet. Tarbell presented herself at Miles's office expecting to find her appointment canceled, but work proceeded as usual. Headquarters was hushed, except for orderlies who conveyed bulletins to Miles: "Two hundred fifty-three unaccounted for, two officers missing, ship in six fathoms of water, only her mast visible, sir." And later in the afternoon: "All but four officers gone, sir." Miles's only reply was to blow his nose while the chief of staff, a man with a bullet hole in his cheek, mourned: "Ain't it a pity! By Jove, ain't it a pity!"[30]

Over the next two months, the country hovered between peace and war. No one was ever sure how the *Maine* blew up (a short-circuit in the electrical wiring, or some remote-control triggering by Spaniards, or even the American press may have been responsible. William Randolph Hearst, publisher of the *New York Journal,* was thought by many to have instigated the war to boost circulation). Tarbell was impressed by the restraint shown by everyone in the War and Navy building—with one notable exception: the assistant secretary of the navy, Theodore Roosevelt. With coattails flying, he thumped up and down the marble halls, bursting in on her sessions with Miles to bark an excited question or give unsought advice. She had heard he was preparing a special unit of volunteers which Western newspapers were calling "Teddy's Terrors," "Teddy's Gilded Gang," and "Roosevelt's Rough Riders." This antagonized her. She wanted peace, and he seemed to her a warmonger or a shameless grandstander. Although Roosevelt technically belonged to the Navy, he was clearly envisioning himself as part of an invading army, and Tarbell felt that if he did not believe in fidelity to his proper job in wartime, good manners, if nothing else, required that he resign his post. Her opposition to Teddy Roosevelt was not new. She believed he had betrayed dissident Republicans in 1884 when he bolted the Mugwump faction to support the party's nominee, the incumbent Blaine, and her distrust made her skeptical even when Teddy waged war on corruption as police commissioner in New York City in the early 1890s.

President William McKinley delayed declaring war against Spain until late April 1898. In the interim, Ida obtained the continuing story of the Senate debate from Senator Hoar's secretary. Dewey won the battle of Manila a few weeks later on May 1. Teddy Roosevelt and his Rough Riders entered Santiago, Cuba, in July, and in August the war was over.

Other *McClure's* editors were excited about the war and knew it made for good copy. In February 1899 they published Rudyard Kipling's poem exhorting Anglo-Saxons to "take up the White man's burden" and instruct—and colonize—"new-caught sullen peoples." Ray Stannard Baker described America's victory as the beginning of the "American Renasance" [*sic*] and claimed the engagement tore away the curtain of provincialism, but Tarbell thought the whole episode could have been avoided.

She saw Senator Hoar grow morose over America's post-victory trend toward imperialism. Hoar felt that helping Cuba toward self-rule would have been a greater manifestation of the Declaration of Independence than the annexation and crushing of the Philippines' own government to guarantee trade. In a spectacular expression of this sentiment, House

Speaker Thomas B. Reed resigned from public life rather than participate in the subversion of American principles.

Watching such men clash with imperialists, Tarbell became involved in the changing idea of America and how journalism might be a public service: "I could not run away to a foreign land where I should be a mere spectator. Indeed, I was beginning to suspect that one great attraction of France was that there I had no responsibility as a citizen."[31] She decided to stay and be of use.

Tarbell had already accomplished much professionally by concentrating solely on her work. Whether in Washington, New York, or on a business trip, the job occupied her to the exclusion of nearly everything else. She answered business letters by return mail, while social notes could take months. She knew there was more to life than work and that those things mattered, but they did not matter enough for her to change her way of life. She sometimes regretted the friends she had not talked to, the plays she had not seen, the walks she had not taken. She was often exhausted, but she seemed not to feel she was misspending her life, nor did she seem to resent that her best energy went into her work.

She once apologized to Herbert B. Adams: "No one has any right to be so busy he cannot enjoy his friends and that I have been. Even here in New York where there is everything I love to tempt me out—pictures, music and the play, I have hardened my heart and hid myself in a boarding house. I am about done, now, however, and shall begin to stretch my legs again."[32]

Ida was much too caught up in working during this period to visit Titusville more than a few times a year, so her family went to her. Franklin Tarbell was fascinated by his daughter's researches into Lincoln. When he went to see her in Washington he would stop off to visit Civil War battlefields in Pennsylvania, Virginia, or West Virginia. He wrote her enthusiastically of Antietam which he toured with a driver: "The National Cemetery is magnificent and there are about two hundred tablets giving a description of the location and maenovers of every core division briggade batter & etc. [sic]. It rained steadily almost all the time we were out and he only charged me $1.50 for horse and drive. I wish you had been along with me Thursday."

Franklin Tarbell apparently introduced himself to his driver, a Confederate veteran named Furss, as the father of Ida Tarbell, for Franklin mentioned in his letter: "He read your Napoleon articles and would like to see you. . . ." He closed saying he'd promised Furss she would send him a copy of McClure's. Ida helped finance her father's trips by sending him the magazine's railroad passes, and he was scrupulous about returning one he did not need so it could be credited to the company.[33]

Franklin may have been too shy to meet many of her new and accomplished friends. Gertrude Hubbard once invited her and Franklin to a Geographic Society reception, but Ida declined, saying that her father asked to be excused since he was "so full of his subject [Gettysburg which they had traveled together] that he couldn't consider another project."[34] None of her surviving correspondence indicates that any of the McClure gang met him, although they seemed to have heard much from her about his fine traits.

When Franklin was away from home, Esther went to Hatch Hollow where she had lived with her parents. The elder Tarbells were not a couple that traveled together. Possibly a part of the value of a break in routine was separation from each other. Esther wrote her daughter she was sure the change would do Franklin good. She said she would love to live in Hatch Hollow except that it would bore Ida's father and the winter would be too severe. She would not turn farmer or hermit in her last days: "I indured [*sic*] enough at Rouseville for all the rest of my life."[35]

Just as it had during their Rouseville days, the oil business continued to rule the Tarbell family. Ida encouraged her father's excursions because they eased his bitterness over the decreasing value of his oil leases. Her brother Will wrote that he shared her concern about their father, but he added: "You couldn't keep him still—he's bound to bang ahead. He gets entirely worn out and almost sick but I don't believe he'll ever stop hustling and his hard luck makes him so much more restless. It's the way with business though, like playing cards. You won't lose with a great temptation to plunge occasionally. We'll keep him off as much as we can, but the trouble is production won't stay up unless you keep fiddling with it and drilling . . . Often I wish I was in some other business and if I ever hit it rich . . . you bet I'll put most of it into something safe."[36]

Despite his words to Ida, safety seems not to have been Will Tarbell's style. He had become a leader in the fight against the Standard through his key role in the Pure Oil Company, a combination formed by independents. As secretary and treasurer, Will was the general auditor of the entire system of accounts in the United States and Europe. Lewis Emery, an oilman and Tarbell neighbor, described Will as "a man upon whom we rely more than on any other person connected with the Pure Oil Company."[37]

Will was apparently quite supportive of his elder sister and proud of her success. He encouraged her to map out a plan to get a percentage of the magazine as well as her salary. Indeed, McClure did give her a small share of the magazine, but whether it was because she asked for it or because he wanted to reward her—he had also rewarded Jaccaci with shares—is not certain.

Will's young son Scott boasted so much about his aunt that one of his playmates, Rubie Ley, decided she must have a picture of Titus-ville's celebrity. Rubie appeared at the Tarbell's front door, bearing her Brownie Kodak, when Ida was there. Tarbell, understanding how important it was to the child, helped Rubie take a professional portrait. "When Miss Tarbell sensed my earnestness, she did not laugh. She said that she would be glad to pose for me, but that she was tired so I must not be disappointed if the picture was not good," Rubie Ley recalled. Tarbell asked her to return the next morning when the light would be better. Dressed as if for the office in a shirtwaist dress with a high starched collar, a watch pinned to her breast—Tarbell folded her hands, looked seriously into the camera, and stood very still. As Ley remembered, "I took two shots [since she said] 'one might not be good.' I bowed awkwardly and said, 'Thank you, Miss Tarbell.' " But Ida had her in for cookies and lemonade which dispelled the child's awe. Having arrived to photograph Miss Tarbell, she departed calling her Aunt Ida.

"Aunt Sarah," Ida's sister, was far less interested in children, according to her grandnieces, and at this time was even removed from Titus-ville itself. Sarah's opportunity to see Europe came in 1897 when she went with Ida, who used this occasion to visit United States diplomats who were veterans of both sides of the Civil War and who might have some firsthand knowledge of Lincoln. Ida was particularly interested in following up a rumor that Lincoln had written personally to Queen Victoria asking her not to recognize the Confederacy. Tarbell pursued this as far as she could, and finally agreed with Lincoln's son that Lincoln would not have undermined his secretary of state by writing to another head of government outside official channels.

Whenever Ida was not working, the two sisters vacationed. They went to England, where they pedaled their bicycles thirty miles from Oxford to Stratford; to Switzerland; to France, where they rendez-voused with Hazen in Loches; and then to Paris, where Ida introduced Sarah to Mme Marillier and Charles Seignobos. Ida's return to Paris could only have been an emotional one. She had left there with a third-class passage and her shoes barely soled. Now she was one of America's best-known writers and her biography of Mme Roland, dedicated to Cécile Marillier, had been published the year before. The Marillier-Seignobos establishment was agog to see her and rejoiced in her success, as letters attest. The talkative Seignobos could not have failed to expound on the major topic of the day—the condemnation of a Jewish army officer for treason in behalf of Germany. Seignobos, along with some of his leading students and Émile Zola, was engaged in the fight to exonerate Captain Alfred Dreyfus, and they eventually succeeded.

After Ida left, Sarah stayed in Paris to study painting. Later she decided she would prefer the Prado to the Louvre and moved to Madrid where, consciously or not, she lived out of the shadow of her elder sister's fame and friendships.

The summer Ida and Sarah went to Europe, they visited McClure and his family in Beuzeval-Houlgate, a spa in northwestern France. McClure was not well. He was suffering from dyspepsia and insomnia, nervous ailments resulting from overwork. To no one's surprise, he suffered a physical breakdown. "It had come to the point where I had either to die or give up my work and go away for a while and I decided to do the latter,"³⁸ McClure explained to a reporter.

John Phillips took over for him. McClure was like a raven—quick-witted, shrewd, and bold, but Phillips was an owl—knowledgeable and quiet. He had wide eyes which gazed through spectacles, thinning hair, and an upturned mustache covering a firmly pinched mouth. Phillips was one of those people most accurately described in the passive voice. Things happened to him, were done to him, but he was seldom the active agent. That was Sam McClure's role. Phillips and McClure had been partners since their days at Knox College when they and Albert Brady, later the magazine's advertising manager, took over the student newspaper. Phillips, a doctor's son, had a comfortable upbringing and, as noted, planned to be a professor until he joined McClure's syndicate. Phillips soon found, however, that although McClure thought he had eighteen hundred dollars to fund the project, he had only six hundred.

Phillips, while seldom the bearer of good news, was essential to McClure because he was practical and willing to stay in place while McClure gyrated between New York and the rest of the world. By the time Tarbell met him, Phillips was possessed of a wife, small children, and a secret—his first wife, a girl from his hometown of Galesburg, Illinois, had hanged herself. The second Mrs. John S. Phillips, Jennie, stayed in the background. A *McClure's* staffer described her thus: ". . . a little woman not without a sort of distinction, tho' it is far from the kind that rests on mental fireworks."³⁹

Phillips installed his family in Duxbury, Massachusetts, for the summer and in Goshen, New York, for the rest of the year. During the week he lived in town devoting himself to the magazine and the lives of the staff.

Phillips, who in his letters exhorted males to be "manly," which in that era was a notion comprising self-reliance, chivalry, and honesty, was also a man possessed by fears. He always remembered his shock upon hearing that one of the finest young men in his hometown was an embezzler, and Phillips feared that he too might break loose and do a shameful act. In his thirties, he took as his motto "Hope little, work much, expect nothing."

Tarbell was at first intimidated by Phillips's seriousness. When he paid her a courtesy call in Washington, she was so flustered that, although it was morning, she offered him a beer. But when McClure left on his extended rest, Phillips and Tarbell began to get to know each other better. They grew sufficiently friendly that he confessed that when he saw her free-lance articles from Paris, written in a self-conscious hand, he had decided she was a middle-aged New England school-teacher and she laughed about how stupid she felt when she realized she had offered him a beer for breakfast.

Tarbell trusted Phillips's caution in ways she never trusted McClure's praise. McClure, bubbling over with love and admiration for her and other writers, could tell Ida when her articles did not work, but the harried and taciturn Phillips knew how to fix them. She felt that this man alone was smart enough to discover her secret—she was really no writer, no matter what everyone said. "You very rarely praised—there was little to praise," she once wrote him. "I can still tell just where you sat when you said the first appreciative word on something in an article. It pulled me up like the Dickens—of course nobody knew that, I was buried in gloom most of the time and I hated and doubted myself and wanted to get back to Paris. I wasn't long in realizing your eye on everything—you were our friendly authority."[40] Indeed, the staff whispered that Sam had three hundred ideas a minute, but only JSP knew which one was not crazy.

Indeed, McClure could drive his associates to near frenzy. After his long rest restored him, he bounced back with such vigor that he overextended himself and his publishing house. Besides the syndicate, the magazine and the short-lived quarterly, McClure prepared to publish an encyclopedia, then abandoned the idea. In 1897, he and Frank Doubleday started Doubleday & McClure Co. to publish books. Each dollar McClure acquired was twice spent—first for settling old debts, then for expansion, which always incurred new liabilities.

A dubious opportunity presented itself in 1899 when J. P. Morgan offered McClure Harper & Brothers publishing house to add to Doubleday & McClure. The financier had purchased Harper to save its textbook division, but found it was not returning a sufficient profit on his investment. "The General," as they nicknamed McClure, leaped at the chance to control *Harper's Weekly, Harper's Monthly, Harper's Bazaar,* and *Round Table* for children, but as new men and new ambitions wedged themselves into the tight circle of old friends, hairline cracks in the organization threatened to fissure. Brady in particular was offended when Doubleday was given a larger share of the business than Brady had. It was all too much for McClure, who went to Johns Hopkins Hospital and then to France to guard his strength.[41]

Phillips, who was diagnosed as having a rapid heartbeat, supervised the complicated dealings with the Harper concern. After several months, business manager Brady convinced others of what he had seen at the beginning: in buying Harper's they were simply buying a debt. The escape clause Brady had insisted on released them from the contract. Late in the year, Doubleday, whose vaulting ambition McClure had started to distrust, resigned to form Doubleday, Page & Co. with former McClure associate Walter Page.

In the midst of all these upheavals, McClure had summoned Ida Tarbell back to New York from Washington to act as editor of *McClure's*. Her actual title was "managing editor," but the staff called the post "desk editor," for she never left the office. Her change in status required her to handle Phillips tactfully, but it did free him for the ongoing Harper negotiations. Tarbell had watched McClure's expansion with alarm. Most men in the firm had neither liked nor trusted Doubleday, but Tarbell thought he was needed. She later wrote McClure from Clifton Springs, where she took her turn at trying to rest: "I do not like to see Mr. Doubleday and Mr. Page go. They are strong men in their way and would relieve you and Mr. Phillips of much heavy care you will have to bear . . . but you know the situation and I do not and you have a magician's skill in pulling things out so I know it will be alright in the end."[42]

Tarbell arrived in New York in mid-May of 1899, in time to settle in for a torrid summer. Her departure from Washington was so hasty that she left arrangements for her apartment to be handled by a secretary. Indeed, it was some time before she was sure that the move to New York was a permanent one.

She found an apartment in Greenwich Village at 40 West Ninth Street, twenty blocks from the office. She chose this quarter, faced in brownstone and graced by foliage, because it gave her a scent of Paris. She frequented two nearby hotel restaurants, the Brevoort, favored by the English, and the Griffou where French was spoken and meals were good and inexpensive. Both places were patronized by a literary crowd, including Mark Twain, who became a pleasant acquaintance, and Mrs. Schuyler Van Rensselaer, an art critic and historian, who became a friend. Born Mariana Griswold in 1851 to an old family in the China trade, she married within her class. After she was widowed at the age of thirty-three, Mrs. Van Rensselaer began to write on such topics as English cathedrals, architecture, and the history of gardening. When her only son died at the age of twenty-one in 1894, she took up settlement work and labored to improve public education. A perfectionist in her writing, Mrs. Van Rensselaer said little about herself but came out firmly against woman suffrage, insisting that women should concentrate on their families. Tarbell was mindful of the difference between her own background and that of her wealthy friend: "She belonged to such a different world, but there was always a bridge over and we came and went naturally on it."[43] It was probably Mrs. Van Rensselaer who convinced Tarbell to become a member, although inactive, of the New York State Association Opposed to the Extension of Suffrage to Women.

Tarbell's home, which she furnished simply but with as much elegance as she could afford, had a large living room with windows reaching to the floor, a small dining room, and two bedrooms, of which the larger became her study. To care for it and her two cats when she was away, she hired an Irish maid.[44]

Her domestic tranquillity was a contrast to the office. Ida's responsibilities as editor were first to see that McClure's instructions were carried out, that production and copyediting departments functioned smoothly, and that the magazine remained lively and vital. Above all, she was not to let a good writer get away. Such judgment is always subject to luck and, like most others at that time, she rejected the work of Theodore Dreiser, but in a very nice way: "I like it very much. I did not consider it, however, a *McClure* article. I should think it a good *Century* or possible *Harper's Magazine* article, and it certainly will lend itself admirably to illustration."[45]

Tarbell's authority was temporary, but it was assured. Viola Roseboro, *McClure's* literary editor, noted: "When I first knew her in the *McClure's* office, remotely enough for she had no idea of letting me close—her life largely consisted in holding people off—one of the things I sharply noted and watched with pleasure was the attitude toward her of the office full of young men. She was above them all in power and had a certain tacit authority over them, tacit because she was not in a [permanent] executive position. Another woman who was with us for a time demonstrated how offensive authority in a woman could be to such males. She was an executive. They all detested her and her assumed masculinity. IMT they doted on and frankly looked up to, accepting her innate power as above all theirs and entitling her to authority. She was with them just as you see her with anybody today . . . I quite thought in those days that she was a good deal older than I was. I am sure she did not look it, but she seemed to the naked eye to have no coquetteries at all."[46]

Ida Tarbell was not one to be cozy in an office atmosphere. Lunches with favorites continued, but she did not allow time for those who would merely sap her energy, nor had she ever. In Paris, once her American friends left, her personal life had centered around Mme Marillier, who was the great-granddaughter of the woman she was writing about. In Washington, Tarbell quit the Patterson boardinghouse which she loved so well because she needed time alone to recoup her strength.

So it was in New York. She was conscious that she hurt other people by her reserve—"I always feel brutal when I don't do what the other person wants,"[47] she once admitted—but she remained quietly unavailable when women on the staff offered chatty friendships.

At this time the McClure enterprises took up a city block on Lexington Avenue between Twenty-fifth and Twenty-sixth streets, two blocks from the city's main shopping thoroughfare on Twenty-third. When Ida Tarbell's desk became the chief operating one, *McClure's* had, in the words of William Allen White, the air of a wholesale silk outlet or a hardware business. He thought the tony *Scribner's* office was like "some ancient volume of forgotten lore" where *McClure's* was an "unexpurgated dictionary of tomorrow." The *McClure's* headquarters was full of clutter and noise and bustle and the latest gadgets of efficiency from typewriters to Dictaphones and pneumatic tubes.[48]

The printing press was so advanced that it had a bell to ring out when it needed paper. The thing nonplussed Mark Twain—almost. When he heard it sounding for help he asked if it could vote. Rudyard Kipling was so taken by the huge elevator which held a delivery truck and horses that he sneaked off to play with the switches by himself and piloted himself to another floor whereupon the printer turned around and feared the prized author had fallen down the elevator shaft.

Stephen Crane often dropped by to perch on Ray Stannard Baker's desk, draw his knees to his chin, and wrap his long arms around his legs. A pale, slim, tired fellow, he was ever cynical, but always interesting. Then there were all the people McClure had hired and didn't need. The more talented eventually slunk away, but at five o'clock the place was overrun by charwomen who had touched McClure with hard-luck stories.

Art director August Jaccaci inspired much speculation. He was rumored to have painted the Havana Opera House murals and to have killed an opponent in a duel in Mexico. A dark exotic man, he looked Italian, Greek, or perhaps Polish. Forty years later it was learned he was a Gypsy. He was affable and so desirous of being helpful that he often interfered with writers and forgot his own duties in the art department. His sudden storms of temper were legendary and sometimes rained on Ida. McClure complained that, unlike Miss Tarbell, Jac constantly needed supervision. He was on his way out for years, saved by one hundred thousand dollars' worth of stock McClure had given him in a generous moment.

Booth Tarkington described the Jaccaci treatment and accent in a letter home. He said Jaccaci had met him with a joyous howl—"Ha, ha! It iss You!" He tossed Tarkington's coat, hat, and stick on a pile of manuscripts and said, "We haf waited for you! And so it iss *you*." Tarbell ("a tall woman . . . a *nice* woman"), Jaccaci, and McClure took Tarkington to lunch. Tarkington observed: "Jaccaci is great and Miss

T. very clever and all very friendly . . . The lunch was long & delightful & when it was over it was almost time to dress for dinner."[49]

They summoned Tarkington to New York because of his tale, "The Gentleman from Indiana," about a small-town newspaper editor's fight against corruption. *McClure's* legend was that when it arrived, Viola Roseboro, with tears streaming from her eyes, approached McClure, saying, "Here is a story sent from God Almighty to save *McClure's Magazine*." Everyone had his or her own version of the quote, but all gave "Rosie" credit for her excellent judgment.

McClure had another reader at this time who also wrote for them. His name was Frank Norris, but he didn't stay long. With McClure's blessing, and faithful salary checks, Norris went home to San Francisco to write *The Octopus*, a realistic tale of California farm life which became an American classic.

Roseboro also published some short stories, but her stronger talent was for detecting the talent of others. A one-time actress whom McClure hired to read manuscripts, Rosie lugged home a suitcase full of them each night and kept two barrels of unsolicited work by her desk. From these she plucked the work of a convict who called himself O. Henry and bought it for the syndicate. Ida allowed her to publish his "Whistling Dick's Christmas Stocking" the first month of her editorship, not knowing that McClure had already rejected it.

Ida respected Roseboro, but was put off by Roseboro's hand-rolled cigars and the coarse Anglo-Saxon words she exhaled with the smoke. Ida was friendlier with Mary Bisland who oozed New Orleans charm. Bisland had worked her way up from health and women's pages—penning such stories as "Is Coffee a Food?"—to a post on the syndicate. She dressed beautifully, scolded Ida for her lack of vanity, and lured her out of the office to try on hats. Tarbell once confessed: "The first time I paid the [exorbitant sum of] twenty dollars for a hat was due to Mary Bisland. I was spoiled for bargains after that."[50] Yet for all her friendship with Bisland, she trusted Rosie's rambunctious bluntness more.

The newest addition to the staff at that time was young Albert Boyden, twenty-three and fresh from Harvard. McClure saw that this dark-haired youngster had a way of keeping everyone cheerful and soon made him production manager so he could jolly editors, writers, and printers into meeting their deadlines.

Ida helped familiarize Boyden with the routine and he caught on so well that soon Tarbell handled only callers and correspondence. Even if he had not been personable, she would have noticed him for the sake of his brother-in-law, John Finley. Finley had worked on *The Chautauqua Assembly Herald* one summer during Ida's tenure and later became president of Knox College, alma mater of Phillips and McClure. Finley went to the *McClure's* organization with the expectation that McClure would buy *Harper's Weekly* and make him its editor. When that plan faded, Finley took a teaching post at Princeton, became president of the College of the City of New York, and then editor in chief of *The New York Times.*

Boyden, eighteen years younger than Ida, quickly moved from the status of neophyte to confidant and sometimes passed secrets of the magazine's inner circle out to the clerks. He had great empathy for women. As a Harvard classmate noted: "His friendships with girls had that unusual touch which marked his relations with womankind through his whole life, and they were altogether free from the element of romance ... There was nothing effeminate about Bert—far from it—yet there was in his make-up something rare among boys and men, a certain sympathetic interest and understanding in all the feminine preoccupations and refinements of life which made him as much at home in the feminine atmosphere as the girls themselves."[51]

Tarbell took Boyden under her wing. When he wanted his first roommate to move out, she gave him the courage to break the news. She practically badgered Boyden into taking his first trip to Europe and, with the McClure gang, saw him off and welcomed him back. He became *McClure's* social director; once his pay increased, Bert and his second and permanent roommate, the Reverend Maitland Bartlett, hosted weekly dinners. No one minded climbing the four flights to their apartment on Stuyvesant Square. One guest recalled: "If [they were] afternoon affairs, there would be gay songs, monologues and imitations ... but it was to Bert's dinners we looked forward to most, dinners alive with discussion of men, affairs and books ..."[52]

The two bachelors served an unvaried menu which included creamed potatoes and cheese, but the food was not important. Talking was a favorite activity for the whole group, but as time passed, Boyden prevailed upon Ida to join him in a cakewalk and other dances as they became the rage.

Ray Stannard Baker left the best physical description of Boyden in noting that his smile was half-ironical and his gestures often self-deprecating. "He was always eager, hurrying, expectant, happy." Baker recalled that Boyden would accept a manuscript with compliments, rush it into print, and return chastising Baker for not understanding the mechanics of putting out a magazine.[53]

Ida Tarbell seemed to rely on the young Boyden as much as she once trusted the young Downer Hazen. Hazen still wrote to Ida, often in melancholy moods: "Fortunately, you are the one woman I have known to whom one doesn't have to explain things. You take things like a man as they come without seeking for *arrière-pensées* [ulterior motives] and without endless analysis. *Que Dieu vous bénisse!*"[54]

One can only wonder how Tarbell received the news, shortly after her forty-third birthday, that Hazen was to marry a twenty-eight-year-old Smith graduate: "The worst has happened and your faith in me is severely tested. I am engaged to Miss Sally Duryea of New York. We are not going to announce our high-handed action just yet but I am writing you in confidence because I wish you to know. . . . Really, Miss Tarbell, I was never in as buoyant and gay a mood as I am now, never as deeply satisfied with the world and all it contains. Only a long series of remarks made to you during the last ten years somewhat hampers my freedom of utterance now, another instance of the tyranny of the past on us."[55]

She did not have much time for regret. *McClure's* and New York were the hub of her life. Witter Bynner, the poetry editor and also a poet, described the Ida Tarbell of this time as "firm as the Statue of Liberty and holding up the lantern of integrity." He said: "Whereas S.S. was the motor, the galvanizer of the staff . . . Phillips and Ida were the control, especially Ida. I can see her still, sitting there and gravely weighing prospects, possibilities, checking errors, smoothing differences. Her interest was mainly factual and moral, rather than literary. She respected Viola's management of the fiction and mine of the poetry under the final say-so of the Chief, but she hadn't the inclusive interest he had in everything we printed. Her concern was honest information and salutary direction. Every fiber of her was firm and true. The rest of us tided around her. And this was not only in matters of magazine policy or contents. It was in personal matters too. She was pacifier and arbiter, guide, philosopher and friend."[56]

Ida Tarbell was not writing very much in those days, but waiting for this woman who had cut through the mystery of Lincoln was an important mystery of a very different kind.

Seven

Lady of the Muckrake

McClure's Magazine had been too dispirited by the end of the nineteenth century to take much joy in the start of the twentieth. The new era saw many changes in the magazine, particularly in terms of its personnel. Phillips was absent several months recovering from exhaustion, Jaccaci moved to Europe. Albert Brady, wizard of *McClure's* business office, died, and McClure, his energy turned to mania, was in France under a physician's care.

Ray Stannard Baker noted: "For most members of the staff, long continued overwork, nervous tension and excitement had begun to extract the price of high-flown ambition and swift success."[1]

The group was under continuous pressure to come up with a circulation-boosting series to meet the boast, "The keynote of *McClure's* is human interest, the record of human activities. John Finley believed he had found just such a subject. McClure was in agreement and wrote to Phillips: "It seems to me that he has found the great feature, and the great feature is Trusts . . . As the Silver Question excited America during the last Presidential campaign. That will be the great red-hot event. And the magazine that puts the various phases of the subject that people want to be informed about will be bound to have a good circulation . . ."[2]

McClure himself had addressed the topic before. In early 1890, his syndicate offered a variety of legal and philosophical opinions as to whether or not trusts were legal, and who derived the most benefit from them. Now the time seemed right for the magazine to do an incisive article.

During 1900, a prosperous year for America, Tarbell, Phillips, and others in New York debated how to show an industry passing from ownership by the many to control by the few. The editors felt that one trust, properly treated, could illustrate the pattern of all others. But which one?

Ida suggested a study of how the Sugar Trust influenced tariff legislation, which in turn affected the price paid by the housewife, but McClure thought that too trivial. The Beef Trust might have become their target, but Philip Armour did himself the favor of dying in January 1901, thus removing a living person on whom to target the exposé. When a letter from Ray Stannard Baker suggested a story on the discovery of oil in California, Tarbell replied:

> Unquestionably we ought to do something in the coming year on the great industrial developments of the country, but it seems clear to me that we must not attempt to do this by describing the discovery and opening of great natural resources such as in the case of the oil. We have got to find a new plan of attacking it. Something that will show clearly not only the magnitude of the industries and commercial developments, and the changes they have brought in various parts of the country, but something which will make clear the great principles by which industrial leaders are combining and controlling these resources.[3]

The result was Baker's article "What the U.S. Steel Corp. Really Is," in November 1901, describing J. Pierpont Morgan's company as a government unto itself. Still, *McClure's* sought something with more impact. In discussions with Phillips, Tarbell offered more vivid examples of the direction the trust article should take. She told him how her father first prospered in the oil business and then was crushed when the monopoly took hold, and how townspeople rose up against the Standard and made revolution seem a sacred thing. As she talked, her own interest in the project quickened. She had once tried to novelize Pithole's boom; now at last it occurred to her that she might treat the story as a documented historical narrative. She grew convinced it could be done, but doubted anyone would care to read it. Phillips prodded her to produce an outline and take it to Sam McClure in Europe.

She sailed in September 1901, a few weeks after McKinley was assassinated and Teddy Roosevelt succeeded to the presidency. She expected to stay with McClure only a week, but her visit stretched on. She and McClure usually managed to have fun together as well as working hard.

This was fine with Hattie McClure, who suffered from rheumatoid arthritis and thought Tarbell had a stabilizing influence on her husband. In fact, Sam McClure had a liberating effect on Ida. Sam McClure was expansive, oversized, and full of ideas for excursions. Once he had her help him collect a thousand neckties in Paris and London. No one can know precisely what was between them. Physical passion seems not to have been Ida Tarbell's style. Most likely, their relationship had the character of courtly love—chaste veneration for the unavailable. Only in this case it was McClure, wed to his college sweetheart long before they met, whose marriage safely limited their involvement.

Tarbell carried her outline for the Standard Oil series to Vevey, Switzerland, where McClure was taking a rest cure. Not unexpectedly, he seized upon her arrival as a chance of escape. He whisked Ida and his wife to Lucerne, the Italian lakes, and Milan before he would talk business. At the spa of Salsomaggiore Terme in Italy, in an area fringed by oil refineries, they baked in mud, basked in steam, and chatted with Cecil Rhodes. At last, McClure approved her proposal of a three-part, twenty-five-thousand-word feature on Standard Oil.

Research, Ida assured McClure, would be a simple task of reviewing and verifying amply documented findings of governmental investigations. In 1872 and 1876, congressional committees had probed the Standard. In 1879, investigators scrutinized it in New York, Ohio, and Pennsylvania. In 1891, an Ohio judge dismantled the trust, whereupon the Standard relocated its headquarters from Cleveland to Bayonne, New Jersey. Tarbell expected to find in the mass of records various charters and agreements by which Standard operated and the testimony of participants in the events. She thought that in a library she could explore the labyrinth that was the Standard Oil Company and map its workings and its plan.

Tarbell professed that she began her work with an open mind. In fact, she said that she was not sure that John D. Rockefeller had done anything illegal. However, she did know the effects he had had on her own family. Franklin Tarbell had been forced to mortgage his home, something he thought tantamount to defiling it. There were people in the town, old friends and business associates, to whom the Tarbells no longer spoke because they had sold out to the Standard, and there was in the Tarbell house the taint of things having gone wrong, promises not kept and hard work not rewarded.

The psychic toll of the Standard was easy to perceive, but about the company itself she knew very little. Informing herself was harder than she expected it to be. Key documents had disappeared. Titusville neighbors whom she thought would help either feared or distrusted her.

Those who sold out to Rockefeller at a handsome profit wanted no further trouble. Those who held out against him still feared what he would do. Her father warned she was jeopardizing *McClure's.* "Don't do it, Ida," he advised. "They will ruin the magazine."

She dismissed as nonsense all warnings that the Standard would kill or maim her; for the Standard to do that would be to indict itself. Finally, she saw that the Standard was indeed aware of her. One night at a dinner party given by Alexander Graham Bell in Washington, Frank Vanderlip, one of the capital's most popular bachelors and vice-president of the Rockefeller-controlled National City Bank, called her into an anteroom. He told her plainly that his bank looked with concern at what she was doing. She was stunned at this tacit financial threat against the magazine, and the implicit threat that she was being watched. "Well, I am sorry," she said, before they rejoined the other guests, "but of course that makes no difference to me."[4]

The Standard did not move directly against her, but Henry Demarest Lloyd did. A decade before, Lloyd had written *Wealth Against Commonwealth* which vilified the Standard. Lloyd was the classic penniless boy who had made good. He married his sweetheart, the daughter of his boss, and was able to live out his days a sincere and comfortable reformer.

Ida had read his book in Paris when her English friend H. Wickham Steed gave her a copy, but she rejected Lloyd's work as a strident argument for socialism, a system she thought more idealistic than practical. "As I saw it," Tarbell later recalled, "it was not capitalism but an open disregard of decent ethical business practices by capitalists which lay at the bottom of the story Mr. Lloyd told so dramatically."[5]

Lloyd's theme had been the malevolent power of wealth. He focused on the Standard to illustrate his arguments, but he did not name it. Tarbell intended to be crisper in her presentation, to go straight to the heart of the story and to tell nothing that could not be proven. She also intended to ask Standard Oil to comment on her findings. This was simply sound journalism, but Lloyd heard about it and warned independents that she had been taken in by Standard Oil. He wrote key people in the oil regions entreating them to avoid Tarbell.

Tarbell, who had cajoled material about Abraham Lincoln from backwoods strangers, could not understand why she could not convince her old neighbors to help her. "It was a persistent fog of suspicion and doubt and fear. From the start this fog hampered what was my first business, making sure of the documents in the case,"[6] she said.

She made a particularly rigorous search for a pamphlet called *The Rise and Fall of the South Improvement Company.* Compiled in 1873, it detailed the exposure and dissolution of the company which had colluded with railroads to obtain rebates (refunds of its own shipping costs), drawbacks (payments from competitors' shipping fees), and illegal information about its rivals' shipments.

No charge was as damaging to the Standard as the accusation that it had grown from the South Improvement Company; Rockefeller always disavowed that he had anything to do with so predatory a scheme. Some insisted that the thirty-year-old document Tarbell sought verified that the Standard had in fact risen from South Improvement's ashes, but all copies had mysteriously disappeared. Reportedly, the Standard had purchased and destroyed them all.

The forces suppressing *The Rise and Fall of the South Improvement Company* had not reckoned with the New York Public Library. After Tarbell gave up on Titusville's archives, she applied there and at last discovered her treasure. Its 126 pages of closely spaced type disclosed a crucial bit of testimony: a John Alexander, asked by a congressional investigator if he sold his refinery to South Improvement, replied, "To one of the members, as I suppose, of the South Improvement Company, Mr. Rockefeller; he is a director in that company; it was sold in name to the Standard Oil Company, of Cleveland, but the arrangement was, as I understand it, that they were to put it into the South Improvement Company."

Thus for the first time, Ida could prove that Rockefeller was a linchpin of an illegal ring whose tactics he transferred to the Standard Oil Company.

Evidence showed that John D. Rockefeller had purchased the charter for South Improvement from an estate in 1871 and asked everyone involved to sign a pledge of secrecy. The charter, a license to operate in the state of Pennsylvania, was quoted in the pamphlet. It granted Rockefeller's group powers of such force and dimension that oilmen felt thoroughly justified in calling it an octopus: "The South Improvement Company could own, contract or operate any work, business or traffic (save only banking), may hold and transfer any kind of property (real or personal), hold and operate on any leased property (operate in any state and territory). Its stockholders, directors included, were liable to the amount of their stock only."

The oil producers were aghast to confront this monstrous thing which today is easily recognizable as a modern corporation. As for being able to engage in any operation save banking, John D. Rockefeller made up for that omission by securing control of the National City Bank of New York. The Pennsylvania Legislature never published this 1870 charter, disclosed who proposed it, or recorded its vote, according to Tarbell who searched for these pieces of information.

While engaged in the affair of the impounded pamphlet, Tarbell realized that she would need an assistant. In her Lincoln work, she had employed a researcher who did only what she directed. What she wanted now was someone with enthusiasm, someone who would enjoy the chase for its own sake. She wanted a reporter, one of the new sort who had gone to college and who had energy, discretion, and polish. To find this prize, she wrote to newspaper editors in Cleveland asking the name of someone who might track down a small bit of information. To each young man—the idea of a similarly qualified young woman seemed not to occur to her—she imposed a challenge. Could he find pictures of some of the principals of the Standard Oil Company and some refineries? She would prefer he set about it at once and that *McClure's* not be mentioned.

Five days later she received an impressive reply: "My understanding is that I have a two-fold duty: first, to follow specific instructions, and second, to make suggestions . . . in the meantime, I shall consult with my brother who is an attorney for Mr. Frank Rockefeller [John's brother] and for an independent oil company. He knows a good deal about prominent figures in the history of the oil business in this city. In the campaign for photographs I shall probably call upon my friend, Mr. Newman, staff photographer for *The Plain Dealer*."[7] Thus John McAlpin Siddall, young associate editor of *The Chautauquan* which had moved to Cleveland after Flood's retirement, got the job.

In the process of investigative reporting, theirs was as illustrious a meeting as that of Holmes and Watson. Only in this case, each was to be Sherlock and no leap of deduction, only clear evidence, was allowed. Ida followed up her telegrams with a letter to Siddall disclosing their actual undertaking: "Perhaps I should say that the work we have in mind is a narrative history of the Standard Oil Company. I am to do it, and shall go about it as I would any other piece of historical work in which I had to draw almost entirely from original sources. It is in no sense a piece of economic work, nor is it intended to be controversial, but a straightforward narrative, as picturesque and dramatic as I can make it, of the great monopoly. We hope it will be something that you will be glad to have been associated with."[8]

To his surprise, Siddall soon found that neither his brother, so happily placed, nor other insiders were willing to assist him. He told Tarbell he doubted he'd be able to help her, but she only added to the list of portraits she required. Siddall, still discouraged, sent in a letter of resignation. Boyden intercepted the envelope while Tarbell was away: he wrote to Siddall that they were disappointed, but could he recommend someone else? Siddall reconsidered, stayed, and allowed Ida to misspell his name for the first year of their correspondence.

He was a young man of twenty-seven, short and plump with an air of excitement and energy. Never having enough to do at work, he led a Lincoln's Boys Club which had adopted as its Bible Tarbell's *Life of*

Lincoln. He also served on reform mayor Tom Johnson's Board of Education.

For Tarbell, Siddall ferreted through photographers' files and volunteered to sort through the stock of deceased photographers who had left boxes of negatives and prints. Onetime Rockefeller neighbors lent him prints, but only for a few days lest they be missed. These he had copied for *McClure's* and for himself so that he could go about the painstaking process of identifying the man in the high hat or the unbuckled spat standing to the left or right of the great John D. Many tableaux were a quarter century old, taken while Rockefeller personally handled most deals that were to make his fortune.

Siddall persuaded a former Oberlin classmate to convince a Cleveland photographer to sell him ten pictures of John D. Rockefeller for fifty dollars each. There was JDR holding his granddaughter, others of his wife, children, father, and even an uncle, taken for family albums and personal souvenirs, and now to be used to illustrate an exposé of his misdeeds. Having taken advantage of the photographer's naïveté, Siddall sought to protect him by having a *McClure's* retoucher erase the background.

Some rumored photos, like prize fish, got away. These included The Great Man on skates and another of him standing next to the hind end of a racehorse he purportedly owned.

After a few telegrams went astray, Tarbell and he communicated only by letter, with Sid at one point suggesting they write in cipher. Sometimes Ida would be on the trail of something so important she could only hint at it through the mails. "I had the other day my first important interview here with their people. I would give a great deal to talk it over with you, knowing your interest. It was in every way amazing to me. Of course, I cannot write it out."[9]

She had planned to confront Standard Oil sources only after she had unearthed documentation they could otherwise have concealed. She explained to a reporter:

> Someone once asked me why I did not go first to the heads of the Company for my information. This person did not know overmuch of humanity I think, else he would have realized instantly that the Standard Oil Company would have shut the door of their closet on their skeleton. But after one had discovered the skeleton and had scrutinized him at a very close range, why then shut the door? That is the reason I did not go to the magnates in the beginning.[10]

She approached Standard Oil when she was ready by venturing into the den of Henry Rogers, one of the Standard's more flamboyant partners, at his home on West Fifty-seventh Street. Rogers had been an early wildcatter, an independent who battled all attempts at take-over until he saw prosperity lay in joining forces with Rockefeller. Rogers himself had at first led New York refiners against Rockefeller and the South Improvement Company: but his boss, Charles Pratt, decided that joining them was the only way to stay in business. Thus Rockefeller acquired the services and capital of two of his ablest foes.

If Frank Vanderlip thought he should warn Ida off on behalf of the Standard, Rogers decided it would be wiser to invite her in. He cared about how people regarded the firm and about what a later generation would call corporate image. While reading his newspaper, Rogers saw *McClure's* advertisement of her forthcoming series. He thought it important that she verify her work with him and asked a mutual acquaintance, Mark Twain, to arrange it.

Their first encounter, lasting two hours, served to introduce magnate and journalist to each other. Rogers, who had gotten his start in Rouseville, remembered Tarbell's Tank Shops and Franklin Tarbell. Ida learned that his had been the white house which she had thought the only beautiful thing in Rouseville. Together they reconstructed the town and the narrow ravine which ran between their hillsides.

When they met, Rogers had just turned sixty-two. Tall and muscular, with a mane of gray hair, he retained a trace of the roustabout despite his grooming and his air of command. As they went over rebates and pipelines, and the independents' struggles and failures, Rogers extolled Standard's achievements, its efficiency and productivity. Ida found herself observing his heavy eyebrows and wondering what the mouth was like behind the drooping white mustache: "I fancy [the mouth] must have been flexible, capable of both firm decision and of gay laughter,"[11] she speculated.

They made a pact—she would bring each case history to him and he would give her documents, figures, justifications. She stressed, however, that she alone would decide how all material was to be used. Future meetings, over two years, often took her to the headquarters of Standard Oil at 26 Broadway. Its atmosphere was Spartan, purposeful, with an efficiency that impressed those used to Victorian geegaws and ornamentation. The air clicked with telegraphic instruments, elevators appeared with a marvelous brisk silence, and within the building, a telegraph key conveyed the instructions of John D. Rockefeller from his Cleveland home. His retirement was active; Rockefeller employed a worldwide work force twice as large as the U.S. Army.

Tarbell was ushered in one door and out another, for company policy decreed that visitors were not to encounter each other. Occasionally, she glimpsed the fabled Miss Harrison, Rogers's private secretary, a woman reputed to earn the staggering amount of ten thousand dollars per annum. Ida was struck by the brusqueness of the efficient business-woman, but she was amused by the attractive, self-important young male clerks piloting her to Rogers's office by varied routes. One thing mystified her. Each time she went there, the same man was stationed at a window, apparently to spy on her. The whole episode delighted Sam McClure. Back at the magazine office, he amused himself by trying to compute the amount of money Rogers contributed to the exposé by giving them so much of his time.

Rogers was always willing to talk to Tarbell, but not necessarily to ad-dress her points. Whether or not he intended to deceive, he did have his own interpretation of events. When she confronted him with false tes-timony he had given under oath, he waved it away saying, "They had no business prying into my private affairs." Both magnate and journalist tried to keep tempers in check. The time Tarbell exploded that one of Rogers's colleagues was a liar and hypocrite, he looked out the window and remarked that it would probably rain. Another time he was so irri-tated that he labeled her remarks un-Christian and advised her to at-tend church more often.

Rogers promised she would interview John D. Rockefeller, but the best he came up with was Henry Flagler, an early partner who, like Rockefeller, had been a clerk and grocery purveyor in Cleveland. In his youth, Flagler was referred to as "the silent, handsome man," but in later years he revealed the aggressive qualities behind that exterior. In about 1870, near the age of forty, Flagler had discovered Florida, estab-lished the Florida East Coast Railway, and experienced a permutation of his personal life. He lost interest in his wife and decided she was de-mented. Flagler confined her to her home, then obtained a divorce under a Florida law he had proposed. By the time Tarbell met him, he was married to a much younger woman and had developed a chain of resorts—including Miami and Palm Beach—to woo passengers to his railroad.

The rambunctious Flagler was at first forthcoming: "John D. Rocke-feller would do me out of a dollar today," he shouted, banging a fist on the table. "This is, if he could do it honestly, Miss Tarbell, if he could do it honestly." With that, his talk turned circumspect and he observed that his old friend, like the Lord in His day, was sadly misunderstood.[12]

What became apparent to Ida was that besides conferring wealth upon his colleagues, Rockefeller inspired intense animosity in them. Rogers told her how he had owned stock in the seventy companies the Standard acquired before 1880, but since transactions were secret, his heirs could not have inherited the company's stock if he had died. Only the organization of the trust under a state law protected for his family what he had acquired.

Along with greater opportunities for profits, Rogers found under the Standard umbrella great opprobrium. In 1885, he was indicted for conspiracy in the matter of how the Standard took over the Vacuum Oil Works of Rochester. He hoped Tarbell would investigate this story thoroughly and vindicate him in his children's eyes. Rogers contended that the Vacuum had been formed solely to trap the Standard into buying it and that judges and lawyers had colluded against the company. When Ida grew alarmed at his paranoia, Rogers thought he had intimidated her into joining his side. He produced a letter thanking her for agreeing to make her story correspond with his understanding. But she explained that he could certainly correct misquotations, if any, in her article, yet he could not reinterpret the facts.

Determined to be impartial, she submitted the case to a lawyer for review and ultimately wrote that Rogers and his codefendants had not deserved to be indicted, as a judge had ruled on appeal.

Reading this article, which was published in *McClure's*, Mark Twain was tickled. He joshed in a letter to Rogers that Tarbell had deprived him of rank as a conspirator. She had plainly been bought, Twain said. But by that time, Rogers had realized that he had to take Ida seriously and decided it would be wiser to end his association with her.

In February 1902, Tarbell spent a week in Washington with the heads of the Industrial Commission, a congressional committee that monitored business practice. They gave her carte blanche to examine their files. On five-by-eight-inch scraps of paper she made notes of what struck her:

"How can I find out just what they manufactured? (Specific) Honorable W. Harkness—who is he? Still alive?"

To Siddall she wrote: "The task confronting me is such a monstrous one that I am staggering a bit under it."[13] Once back in New York, she sent Martin Knapp, chairman of the Interstate Commerce Commission, a copy of her *Life of Lincoln*. That apparently expedited matters because Knapp responded with the schedule of petroleum tariff rates beneficial to Standard Oil. He also referred her to specific testimony before the Industrial Commission and to an article on railway discriminations. He advised her to pay particular attention to the location of Standard plants versus those of the independents. Independents had the advantage of being at the site of the wells, but railroads manipulated rates to eliminate their edge. Knapp closed by saying he preferred she not mention his name.[14]

Whatever Tarbell could pry loose by charm, she reviewed and cross-referenced. The Industrial Commission had published in 1900 a digest of evidence on rebates, and quoted Rockefeller as saying that the Standard had refunded illegal rebates before a suit was brought. She checked the records of a circuit court in the Southern District of Ohio and found Rockefeller was correct, but only technically. He had made refunds just twelve days before the judge looked into the case.

In the first several months of 1902, Tarbell concluded drafts of the first three articles of her series. She opened with the discovery of oil and mentioned one entrepreneur: "A young Iowa school teacher and farmer, visiting at his home in Erie County, saw his chance to invent a receptacle which would hold oil in quantities . . . " She told how he worked himself and his men night and day. That man was her father.

Her second installment dealt with the formation of the Standard, and the third with the oil war of 1872 where independents defeated the South Improvement Company. She wrote to Phillips, who was vacationing with his family in Duxbury, Massachusetts, that she wanted to show him her work as his judgment and criticism meant more than anyone else's. Phillips's comments were sufficiently critical that he postponed her articles. Just before her European vacation, she wrote Siddall a letter which showed that the investigation was wearing her down: "I have three articles finished, practically, and as we shall not begin now before November, probably, I am going off on Thursday, feeling moderately comfortable. At all events, I know that it will be a good thing for the work for me to drop it entirely for a while. It has become a great bugbear to me. I dream of the octopus by night and think of nothing else by day, and I shall be glad to exchange it for the Alps."[15]

What she found on the other side of the Atlantic was the *McClure's* staff at play and her sister Sarah who was still painting abroad. The sisters went to Reims and Geneva to see Charles Borgeaud. Then Ida went off with the McClure party to Feisch, stopping a few days at Interlaken where she nursed a poet in the group named Edith Wyatt who had injured her foot in a fall from a bicycle.

Tarbell capped her European holiday by researching animals in Paris, Berlin, and Leipzig. On a whim McClure had ordered her to Germany to gather material for a prospective animal magazine. She spent several weeks interviewing trainers, tracking hunters and keepers, and visiting zoos, all to compile articles for a project which McClure never mentioned again.

But with all the distractions, the octopus would not leave her in peace. After an ecstatic Sunday spent in the Cologne Cathedral listening to organ music and basking in the light of stained-glass windows, she wrote Boyden:

This is the first day since I left New York when I have been alone! It is practically my first opportunity to remember that I am down for a series of articles on the Standard Oil Co.! . . . I left Paris and my charges last night and I was hardly in my sleeper before I began [to] think of that terrible Introduction. My plan is to have it ready when I reach New York. That and the first article. I shall sail with Mr. McC on the "Graf Waldersee" and I want to persuade him to let us go ahead [with publication] in Nov. I may not succeed but I'll do my best. I have been busily enough at work now for ten days but it has been other matters. You know how the Gen'l absorbs me . . . I am actually on my way to Berlin and Leipsic [sic] to get on track of what they are doing there—as well as to see Mr. [Andrew D.] White whom I may miss— He's off north and was not sure of getting back but I hope to catch him. [16]

In the meantime, she had requested Andrew D. White, the U.S. ambassador to Germany, to write her in Hamburg care of the Pure Oil Company, her brother's organization. Quite possibly, Tarbell wanted to monitor the Standard's efforts to take over the market for oil in Germany, a market her brother was trying to develop for the Pure Oil Company. Tarbell probably used the opportunity to trace the story of a Herr Poth, the independents' foreign agent. Poth had sworn an oath of loyalty to them and successfully pleaded their case before German officials, but then had been tricked into selling to the Standard just before his death. In Berlin and Hamburg, she could have verified the story with Poth's family and with concerned Germans.

She never did see the ambassador. She wrote him from her ship: "I called at the Embassy in Berlin and your people were very courteous and helpful in securing me the prompt attention in a matter I was interested in."[17]

Their failure to meet may have been convenient for both. White did not appear to put the weight of the U.S. government behind her investigation and Tarbell did not have to make editorial promises. For some time, they had been discussing publication of his articles, some of which, including an interview with Tolstoy, had already appeared in *McClure's.*

Back home, she knitted together more of the Standard Oil story. Henry Demarest Lloyd's *Wealth Against Commonwealth* told of a widow defrauded by Rockefeller. Tarbell thought the story delicious and applied to Lloyd for documentation. He wrote that court records had been stolen in his day but were since returned to Cleveland. She searched for them herself several weeks before turning up a copy.

The relationship between Tarbell and Lloyd assumed the character of a complicated dance. Each bowed before the icon of the subject and bobbed before the idol of professional courtesy. Lloyd, who now saw she was a formidable critic of the Standard, was probably curious to meet the woman about whom he had warned western Pennsylvania, and she probably wanted to see the suspicious Jeremiah of the Standard.

In late September 1902, she went to meet him at his estate in Seaconnet, Rhode Island. She found him a charming, silver-headed gentleman in his mid-fifties. As she outlined her series, he shared his research, including the case of the widow Backus, and recommended persons and lines of inquiry to be followed in Titusville. The two journalists were of one mind toward their prey: Rockefeller was a great man. They differed only in the degree of greatness they would accord him. Lloyd placed him among the five greatest of history, something Tarbell averred was a little strong.

Tarbell impressed him favorably, but her balanced presentation continued to concern him. For her part, Tarbell was charmed by Lloyd's passionate commitment to social change. Despite his egalitarian philosophy, Lloyd had the advantage of a seaside estate, yet he was able to make her feel guilty for her love of fine silver and well-wrought goods. Tarbell was humble in her bread-and-butter note: "I cannot tell you what a good time I had and what an impulse you gave me. With my radical leanings I sometimes grow very restive in my practical and rather conservative—though I think entirely sincere—surroundings. It does me good to rub up against the people in the advance line where I believe most of us will be one day."[18]

Tarbell's rendering of the widow's story was consistent with what Lloyd had reported, but less passionate. She depicted a successful businesswoman who allowed herself to be frightened, who clutched at Rockefeller and refused to see the seriousness of the contracts she was concluding. Siddall urged Tarbell to omit it, but she defended its inclusion, saying that it illustrated how Rockefeller could terrorize and eliminate successful refiners.

Lloyd approved of her article and wrote her: "When you get through with 'Johnnie' I don't think there will be very much left of him except something resembling one of his own grease spots."[19]

Tarbell worked at home in her study, sitting on a bentwood chair before a partners desk with baskets of material in messy heaps before her and framed photographs of Phillips and McClure overhead. In one day she would accomplish a great deal, only a little the next, but she worked continuously, constantly aware of approaching deadlines and the amount of work to be done. By having Siddall at work in Cleveland, new access to the oil regions, and the cooperation of government officials, Tarbell and *McClure's Magazine* became a Hydra stinging the uncovered flesh of the country's great monopoly.

Month after month for the next two years, Tarbell turned out *The*

History of the Standard Oil Company. She gathered about her as many pertinent books, transcripts and clippings as possible, arranged them in order and wrote. When one envelope was emptied of notes, enlarged into a chapter and handed in, she reviewed her material and rearranged what she needed for the next installment. When some fact or verification eluded her, she mailed off a query to Siddall. One such inquiry related to the trustworthiness of one of Rockefeller's many foes: "Can you find out for me the standing and character of Charles T. Morehouse, who was a manufacturer of lubricating oil in Cleveland up to 1877? I want to know if he was a thoroughly reliable person."[20] In 1879, Morehouse had told the New York Assembly how Rockefeller drove him out of business by choking off his supply of crude oil. It was for Tarbell's purposes a piquant tale, but she wanted to make sure it was true.

Her editors were as scrupulous as she. Every *McClure's* story was rewritten three times at the direction of the editors—a routine process which unhinged many writers, but not Tarbell. She picked up her pen, rewrote, and for good measure, sent this copy to Siddall who read each installment as many as thirty times before commenting in multipaged, single-spaced critiques. She also submitted her work to economists. McClure paid John R. Commons—who later became a dean of both American labor historians and Wisconsin Progressivism—and John Bates Clark—who had studied for the ministry as well as becoming a social scientist—to assist her. Both were as concerned with ethics as with economics, which suited Tarbell perfectly.

Roseboro said of the editing process: "She had to fight her equals to say the least there, and she did it with Sam McClure and JSP demanding that they be satisfied and thrilled; they pounded her and her stuff to make the best of it page by page, and of course never [did] a big person [take as] much merciless help as she did."[21]

In Roseboro's opinion, this brought out Tarbell's best, wrought a perfection she would not elsewhere allow herself, and moderated her tendency to preach. Phillips and McClure found that Tarbell was presenting a much greater story than they had bargained for. McClure originally envisioned a three-part series. Phillips, on reading her first manuscripts, increased it to six. Once publication began and reaction poured in, they expanded it further to twelve.

Once a day, morning or afternoon, she went up to the office. The atmosphere of the magazine was a tonic to be sipped in careful drafts. Enough would revive, an extra drop exhaust. Boyden was ever primed with the latest gossip on who said what to whom. Viola Roseboro usually wanted to tell Ida about new authors and describe them with a curse word or two. Then there were the new people. A clerk named

Molly Best habitually arrived so disheveled that Boyden was forced to
pin her clothing together to hide the considerable sum of cash she had
sewn in her stocking.

There was also a new writer on the staff, a former teacher in her late
twenties, who had lived in Virginia and Nebraska and acquired the
worst accents of both. Only McClure and Roseboro liked her. The rest
thought Willa Cather a disgruntled "yes-man," according to Curtis
Brady, one of several Brady brothers on the business staff. Cather
wanted to meet Ida Tarbell, the woman writer who had made a name
for herself, but Tarbell had no time. Ida "didn't cotton to her, nor discount her either," according to Roseboro. In later years, Tarbell expressed great admiration for *Death Comes for the Archbishop* and
defended Cather's way of guarding her privacy to protect her working
hours.

Unlike Cather, Finley Peter Dunne was popular. He was not actually
a staff member, but he was a presence at *McClure's*. The syndicate dis-
tributed his essays after 1904 and paid Dunne a thousand dollars apiece
for the privilege. Dunne wrote the famous Mr. Dooley stories which
centered around barkeeper Martin Dooley, an Irishman who lacked
education but possessed the ability to smell a rat.

The child of Irish immigrants, Finley Peter Dunne was, like most
others at *McClure's*, Midwestern. His hometown was Chicago, where
he created Mr. Dooley. In 1898, when Dunne was thirty-one, Mr.
Dooley began to comment on the coming conflict with Spain. As politicians grew more melodramatic and jingoistic, Mr. Dooley grew more
cynical. When President McKinley considered buying Cuba, the Irishman commented to his friend Hennessy: "Ye cud never be a rale
pathrite [patriot]. Ye have no stock ticker in ye'er house." After Admiral Dewey sank the Spanish fleet at Manila, Martin Dooley claimed
him as his cousin: "Dewey or Dooley, 'tis all th' same," said he. Dooley's monologue painted Dewey as somewhat of a braggart. "I'll bet ye,
whin we come to find out about him, we'll hear he's ilicted himself king
iv th' F'lipine Islands. Dooley th' Wanst [Dooley dialect for First]."
Later Mr. Dooley disowned Dewey.

Dunne liked nothing better than to ridicule cant with his acid
green pen. Senator Henry Cabot Lodge spoke of the nobility of beating
back Spain's decaying empire to which Mr. Dooley replied, "Hands
acrost th' sea an' into somewan's pocket." Dooley quoted Kipling—almost: "Take up th' white man's burden an' hand it to th' coons."

Even Theodore Roosevelt had to acknowledge Mr. Dooley's sagacity:
"As you know, I am an Expansionist," Roosevelt wrote Dunne, "but
your delicious phrase about 'take up the white man's burden and put it
on the coons,' exactly hits off the weak spot in my own theory; though,
mind you, I am by no means willing to give up the theory yet."[22]

Dunne himself hated writing. Sad and serious, he procrastinated until the pressure built and escaped in a flash of brilliant wit. In his mid-thirties, Dunne had a workingman's fleshiness, a dandy's vest with watch fob, and slicked-down hair; and the pince-nez of a man who reads long hours into the night.

One final interesting specimen of *McClure's* menagerie was a journalist named Lincoln Steffens. Originally from a moneyed San Francisco family, Stef had cultivated an artistic flair during his student days in Germany and France. He was short with a tufty beard and an upturned mustache and he kept his fine brown hair cropped high above his forehead.

Stef was hired because Ida Tarbell was too busy with the Standard to pinch-hit as managing editor. McClure's offer was a lifeline to Stef. He was at a dead end both in a novel he was attempting and with his job as city editor of the *Commercial Advertiser*. His bosses felt he was used up, too worn out at thirty-five to be a journalist anymore. They were wrong. Muscular and alert, Stef was the antithesis of what was needed in a desk editor. McClure soon saw this and sent him out to report.

According to McClure's autobiography, Ida Tarbell suggested that Stef visit Cleveland where Siddall could introduce him to Mayor Tom Johnson. She thought it might be a good idea to have an article on the admirable aspects of that city's government. He visited that and other cities, but instead of finding what was admirable, he found evidence of widespread corruption. He produced "The Shame of the Cities" series which began to run in October 1902 as "Tweed Days in St. Louis." Steffens was listed as coauthor with a local newspaperman named Claude Wetmore.

McClure's Magazine was now on the cusp of greatness, but Sam McClure in the days stretching beyond 1900 was less editor than menace. He would steam in from Europe with last-minute orders which upended months of work. Ellery Sedgwick, later editor of the *Atlantic Monthly*, wrote:

There were despondent attempts at self-protection. Schemes were constantly made to circumvent [Sam McClure's] activities. Since the office could not harbor a quiet desk, by collusion with the cashier, the staff would hire a secret room in some hotel and then until the hide-out was discovered, a systematic effort would be made to finish an article before the deadline. The device never served for long. All New York was within too easy reach, and there were occasions when staff articles could only be written in the precarious security of a Washington bedroom . . . it was miraculous how in the incandescent office the forces of attraction and repulsion were kept so nearly in balance; that with all the subterranean

rumblings and occasional little spurts of flame, the explosion was
so long in coming . . . "[23]

Steffens privately considered Tarbell the only dependable journalist
there and the only good-humored person at *McClure's* besides himself.
"She was another fellow, a nice fellow—we didn't have a feeling of man
or woman in that office," he recalled. "There was never any doubt of
her copy. It was so reliable, always on time, the rest of us were all unreliable."[24]

When the Standard Oil series debuted in November 1902, the time
of Ida Tarbell's forty-fifth birthday, the nation had a rueful example of
how a millionaire's business could affect their lives. A coal strike
gripped the country. Pennsylvania's National Guard had been ordered
to the anthracite regions to quell riots, the mine operators refused a
presidential request that work resume pending an investigation, and finally the matter was settled by arbitration.

William Randolph Hearst's populist *Journal* at first covered the story
in terms of "coal barons" and "strikers," but as people began to read
and talk about *McClure's* series, Hearst peppered his headlines with the
phrase COAL TRUST. Among stories of eloping princesses, fat ladies who
sat on burglars, and society divorces, he trumpeted "Book Trust" and
"Asphalt Trust" as well. "Trust" became the catchword that could be
counted on to attract the reader's eye. When J. P. Morgan formed International Harvester, it was reported under MORGAN FORMS ANOTHER
TRUST. An account of Standard's operation in Illinois proclaimed CHI-
CAGO IN GRIP OF TRUST.

Standard Oil itself began to receive much more publicity. Joseph Pu-
litzer's New York *World* asked on Christmas Day of 1902: BILLION $
YANKEE TRUST IN EUROPE? referring to Rockefeller and others said to be
interested in a GIGANTIC GAS DEAL. This followed a story headlined J. D.
ROCKEFELLER'S $4,000,000 CHECK/HIS SHARE OF STANDARD OIL DIVI-
DEND FOR LAST QUARTER IN 1902.

In the second installment of "The History of the Standard Oil Company," appearing in December 1902, Tarbell served notice that what
Rockefeller had concealed was about to be revealed. She disclosed that
the Standard's original capitalization had been one million dollars, and
she provided the names of those who had joined—John and William
Rockefeller, Henry Flagler, Samuel Andrews, and Stephen V. Harkness—when Standard consolidated in 1870. Worse for Rockefeller, the
articles declared him to be the force behind the South Improvement
Company and raised the nasty issue of rebates: while a discount for
quantity is considered reasonable in most business arrangements, such
practice in this case was expressly forbidden by law.

The situation was as Ida's father had described it to her so long before. Railroads had begun to develop when Ulysses Grant accorded rights of way and government aid to certain men on the condition that they would operate railroads as public utilities. They were to be open to all at equal rates with no consideration given to the volume of business. Many abused this rule, including Rockefeller. Tarbell uncovered testimony revealing how he first made a deal with the Lake Shore Railroad which allowed his refineries in Cleveland to have a discount or rebate while those who had the advantage of being closer to the wells were to pay a higher freight. To further substantiate her charges, she listed the system of rebates reported by the House Committee on Manufactures when it investigated the Standard in 1888.

Even more than the rebate, news of Rockefeller's attempt to destroy competitors through the discredited South Improvement Company was a great embarrassment to him. Tarbell told her readers that Rockefeller convinced independents in Pittsburgh and Philadelphia to join in the South Improvement Company. Then together they moved against rivals in two centers—refiners at the Cleveland port and those in the oil regions.

Her source was that most valuable pamphlet, *The History of the South Improvement Company*, which listed Standard Oil as the biggest shareholder. With South Improvement as their shield, Rockefeller and his colleagues sought such advantageous treatment from railroads as to destroy competitors until they were unmasked and South Improvement was forced to disband. Tarbell's bombshell was that the Standard still operated according to this outlawed plan. All this was served up with illustrations furnished by Siddall.

It is not difficult to imagine the secretive Rockefeller's surprise when he saw photographs of himself and his associates displayed like mug shots in the pages of *McClure's Magazine*. *McClure's* mailbags swelled with praise of her and indignation at the Standard. Even an astrologer joined in. He foretold that 1903 and 1904 would be critical for the Standard in the legislature, predicting that its outlays would be increased and there would be an impediment to its "grasping the reins of power to control business and legislation in the United States."[25]

In Titusville there was great excitement. Those who fought the Standard at last trusted Ida Tarbell. She observed: "I have been having a very interesting time here with the Standard work. It is very interesting to note now, that the thing is well under way, and I have not been kidnapped or sued for libel as some of my friends prophesied, people are willing to talk freely to me."[26]

One of these was Lewis Emery, who had known Ida Tarbell since she was a baby. Emery was a hero in the oil regions because he had thwarted Rockefeller's control of railroads by building a pipeline to transport oil. He was one of the most successful independents, but he amused Tarbell by describing himself as Rockefeller's helpless victim. After Emery read her early installments in the pages of *McClure's*, he wrote Lloyd: "I shared your misgivings relative to the motive prompting Miss Tarbell to write such a history: I have been watching her articles closely and have expressed to her personally my doubts as to her sincerity in writing a truthful history of the acts of the men composing that company . . . " But, Emery said, he had gone to see her in New York, and they spent several hours talking about her work. After looking over her future articles he decided to help. Emery told Lloyd: "I shall assist her as best I know how to prepare certain articles on the independent movement . . . " Emery closed by asking Lloyd to return photographs of refineries dismantled by the Standard, photos he had sent Lloyd and now wanted to pass to Tarbell.[27]

Lloyd, however, retained reservations. Tarbell had won his confidence; her publisher, McClure, had not. He found the advertisement for the series too even-handed and feared the magazine might still come out on the side of the Standard. Lloyd sent Emery his photos, with a worried letter to which Emery replied: "I have not the least doubt as to the honesty and good intentions of Miss Tarbell but you have opened my eyes to a certain extent relative to the publishers and the whole milk in the coconut."[28] Emery asked permission to send Lloyd's letter to Tarbell, which Lloyd granted—provided there seemed to be no turn of phrase which implied criticism of her.

Happily for Tarbell, her purpose was not to win the wholehearted approval of these two. She secured their materials which documented and elaborated the independents' side of the story. Lloyd did not live to see "The History of the Standard Oil Company" completed. He died suddenly six months after this last correspondence with Emery.

As Tarbell hammered at the Standard, Lincoln Steffens was peppering away at political corruption and Baker was investigating union abuses. The third installment of the Standard Oil story—describing the oil war of 1872 and how the independents defeated Rockefeller's South Improvement scheme—appeared in January 1903, and was accompanied by Steffens' exposé of Minneapolis, and Baker's "The Right to Work" about miners who were harassed, beaten, and murdered for refusing to strike. Baker was sympathetic to the workingman and was concerned over the way unions were abusing their growing power.

As McClure looked over the issue before it finally went to press, he was inspired to insert a last-minute editorial comment:

> The leading article, "The Shame of Minneapolis," might have been called "The American Contempt of Law." That title could well have served for the current chapter of Miss Tarbell's "History of Standard Oil." And it would have fitted perfectly Mr. Baker's

"The Right to Work." All together, these articles come pretty near showing how universal is this dangerous trait of ours . . . Capitalists, workingmen, politicians, citizens—all breaking the law, or letting it be broken. Who is left to uphold it? The lawyers? Some of the best lawyers in this country are hired, not to go into court to defend cases, but to advise corporations and business firms how they can get around the law without too great a risk of punishment. The judges? Too many of them so respect the laws that for some "error" or quibble they restore to office and liberty men convicted on evidence overwhelmingly convincing to common sense. The churches? We know of one, an ancient and wealthy establishment, which had to be compelled by a Tammany hold-over health officer to put its tenements in sanitary condition. The colleges? They do not understand. There is no one left; none but all of us.

McClure's editorial introduced a new chapter to the literature of exposure. The January issue sold out. Subscriptions soared. Editors took note. Leslie's began a fight against railway accidents. Everybody's announced "Frenzied Finance" by Thomas Lawson, which delved into Standard Oil's copper interests. The Ladies' Home Journal opened fire on patent medicines.

McClure's knew it was on to something, and the staff was united as never before. "Anyone who thought we sat around with our brows screwed together trying to reform the world was far from the truth. We were after, as McClure always insisted, interesting reading material and if it contributed to the general good, so much the better,"[29] Tarbell maintained.

McClure liked to jolt people, but the Scotch-Irish immigrant also felt a sense of mission. He wrote Richard Gilder of The Century: "I hope the people will rouse themselves. It is up to magazines to rouse public opinion and newspapers have forfeited their opinion by sensationalism and partisanship."[30]

McClure's band could not claim to be the first investigative reporters. Henry Demarest Lloyd preceded Tarbell and Thomas Nast's cartoons limned the corruption of city government before Steffens came along. Josiah Flynn had written of the criminal class for McClure's in 1901 and 1902. Other McClure writers such as Hamlin Garland showed through novels the venality of politicians and the victimization of omnipresent little people.

But Tarbell and her colleagues hit with combined force. Their reach and scope were national. They not only exposed miscreancy, but they pointed to the specific perpetrators. No one was surprised if New York was a den of iniquity corrupted by foreigners, but McClure's made it clear that crime crisscrossed Minneapolis, St. Louis, Pittsburgh, Phila-

delphia, and Chicago. This sweep may have accounted for their success.
It was not because they found lawbreaking in Cleveland, Titusville,
Colorado, or St. Louis that they were read; but because they went to
those cities and states and regarded them as equally worthy of attention
and colorful description as Paris or Moscow.

One young staffer named Mark Sullivan, who went on to become a
noted conservative journalist, took a dim view of the goings-on at
McClure's: "Steffens was so busy finding shame here, there and elsewhere that he could not cover all the cities that clamored for his attention . . . a remarkable feature of that series was that cities, or many
citizens in them, seemed to take a morbid pleasure in being included.
They wrote letters to *McClure's* crying 'Expose us next!' Many enclosed briefs or fragmentary manuscripts or 'leads' to the mine of
shame."[31]

Why were Americans, proud of their growth and sure of their moral
superiority over the rest of the world, ready to see the dark side of
themselves? Perhaps it was because these writers believed in the ideals
of the country at the same time as they exposed its hypocrisy. All were
from pioneer stock, reared by hardworking parents on the principles of
plain living, inspired by American history, and reverential toward Lincoln. They had the American penchant for facts over philosophy and
they not only searched for corruption, but they also unmasked power in
America and found that that power did not rest with the people.

With like-minded people, Tarbell joined a larger stream that was to
be known as the Progressive Movement. Confident of their moral
values and the perfectability of the world, Progressives pointed out what
needed to be changed, and fully believed in the fundamental rightness
of things as they had been when the individual entrepreneur and the
farmer were America's kings.

As journalists, she, Baker, and Steffens spearheaded a popular investigative movement. Already renowned, their work would braid them together in American history books. They would be known as
"Muckrakers," and the man who would give them that name, President
Theodore Roosevelt, did not like the discontent he saw them effecting.

Roosevelt thought the abuses of the trusts needed to be curbed, but
he feared that if the public were encouraged to hate business combinations, more harm than good would result. In his first annual speech, a
year before Tarbell's work was published, he tried to minimize public
alarm by saying the trusts would be controlled by making public facts
about the ways they bent the law. He said:

> There is a widespread conviction in the minds of the American
> people that the great corporations known as trusts are in certain of
> their features and tendencies hurtful to the general welfare . . . It is

based upon sincere conviction that combination and concentration should be, not prohibited, but supervised and within reasonable limits controlled, and in my judgment this conviction is right
. . . The first essential in determining how to deal with the great industrial combinations is knowledge of the facts—publicity . . .
What further remedies are needed in the way of governmental reg-
ulations or taxation can only be determined after publicity has
been obtained.[32]

Roosevelt felt the federal government should oversee the trusts by
means of commissions and a new cabinet officer, the Secretary of Commerce and Industries. In this speech, Roosevelt also noted that railroads
abused some privileges. He said the Interstate Commerce Act of 1887
had been in some provisions wrong, in some weak. He declared that
many citizens complained that rates were not maintained, and rebates
were habitually offered to the large shipper at the expense of the smaller
competitor. "The act should be amended," he said. "The railway is a
public servant. Its rates should be just to and open to all shippers alike."
    Roosevelt did take action. In his first year in office, while Tarbell
worked on her articles, Roosevelt charged the Beef Trust with restraint
of trade and brought suit against the Northern Securities railroad combination which monopolized transportation in the Northwest. Northern's principals—J. Pierpont Morgan, James J. Hall, and E. J.
Harriman—were so powerful that their battle for control in 1901 had
caused a stock market panic, so Teddy Roosevelt sought to clip their
eagle wings. As Republican party leaders told him to go slowly, the
public agitated for more legal action against the trusts. Teddy, mindful
of reelection and fearful of the mob, began to backpedal.
    Tarbell's series made it even harder for him to avoid the issue of
trusts. In his annual message on November 11, 1902, he assured congressmen who clamored for a constitutional amendment to curb business combinations that they already had the power to regulate trusts.
Taunted by Democrats who wanted to appropriate a quarter million
dollars to the attorney general's office to prosecute the trusts, House
Republicans felt compelled to show they too were with the people on
the suddenly visible issue. They voted half a million dollars for the purpose without one dissenting vote. MADE GOP POSE AS TRUST-BUSTERS[33]
the *New York World* shrieked.
    Whatever Tarbell thought of Roosevelt's handling of business com-
binations, she found the president a fascinating figure, worthy of her
microscopic vision. One night at a White House musical she watched
him and thought he looked as if he were about to burst out of his suit.
"I felt his clothes might not contain him, he was steamed up, so ready
to go, attack anything, anywhere."[34]

That thought may have returned to her when Roosevelt went after the Panama Canal. Viola Roseboro described Tarbell's reaction on the day in November 1903 when the United States acquired it by treaty: "The morning we got the word at *McClure's* that Roosevelt had snatched Panama there were gasps and amusement and excitement, but IMT was very grave. That was a dishonorable outrage of strength and she got a line on Teddy that she never lost sight of thereafter. Also she always thought him a delight and a wonderful person and of great value as well as of some disadvantage to his country."[35]

Teddy Roosevelt did his best to beguile the press. He sent Baker an advance copy of his annual address, made Lincoln Steffens feel as though he were an adviser, and summoned them all individually to lunch. When Ida Tarbell's turn came, Finley Peter Dunne commented tartly, "If he can't convince the lady, he'll vamp her."[36]

Perhaps it was at that White House meeting that she insisted that *McClure's* was only concerned with reportage, not revolution. "I don't object to the facts," Roosevelt exclaimed, "but you and Baker are not *practical!*"[37]

As for John D. Rockefeller, within twelve months of Tarbell's first exposé, the Rockefeller Institute for medical research announced a pension plan for his employees and made gifts of land to benevolent institutions. Newspapers reported his largess, but highlighted other events as well.

William Randolph Hearst in particular thought the Rockefeller story could boost his newspaper's circulation. His *Evening Journal* fairly smacked its figurative lips in a story headed OIL KINGS DIVIDE $20,000,000 MORE. It said: "JDR went down to his office at 26 Broadway to-day and a few hours later emerged $8,000,000 richer than when he entered. Standard Oil had declared its quarterly dividend of $20 per share. This was an increase of $10 over the dividend declared last November."[38]

In April 1903, a reporter for Hearst's *Journal* asked Ida about Rockefeller's father, William, insisting he was still alive. She had thought his parents were both in a Cleveland graveyard, but now she began to fear that Hearst would scoop *McClure's*. She was so rattled that she got the publication's name wrong when she wrote Siddall: "I think *The World* is contemplating an interview with the old gentleman. I am sure we would have done that long ago if he had been in a land where he could be interviewed."[39]

The race was on to find the elder Rockefeller. Ida had that most useful of assets, a friend in the enemy's camp. Through her Lincoln research, she had met Hiram Brown, a former Rockefeller neighbor. Siddall talked to him and learned that Rockefeller's father had been a dubious character who spent long stretches of time away from home, had been charged with rape, and had quite possibly started a bigamous family.

Tarbell was enchanted: "As to the story of the 'Old Gentleman,' I do not know how much I can use of it; that I can use it, however, in some form, is evident, when I come to the character sketch." She coaxed Siddall to hurry: "I am beginning to be mortally afraid that he will die before we have his photograph."[40]

Month after month, Rockefeller and Standard Oil were pilloried in *McClure's* but did not respond directly. Craving to know Rockefeller's reaction, Siddall dispatched Brown to visit the multimillionaire. Brown discovered him physically fitter than in years. In an observation indicative of some humor as well as their attention to detail, Brown told Siddall he was wrong to think an ailment had cost Rockefeller his hair—he still had his eyelashes. However, Rockefeller was openly preoccupied by business despite his "retirement" and in constant touch with the telegraph office in his home which connected him to New York. Possibly, the extremely cautious Rockefeller also smelled a trap. At last, in response to Brown's questions, he revealed that his father was senile and living on his farm in Iowa, cared for by nieces.

Brown mentioned his "lady friend," Ida Tarbell, and Rockefeller countered that he should read a book by Gilbert Montague which had been done with the help of S. C. T. Dodd, Standard's corporate counsel. Free copies of this work, *The Rise and Progress of the Standard Oil Company*, were turning up in libraries, newspaper offices, and church rectories around the country.

At length, Rockefeller said of Tarbell's series: "I tell you, Hiram, things have changed since you and I were boys. The world is full of socialists and anarchists. Whenever a man succeeds remarkably in any particular line of business, they jump on him and cry him down."

Siddall reported this to Tarbell and concluded: "Brown says that [Rockefeller's] whole attitude is that of a game fighter who expects to be whacked on the head once in a while. He is not in the least disturbed by any blows he may receive. He maintains the Standard has done more good than harm."[41]

A few weeks later Ida journeyed to Cleveland to have a look at Rockefeller for herself. She feared what might happen if Rockefeller discovered her. She arrived early, went to the Euclid Avenue Baptist Church, and slipped out later that same day. Meeting her at the morning service was the illustrator George Varian who sketched surreptitiously, flanked by Tarbell and Siddall, blocking the sight of his sketchpad. Tarbell was intent on Rockefeller and surprised by his attempt to hide his baldness under a skullcap. As his eyes scanned the crowd she was sure he would recognize her and throw them all out. She later described him as dry and massive, an amphibian creature with the neck of a bull and the skin of a snake. She thought him the oldest man in the world. He was sixty-six.[42]

Once her series began, those with a grievance knew where to apply for redress. Frank Rockefeller, an estranged brother, sent word he would give her documents about the oil man if she would come to him secretly. Somehow disguised with Siddall's aid, she appeared in his Cleveland office. Frank Rockefeller was vituperative about the way he and a family friend had been relieved of Standard Oil stock; he said venomously that he planned to disinter his children from the family plot lest they ever be forced to lie beside his brother. Tarbell thought his hatred so ugly she left, sympathizing for once with John's point of view, but carrying away with her information about the stock deal nonetheless.

Standard Oil's wastebasket, not the courthouse or family friends, furnished her with the most sensational article. According to Ida, a man called on her late one evening bearing an armload of records which proved that the Standard systematically spied on competitors by exploiting access to confidential shipping records.

Over the years, Rockefeller's firm had evinced an uncanny ability to move ahead of its rivals. Pennsylvanians ruefully called the Standard "The Great Invisible Oil Company." Many of the independents claimed that their secrets were being leaked via railroad freight offices around the country; but when the charges were investigated, Rockefeller's men always produced plausible explanations. One told the Interstate Commerce Commission in 1887 that his employees simply inspected public lists of incoming cars, their contents, and consignors at the depot and that anyone might have done the same.

Ida's nighttime visitor told her this: a boy he had taught in Sunday school worked for Standard Oil and had had the regular monthly duty of burning records. One day he noticed a familiar name entered repeatedly on forms and letters. Sorting them, he realized the local railroad office was sending the Standard full details of his teacher's dealings and that the Standard was using this information to pirate his trade. Amid the rest of the refuse the boy found were similar tabs on other businesses and lists of all competitors' shipments gathered from confidential freight office books. Much information was on plain white paper, but sometimes recorders carelessly used railroad stationery or signed their names.

The boy took the material to his teacher who conveyed it to Tarbell. When she examined it under her lamp she found so many states represented in detail that it showed that the practice of spying on competitors was not random but was in fact a function of Standard Oil's marketing division. Using this data, the Standard could decide where to cut prices and by how much so as to drive a competitor from an area; then it could raise prices once a monopoly was secured.

To have come upon this was a great coup, but it revealed that Rogers had lied to her. Sometime before, at his invitation, she had visited the Standard canning works in Long Island City, New York. Its capacity was an astounding seventy-five thousand gallons, yet it was run with an economy that oil region boomtowners never would have considered. Always as captivated by machinery as a mystic by the divine, Tarbell had watched as flat sheets of tin were twirled into containers, filled and capped with the turn of a valve, then boxed, nailed, and carted to the river and on to ports as far away as China. In her enthusiasm, she had decided to write a chapter on the legitimate greatness of the Standard Oil Company.

In this article, which ran in July 1903, Tarbell mentioned "The Standard Information Bureau"—a widespread system of reporters who picked up gossip about competitors for the Standard: "Spies they are called [in the oil regions]. They may deserve the name sometimes, but the service may be perfectly legitimate."

Now she saw she had been duped. The Standard learned about competitors not from snatches of gossip and publicly posted freight lists, but from an organized illegal strategy. "Some way the unravelling of this espionage charge, the proofs of it, turned my stomach against the Standard in a way that the indefensible and robust fights over transportation had never done. There was a littleness about it that seemed utterly contemptible compared to the immense genius and ability that had gone into the organization. Nothing about the Standard had ever given me the feeling that did,"[43] she told a women's group.

Siddall produced testimony which corroborated the spy charges. A Mr. Wall told him Standard employees had come forward in Baltimore, Louisville, and Toledo to confess that railwaymen were being paid to provide shipping information. Siddall said a Baltimore oilman awaited her arrival to produce more information and off she went.

In truth, the cloak-and-dagger tale about a Sunday-school teacher that Tarbell reported may have been a cover. She sought always to protect the identity of her informant and the one to tell her about the espionage may well have been Siddall's man from Baltimore. His name, Fehsenfeld, appears in her correspondence but is not used in *The History of the Standard Oil Company*.

After she had studied the Baltimore shipping records, she again asked Rogers if the Standard engaged in any espionage with the help of railroad agents. He reiterated that they did everything they could to get information legally and fairly, and called her idea of spying nonsense.

Tarbell knew better. She published the story of Standard's espionage network in February 1904, and since she showed how it undercut rivals, she called it "Cutting to Kill." "The only time in all my relations with him when I saw his face white with rage,"[44] was the way she described

Rogers's demeanor after it appeared. He ended her visits to 26 Broadway.

The animus of Rogers, the spleen of Rockefeller's brother, and the wreck of many lives weighed upon her. Her respite was the continuity of her family. Because of research, she spent more time in Titusville than she had since college, but only one description of her visits survives: "When I was forty years old my father, catching me reading a volume of a certain Congressional trust investigation on a Sunday afternoon, reproved me in this gentle way. 'You shouldn't read that on Sunday, Ida.' I quickly exchanged it for *Pilgrim's Progress* which is not without a suggestion for a student of the trust."

Ida and her father shared a dry and quiet wit. Once when he was confined to bed he wrote her: "I have studied up sciatica some and the authorities contradict one another so much I don't know what to do. One says exercise all you can. Another keep still. One doctor here in town says rub it like sixty. Another says don't rub it it will make it worse so I have tried to average it. . . . Your mother is around, was downtown yesterday and over to Will's three times. She is keeping busy looking after her flowers and *dog*. The dog gives her more trouble than I do but she spends all her breath scolding him and I am let down easy."[45]

To keep in still closer touch with her family, Ida invited her nieces to visit her in New York. When they were children, she hired a Frenchwoman to show them the town while she was at work. They went to museums, Coney Island, Wall Street, and department stores: "Aunt Ida planned for us to do everything a child never having been out of a small town would want to do in New York City," Clara said. In the evenings, Ida took them to dine with friends, especially the Phillipses. She probably also took the girls to see melodramas. She told a reporter from San Diego that she had developed a taste for them while writing about Standard Oil: "I love to hiss the villain," she said.

Clara remembered Ida's enthusiasm: "Her interest and joy in [our] daily experiences were as great as ours," but Clara also remembered how displeased Ida was when they criticized others and when Esther allowed herself to get fat. Considering this a weakness of character, Ida scolded until Esther cried and Ida contritely bought her a present. However Ida lectured the girl thereafter, she made it a point never to mention Esther's girth to others.[46]

Ida frequently saw Will who was now living in Philadelphia where the Pure Oil Company was headquartered. A friend recalled the evening Ida arranged a dinner for four at the National Arts Club on Gramercy Park. While three of them waited for Will, Ida boasted that her brother was the only man who had successfully fought the Rockefellers and that he was often so busy they had to make an appointment three weeks in advance. Then, after dinner, Will entertained them by reading from a Southern newspaper that he had found on the train. It was a poem describing the harm Ida had done John D. Rockefeller. The refrain—"Oh, Ida, how could you do such a thing?"—had them in fits of laughter, but Ida seemed embarrassed and wriggled restlessly in her chair.

Handsome in his youth, Will Tarbell in middle age was balding and dependent on eyeglasses. Although he was much occupied by his work which had taken him to Germany to set up oil markets, he was still an avid outdoorsman. He even wrote verses about his hunting dogs. Ella Tarbell Price, his granddaughter, recalls coming across a box of his treasured photographs of dogs, fish, and game. There were none of his children, and only one of his wife.

Will was proud of Ida's success and seemed to feel no surprise that his sister had become a national figure. They traded information about the Standard; Will reviewed her manuscript, gave her leads and introductions, and was most devoted when she needed encouragement.

There is no sign that he felt the same about Sarah. As Franklin and Esther Tarbell grew older, it became apparent that they needed someone to take care of them. Once Will moved to Philadelphia, he couldn't see that they were cared for, so, as head of the household, he chose between his sisters. He decided that Ida was necessary where she was, and summoned Sarah home from Europe. She closed her studio and returned dutifully to Titusville's cloudy days. She painted a portrait of Esther reading by gas lamp which is now in the home of her grandniece Caroline Tarbell Tupper. Overall, the painting evokes the maternal roundness of a Mary Cassatt.

For Sarah's sacrifice, Ida was ever grateful and guilty, according to her grandnieces. In earlier days, Ida would exorcise some of her concern through work, but as the series dragged on, it took her to the heart of all she had been avoiding. Writing, even when it was not going well, had once been her drug and tonic, but now she was writing of her own people, of their impotence, gullibility, and defeat.

The more Tarbell became celebrated, the more she felt beset. "In writing my Standard Oil chapters my sympathies have been mightily worked upon until I have suffered over again the defeats of these independent refiners," she admitted.

She said this to Gilbert H. Montague who published it in the January 6, 1904, *Boston Transcript*. Montague was the young Harvard law student who had written the defense of the Standard. The two met in an atmosphere of friendliness, probed the rival's sources and intentions, and parted determined to discredit the other. Tarbell saw that Montague had not researched as fully as she had and alluded to this in

McClure's. He dismissed her as a journalist who could not see the historical growth of the oil industry as the development of the Middle States through the agency of the railways.

The controversies brought her continuing attention. At one point an impetuous, and perhaps not too stable, stranger showed up at the office announcing she must get her hat—he was marrying her and taking her to live in the Midwest. But even those who knew her well began to see her in a new light. Hazen wrote that she was becoming as much a household word as "Hamilton or the Only Theodore . . . the one false note you strike is in your innuendo against marriage, the one perfect institution in the world." He said that he and his wife bragged a bit about their friendship with her. They had placed their author's copies of her work where everyone could see them and they could nonchalantly say they knew the author.

McClure professed awe: "Your articles are the great magazine feature of recent years. The way you are generally esteemed and reverenced pleases me tremendously. You are today the most generally famous woman in America. You have achieved a great distinction. People universally speak of you with such a reverence that I am getting sort of afraid of you." Later he reported from Europe: "Everywhere even in obscure local journals your work is constantly mentioned—both in Geneva and Lausanne papers have arrived on your work in connection with Standard Oil."[47]

Even her fame did not bring her invitations to all events. An exclusion which rankled her was the Periodical Publishers' Dinner, a stag affair. McClure, Baker, Steffens, Phillips, and Boyden dined with the president, the secretary of state, foreign ambassadors, and senators, but the celebrated Ida Tarbell was not even present. "It is the first time since I came into the office that the fact of petticoats has stood in my way and I am half inclined to resent it,"[48] she grumbled.

At this same time, the air warmed, bubbled, and simmered with crisis. Sam McClure was having an affair. It did not remain his personal dilemma nor a private problem for his wife; the entire office became embroiled. As Sam McClure grew more successful and his own youth faded, he established his French summer home as a way station for young writers. In 1903, he had invited Cale and Alice Hegan Rice, he a playwright, she the author of the best-selling *Mrs. Wiggs of the Cabbage Patch*, to spend part of their honeymoon on a walking tour of the Alps.

For the first part of the trip, as Mrs. McClure shopped in Paris, a young poet named Florence Wilkinson joined the Rices and McClure on the hike. They went to Chamonix where McClure arranged for the honeymooners to be on a different floor so that all might have a view of Mont Blanc. Just before Ida joined the party, McClure's "Firenze" left.

The re-formed group donned rucksacks at the foot of the Rhone glacier and hiked along the river, sleeping in farmhouses and tramping Alpine roads. Ida always described herself as happiest in the mountains, but McClure's dalliance weighed so heavily upon her that when they parted in Bergamo in the Italian Alps she was holding back tears. McClure joined his wife at Divonne-les-Bains near Geneva and Ida accompanied the honeymooners to Venice. At some point she and the Rices must have broken down to gossip about the General, for reference to "Firenze" spiced their correspondence for decades. The couple, who became Ida's dear friends, nicknamed the writer "Julie" for reasons no one knows today.

After Venice she sailed home with McClure and his wife and helped them celebrate their twentieth wedding anniversary. However calmly she seemed to take McClure's behavior, inwardly she had much to think about. For years, by turns brotherly and worshipful, McClure had been rhapsodizing over her smile and telling Tarbell he loved *her*—"I have always cared for you in a special manner, as much as a man can care for a woman without actually loving her,"[49] he wrote.

Just before that summer, in March 1903, he had written her a solicitous letter from Europe saying that he missed her and wanted to live near her and be with her during the coming years. He professed, "I want you to live *your* life and be just as happy as a woman can be in your way. I am so anxious about you I want to see you better circumstanced."[50]

If she had ever read more into such communications than they warranted, she could not now. Ida probably would not have wanted an affair with McClure, but she had to note that in Florence Wilkinson he found a woman who swept aside all his scruples.

Normally Europe revitalized her, but Ida returned home tired and rapidly became more and more exhausted. The Standard Oil series was published as fast as she could write—and rewrite—it. Each installment was a wonder of transition, one flowed into another and was made to amplify the preceding one whether it did naturally or not. As her energy flagged, Tarbell was so late in handing in some chapters that Siddall had no time to review them.

More and more Ida Tarbell leaned on Phillips and transferred to him the affection she had felt for McClure. Phillips, in turn, unburdened himself to her. His wife, following the birth of their fifth child and only son in 1900, was often ill. To this was added the weight of McClure's absences, orders, and criticisms. As the two partners became estranged, the staff, especially Tarbell, sided with Phillips.

At Christmas, Ida gave Phillips her photo. She said she felt embarrassed, but he had asked for it and he was the one person she took at his word. She was emboldened to declare her feeling: "It [the photo] car-

ries with it my profound wish for your happiness. You deserve happiness if anyone does for your courage, your truthfulness and your gentleness. You unconsciously strengthen everybody who comes near you.
Someday I hope you will get what you deserve in freedom of care and in
joy of life. I wouldn't have dared say this to your face perhaps but it is
often in my heart to say it. If it sounds expansive, please remember it is
Christmas and that expansion is one of its effects."[51]

The letters she wrote McClure when she was fond of him—as least
those which have survived—radiate with self-assured admiration, but
her letters to Phillips after her disillusion with McClure shyly offer her
heart.

She knew Phillips well. They had seen each other daily for years. She
knew his footsteps, the tilt of his head, and could anticipate his reaction
to every situation. Moreover, they shared what was most vital to
them—their work. This bond held her as no other, although it is clear
she could have forged ties to other men if she had wished.

Even beyond the McClure set, she had a rich social life: "It is doubt-
ful whether any other woman in New York is welcomed in so many or
so varied social circles as she," noted one profile in *The Reader*. A few
months later this same magazine added: "It has been said that Miss Ida
Tarbell is the most popular woman in America, and even dissenters
from that opinion will admit the choice lies between [sic] her, Miss
Jane Addams and Miss Helen Gould [a philanthropist]."[52]

Men liked her very much. One admirer was Albert G. Robinson, a
newspaperman two years older than she. Orphaned as a boy, he was
self-educated but polished. He had reported on the Spanish American
War for the *New York Evening Post* and went on to become an editorial writer for the *New York Sun*. When he was transferred from New
York to Washington, he said his chief regret was the interruption of his
friendship with Ida Tarbell. He wrote her: "The move entails certain
losses, and I count among them a certain number of evenings which I
had hoped and expected to spend on West 9th Street this winter, getting better acquainted with   your cat."[53]

Her own success had given Ida Tarbell the confidence to be as much
at home with notables as with the people of Titusville. Evenings of
lively conversation were happy antidotes to work. She was charming,
avid to hear what others had to say, and to comment on it—sometimes
she felt at too great length.

Roseboro thought Tarbell often led a conversation in order to steer it
from personal matters. She observed: "She has got in the habit of protecting herself from people that way, and the other side is that when she
gets with the people who have what she wants [to know about] she is
masterly in keeping them talking." Roseboro lamented that Tarbell ex-

pressed herself less forcefully as a writer than she did in someone's parlor.[54]

Tarbell also was greatly empathetic. She had the intuitive gift of understanding others' feelings. Henry S. Pritchett, a noted astronomer and
president of the Massachusetts Institute of Technology, was a great admirer. Among her family papers are several letters from him in which he
attempted to rearrange his schedule so they might have a friendly chat.
Possibly for propriety's sake, he always took care to mention his wife's
hopes to see her as well. Pritchett was especially warm after she wrote
him a note on the eve of his installment at MIT. He wrote: "I am taking a moment from the preparations of tomorrow to thank you for a
helping hand-grasp. After all, we know some friends better in months
than others in years and to them we instinctively give our confidence. I
like to consider you as on that list. . . ."[55]

Ida's friendships with males were sufficiently numerous that the novelist Mary Austin took note. Austin, much admired for her stories of the
West, was so confident of her own genius that a critic carped that she
had an empress complex. Eleven years younger than Tarbell, she was
quite round, divorced, and very vocal about her hopes of finding another husband. In fact, at one point she went after Lincoln Steffens. Ida
had seen many men fly from Austin's attentions, and she was taken
aback when Austin told her: "You often have men to lunch. Different
men. I don't know men. Why can't you take me and introduce me?"
Tarbell was very matter-of-fact about her business lunches: "Men were
as impersonal as the pitcher on the table," she said, then added, "but
they always had a good time."[56]

Her private life did not ease her struggles with the Standard articles.
She uncovered one letter showing that Mark Hanna, President McKinley's closest adviser, had intervened to protect Rockefeller from prose-
cution in Ohio, but she let one of her sources persuade her that
disclosure would literally kill Hanna. She capitulated and instantly
knew she had degraded herself.

She made a report on the matter for the McClure's files and said:
"He [her source, David K. Watson, an Ohio lawyer] got me where he
could make a plea to me on the ground of my obligation to him and I
have a sense of defeat that I have not had in any other single incident in
the conduct of this work." Hanna died in February 1904, but
McClure's honored Tarbell's promise and withheld a sensational disclosure. Out of respect for the dead, they delayed one of Steffens's articles criticizing Hanna. After such a glorious romp of exposé, the editors,
especially the young ones, felt they had been reined in. Boyden wrote
Siddall: "We are all much depressed over Hanna."[57]

In early spring 1904, Ida began a study of the price of oil to show

how Standard's control allowed it to create false shortages and boost its prices. To her dismay, she found she could not condense and arrange all the material with her old skill. Scheduled for May, the article was postponed until June and finally ran in September. Will, whose help and advice she had sought throughout the project, wrote her sympathetically: "I guess you are something like me, a little stale and need a few days fishing. Don't be at all discouraged over your article. It's going to be good. [It's] strong now as it is, but you can get it stronger."[58]

In November 1904, as the series finished, *The History of the Standard Oil Company* was published in two volumes—complete with 64 appendices of documentation filling 241 pages. Seemingly every newspaper in the country carried Tarbell's picture and an article about her. She pasted reviews into a big scrapbook so that columns of the *Topeka Herald* and the *Richmond Gazette* and the *News* of Portland, Maine, ran side by side. *The New York Times* said: "As readable as any 'story' with rather more romance than the usual business novel . . . honest the writer has tried to be to both sides of the controversies . . . " *The Critic* wrote: "Miss Tarbell has beaten upon facts rather than upon a gong, and her *History of Standard Oil* is to the present time the most remarkable book of its kind ever written in this country." Others continued in the same vein, praising her as restrained, dispassionate, and factual.

Her scrapbook even included a clipping describing how Samuel McClure had been blackballed from the Ardsley (New York) Country Club by Standard supporters; a notice of Rockefeller's gift of half a million dollars to Johns Hopkins University; a defense of JDR in the *St. John-New Brunswick Globe* signed "Ignoramus"; and cartoons. One depicted Ida shooting the entire Rockefeller family with a bow and arrow; another captioned "Let your light shine before men" showed her stoking up a fire. *Harper's Weekly* ran an open letter from "Satan" which an editor said they had reason to believe was from Mark Twain. "Satan" detected hypocrisy and asked why charities which accepted guilt money in wills were too good to take from the living Rockefeller. The *Oil City Derrick*, now a Rockefeller organ, ran page after page against Tarbell, calling her work a freak story and saying that she wanted no one but her precious independents to succeed. Next to this, Ida pasted an advisory from the S. S. McClure Company thanking the *Derrick* for the notices.

One publication she and *McClure's* took very seriously was *The Nation*. An intelligent, principled weekly which crusaded for reform of the tariff and the civil service systems, it had helped form Tarbell's thinking; but the essentially patrician publication began to feel the breeze of revolution and chastised Tarbell. Ignoring her 241 pages of careful documentation, the reviewer wrote:

. . . This book seems to have been written for the purpose of inten-sifying the popular hatred. The writer had either a vague concep-tion of the nature of proof, or she is willing to black the character of Mr. John D. Rockefeller by insinuation and detraction.

Tarbell had been plain-spoken in pointing out the independents' follies, but *The Nation* claimed she portrayed Standard Oil as evil incarnate and the oil regions as powers of goodness. It condemned her and other reform-minded journalists as hatemongers:

> We need reforms badly enough, but we shall not get them until we have an electorate able to control its passions, to reserve its con-demnation, to deliberate before it acts. When that time comes, a railing accusation will not be accepted as history.[59]

Tarbell and McClure were outraged, but the Standard was delighted and reprinted it with *The Nation's* permission, for circulation to li-braries, ministers, and other avenues of public opinion.

McClure's did not let up. The editors sought to compound the suc-cess of *The History of the Standard Oil Company* by profiling its foun-der, and Ida Tarbell was ready. She had said it would take a Balzac to portray the oil business, and the profile she wrote was a Balzacian de-scription of rapacity and greed. She had been gathering anecdotes for it from the very beginning of her investigations and when she wrote, her tone was quite different from the cold arraignment that had character-ized her previous articles. It was as if a rich, strong underground pool had been tapped and had come forth in a rush.

In John D. Rockefeller she found an object worthy of her fury. She found him guilty of baldness, bumps, and being the son of a snake oil dealer. She took his appearance, affected by a stomach ailment and the alopecia which rendered him hairless, as a moral sign.

Not for the sake of the oil region was she angry. The victims, buck-shot to his bullet, had victimized themselves. She was furious that such an unscrupulous man could live and act and triumph and she showed no mercy. John D. Rockefeller was a Tarbell hero gone wrong. He was totally self-made, the self-educated child of poor people who had made himself a man of great power. But Rockefeller's motive had been greed, and his methods those of the bully. Rockefeller possessed superior powers and, to Tarbell's mind, no circumstances mitigated his misuse of them. In "John D. Rockefeller, A Character Study," she inveighed:

> Rich indeed should be the returns to the public for what it has cost to built up a fortune like Mr. Rockefeller's . . . Cheap oil? Mr.

Rockefeller's fundamental reason for forming his first combination was to keep *up* the price of oil. It has been forced down by the inventions and discoveries of his competitors. He has never lowered it a point if it could be avoided, and in times of public stress he had taken advantage of the very misery of the poor to demand higher prices. Nobody has yet forgotten the raising of the price of oil in the coal famine of 1902. Even the coal barons themselves in that winter combined to see that the poor of the great cities received their little bags of coal promptly and at reasonable prices and in preference to rich patrons. But the price of oil and the price of oil-stoves went up. Does it pay the public to trust the control of a great necessity of life to such a man? . . . Mr. Rockefeller, much as he dislikes the light, cannot escape the fate of his own greatness. All his vast wealth spent in one supreme effort to evade the judgment of men would be but wasted . . . the greater the power to which he has risen the stronger the light in which he must finally and eternally rest.[60]

To fill out the page, *McClure's* excerpted Ruskin on Judas Iscariot.

Ida's profile revealed that John D. had driven his brother Frank and a boyhood friend named James Corrigan from the business by needlessly calling in loans. Because of John D. Rockefeller's scandalous conduct toward his brother and friend, and because of Tarbell's personal attacks, both author and subject came under fire. Both had to issue statements.

Silent against every charge until now, John D. Rockefeller instructed his Cleveland attorney Virgil P. Kline to point out that while he may have driven his brother and boyhood friend from the business, an arbitration court had sided with him against Corrigan. Newspapers around the country announced that Tarbell stood by her statements. She insisted, "He presents himself to the public in two phases—as the richest man in the world and as an active adherent of the Christian church. If Mr. Rockefeller did not and had not all his life declared that the church and the Bible were the most precious things in his life, I should hesitate to apply the golden rule to the Corrigan case. As it is, I claim I have that right."[61]

Tarbell, quite pleased with her reply, flattered herself that she came out ahead. Her brother praised her lavishly and John Phillips said she had never handled herself so well, but self-congratulation over the character sketch abated when Siddall received word that Frank Rockefeller was out to get him. Reportedly, Frank was bringing suit against the magazine because *McClure's* had smeared their father's reputation. Frank had only intended to attack his brother, John D.

Tarbell, who had taken the precaution of submitting the piece to Corrigan for correction, gathered their correspondence. She also dictated an internal report defending her inclusion of the misadventures of Rockefeller *père* as a key to the character of his son.

They were in the midst of contacting lawyers and summoning Siddall to New York when Tarbell received an anonymous phone call from a person who said he had come from Cleveland expressly to meet her. Curiosity triumphed over apprehension. She went to the Fifth Avenue Hotel, and found Frank Rockefeller. Reports of his anger had been highly exaggerated. He was there to offer her fresh evidence of his brother's perjury. She interrupted his diatribe to ask if he planned to sue her or *McClure's*. Rockefeller admitted he had never expected her to attack his father, but said he was sure he'd get over his hurt.

After the sketch, some members of the press set about to do to Tarbell what she had done to Rockefeller: "Is it envy, uncharitableness or what not that induces spasms of attack upon men who get rich and give away money?" *Harper's Weekly* asked. *The Presbyterian Banner* called the work "Sinister and indecent." In Michigan, *The Gateway* questioned how Ida Tarbell would feel if she were denied her eyebrows and said a man should be judged by his acts. It said the monster was Tarbell herself and blamed her spleen on her "single blessedness" or spinsterhood.

What made Tarbell forget judiciousness and objectivity in her all-out attack? Some said she was embittered because of what the Standard had done to her father. Actually, she always realized that people, especially those she loved, had collaborated with their fates. When she sat down to write the Rockefeller profile, her father was lying in the agonies of stomach cancer in Titusville. It is likely that her personal anguish overpowered the governing mechanism which usually made her weigh all sides of a question. She finished her assessment of Rockefeller and hurried to her father's deathbed.

Franklin had become ill while visiting Will in Philadelphia. He was taken to Clifton Springs for treatment, then brought home. Fearfully, Ida returned to Titusville. She was so relieved to find him still alive and capable of recognizing her that she allowed herself to hope that her father, who was seventy-eight, might still live.

Throughout February 1905, she alternated between hope he would recover and certainty that he would not. Finally, on March 1, after a two-month ordeal, he died, and family life as she had known it was sealed in her father's grave.

Sarah, just past forty, stayed with Esther in Titusville while Will and Ida returned to their jobs. Work was always Ida's antidote to sorrow. She did not stay home long after the funeral. Instead, she took her grief to Kansas where she could throw herself into a report on Standard Oil's war against a new generation of independents.

The Kansas and Indian Territory oil fields were the richest and most spectacular pools ever discovered in the country. They signaled the shifting of the petroleum boom from western Pennsylvania to the Southwest. This fact was not lost on Standard Oil. Kansas independents and the schoolteachers who invested in the fields were so irate over John D. Rockefeller's encroachments that the state opened its own refinery in a state prison.

For ten days Ida Tarbell toured rambunctious Kansas oil lands in a buckboard encrusted with dust. Then, after a night in a boomtown hotel so unsavory that she felt she had to push the bureau against her door, she was discovered by the populace. Everyone knew about her articles.

Thirty or forty wildcatters, Indians among them, serenaded her while she sat talking with a newspaper editor. Then, to her horror, they requested a speech. She passed out cigars which some tied to their lapels as souvenirs. Ida Tarbell, foe of the Standard, was hailed everywhere. She described the furor to Boyden in a letter from Independence, Kansas: "Nothing more grave and more laughable, deeper or shallower, have I ever struck. I'm gradually making my way through the state but there is so much to do. I hope to Heaven that all the foolishness about my respected self which has been published in these papers out here will not reach the office. Believe nothing until I have a hearing."[62]

She added that she would be glad to leave the ruckus of Kansas, where every move she made hit the newspapers and every word she uttered was printed by reporters, sometimes erroneously. When she did agree to speak, Ida urged the Kansans: "You must make yourselves as good refiners, as good transporters, as good marketers, as ingenious, as informed, as imaginative in your legitimate undertakings as [the Standard is] in both their legitimate and illegitimate." This was not popular. They did not want to hear they might have something to learn from Rockefeller. They wanted to hear something more rousing and less practical. "You have gone over to the Standard!" was one Populist accusation. Meanwhile, Standard Oil sympathizers denounced her as "an enemy to society."[63]

As she traveled home through Missouri, she spoke in a few towns where she was a great success. The Knife and Fork Club of Kansas City was particularly impressed. The *Star* reported that sensational as her message had been, she herself was the attraction. The Knife and Forkers had expected a masculine old maid. Instead, she, the first woman ever invited to speak to them, arrayed herself in a low-cut mauve gown, threw a silk scarf over her shoulders, and clasped a string of pearls around her neck.

The Paris, Missouri, *Herald* indicated that Tarbell had vamped her audience: "Instead of sober garb, straight lines and stern simplicity expected . . . the lines were circles! . . . Above all, imagine a woman, hated and feared by John D. Rockefeller and his fellow oligarchs, being so feminine as to appear décolleté in order to make her assault more effective!"

Success wore her out: "It brought fantastic situations where I was utterly unfit to play the part. A woman of twenty-five, fresh, full of zest, only interested in what was happening to her, would have reveled in the experience. But here I was—fifty, fagged and wanting to be let alone while I collected trustworthy information for my articles—dragged to the front as an apostle."[64]

So much was happening that even she, who said she always shrank from self-knowledge, felt that she somehow had to sort things out. She was overwhelmed by reaction to the Standard story—especially since she originally doubted that anyone would care to read it. She was shaken by the death of her father and the hedonism of Sam McClure. Tarbell felt the need of a faithful companion, and so she bought a diary. In the next year, much would be written there.

Outwardly, she was still unflappable: to Lincoln Steffens, the twentieth-century radical with the nineteenth-century gallantry, his colleague's chief merit was settling the boys' rambunctious disputes: "Sensible, capable and very affectionate, she knew each one of us and all our idiosyncrasies and troubles. She had none of her own as far as we ever heard." Upton Sinclair recalled: "Ida Tarbell was largely a conventional-minded lady, sweet and gracious." Virgin mother, Joan of Arc, exhausted spinster. Perhaps only Mr. Dooley held the key: "That Idarem's a lady, but she has the punch."[65]

However chaotic her emotions may have been, her professional "punch" was indeed potent. *The History of the Standard Oil Company* had long-ranging effects. In nearly forty years of history, the Standard Oil Company had a seemingly charmed manner of eluding the slippery fingers of government investigation. Even when the state of Ohio dissolved Standard Oil of Ohio because its charter violated state law, the Standard survived because its trustees did not surrender their certificates. Ida Tarbell's exposé broke John D. Rockefeller's luck.

Let us consider her *History* apart from the character profile: Other men of wealth had been scrutinized, but the founder of Standard Oil was the one who struck people's imagination. Rogers was a gambler, Morgan a potentate, and Carnegie a tyrant, but all were public about it. Rockefeller was the wolf in a prayer shawl. "There are worse men than John D. Rockefeller," said *The Arena*. "There is probably not one who in the public mind so typifies the grave and startling menace to the social order."[66]

If Tarbell had been writing an analysis of all the economic forces of the era, she might have judged that Rockefeller was no worse than some others, but her ethics were not relative. She made Rockefeller's Standard Oil a case history of the trust. Despite his superior ability and purpose, she claimed that the rebate was a major component of his success. Rockefeller was the villain of her piece, but there were no heroes. She portrayed independents as having defeated themselves time and time again in their efforts to work together or to believe that they could win, but it was not her nature to tell a hopeless tale. She hoped to inspire. Toward the end of her series, she showed how they were fighting back.

Critics through the years have sometimes termed her quaint and schoolmarmish for applying "Do unto others as you would have them do unto you" to the battleground of business, but in this she was a product of her time. American economists of that day felt ethics were to be factored into their science. Even the American Economic Association, founded in 1885, included among its members twenty-three ministers. Rockefeller offered one justification of his questionable practices: "Everyone was doing it. We were not the only ones." This was not acceptable to the ethically-minded, nor to the Supreme Court of the United States.

The case against the Standard began in St. Louis on November 15, 1906, when Attorney General Charles Bonaparte (grandnephew of that military Bonaparte who was Tarbell's first successful biographical subject) filed a petition under the Sherman Act against the Standard Oil Company of New Jersey, its seventy affiliated corporations, and seven trustees, charging that the defendants had combined and conspired to restrain and monopolize interstate commerce in petroleum. The government charged, as had Tarbell in her book, that Standard Oil conspired to monopolize trade by securing rebates and preferences from railroads by controlling pipelines, by local price cutting, by espionage, by operating under the guise of sham companies, and by eliminating competition.

The judge affirmed these contentions. The Standard appealed; then, in May of 1911, the Supreme Court upheld the decision. The Standard Oil Company was dissolved. Tarbell was never triumphant over this turn of events. She saw that while the mighty octopus had been chopped into thirty-eight bits, the group continued to function in concert. Moreover, the decision promulgated the rule of reason, which left companies free to operate in restraint of trade as long as it was "reasonable."

Among the divisions created by the dissolution were Standard Oil of New Jersey which became known as Exxon; Standard Oil of New York, or Mobil; Ohio, marketed under the trade name of Boron; Standard Oil of California or Chevron; and Standard Oil of Indiana with its Amoco pumps.

Extraordinary demand, not legality, eventually promoted rivalry among the Standard Oil companies. Oil became the national source of energy and the acceptance of the automobile created a need far greater than any one group could control. The U.S. Navy's requirements were so great that Standard's rivals took on a large share of the business. The industry, however, was destined to be one of cooperation and "enlightened" restraint of trade. During World War I, a Petroleum War Service Committee was formed with the president of Standard Oil of New Jersey as chairman. He and his members recommended that, in the interests of the war effort, they pool production and coordinate all efforts. Thus, emerging rivals from California and the Southwest were soon working in concert with the Standard. The government of the United States, which was to have regulated the oil business, became the client of petroleum interests.

Tarbell saw that Rockefeller had triumphed and that her own victory, however moral, was hollow. It was this she recognized, not that nine justices of the Supreme Court of the United States had ruled in favor of her life's work. She went on to new subjects, but she released information damaging to Rockefeller whenever she could. Three months after her series ran, the Bureau of Corporations, later known as the Federal Trade Commission, investigated petroleum transportation and she made some of her papers available to Commissioner James R. Garfield.[67]

His report of May 1906 elaborated on her exposé and found the railroads had indeed discriminated on behalf of Standard Oil, crushing its rivals and allowing the oil trust to harvest three-quarters of a million dollars a year from the railroads. President Roosevelt fumed in a broadside to Congress: "Of course the ultimate result is that it obtains a much larger profit at the expense of the public . . . This immediate correction, partial or complete, of the evil of the secret rates is of course on the one hand an acknowledgment that they were wrong, and yet were persevered in until exposed; and on the other hand a proof of the efficiency of the work that has been done by the Bureau of Corporations." The president did not see fit to give credit to the work done by independent journalists.[68]

Tarbell exulted when religious and educational institutions questioned taking money as tainted as Rockefeller's. She gladly armed the Reverend Washington Gladden, the influential Congregational minister, with facts she had gleaned about Rockefeller's character and business methods.[69] She jumped in when Congress investigated Rockefeller's role in developing the Mesabi iron range in Minnesota. She wrote Congressman William Kent: "A whole pipeline system, the Mellon Pipe, from Pittsburgh to the seaboard was swept into the Standard by the same kind of operation. They never made such a hauling. I wish the committee would get this before the public—of course this is confidential to you. I would not be willing to appear in it in any way."[70]

Never did she seem to understand that her cry against predatory competition was finally turned into law. The Hepburn Act of 1906 provided for more efficient control over railroad rates and classified pipeline companies as common carriers which were to treat all customers equally. The Mann-Elkins Act of 1910 gave greater power to the Interstate Commerce Commission to control pipeline rates. In 1914, the Federal Trade Commission Act was created to police business practices and the Clayton Act prohibited unfair competition which tended to promote monopoly. Within a decade, virtually all the abuses she had pinpointed were proscribed.

As the years passed, *The History of the Standard Oil Company* lost its immediacy, but the urgency never receded for Tarbell. In the 1930s, she took a young history professor, Dr. Paul Giddens, and his wife to lunch at the National Arts Club. "Tell me," he asked, making conversation, "if you could rewrite your book today, what would you change?" Fifty years after their conversation, he vividly recalled that her eyes flashed. She emphatically set down her knife and fork and answered: "Not one word, young man, not one word."[71]

Ida at age thirty-six in London wearing the dress she had styled for transformation into an evening gown.

Rouseville in the 1860s. The Tarbell home (upper right-hand corner) was on a hillside where, in season, leafy branches could obscure the derricks below.

At home writing *The History of the Standard Oil Company* series—behind a desk made neat for the photographer.

Ida with her mother Esther and sister Sarah at the Titusville home after the death of her father.

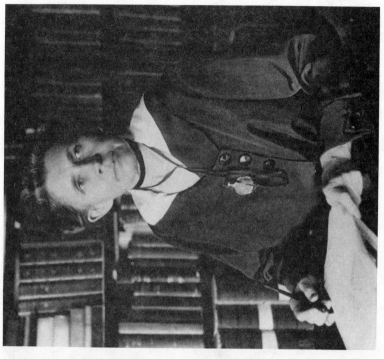

Ida at age sixty, before she was diagnosed as having tuberculosis.

Ida's Redding Ridge, Connecticut, farm that became the family headquarters.

Surrounded by work at seventy-six, upon completion of *All in the Day's Work*. Portrait by Feodor Zakharov

Eight

Unexplored Land

John D. Rockefeller was not the only one to feel the brunt of Tarbell's anger; there was still some left for Sam McClure. She, Phillips, and Boyden took it upon themselves to try to curb his philandering. They felt his conduct made the preeminent journal of exposé a target for exposure itself. By loosening his morality, McClure had stepped outside their circle and seemed to be betraying *McClure's Magazine*. Tarbell, Phillips, and Boyden were by turns a cabal promoting their own views and a vice squad of Keystone Kops.

McClure's dalliance became an office scandal after he directed poetry editor Witter Bynner to publish Florence Wilkinson's work and to deliver personally the acceptance letter with a bouquet of flowers. On Bynner's return from the lady's doorstep, Ida summoned him into her office for a counsel of war. Phillips, Boyden, and she chastised him for helping McClure deceive his wife, then they turned on McClure. Under their questioning, the General admitted he had written compromising letters which, in the hands of someone like William Randolph Hearst, could damage the magazine and its moral credibility.

Phillips hurried to Wilkinson, then vacationing in upstate New York, and extracted her promise that all correspondence would be returned. Wilkinson also offered to send future letters to McClure in care of his wife. When Hattie McClure agreed with this plan, Tarbell was shocked into expressing herself in bold language: "My dear Mr. Phillips—The Lord help us! I'm too small for this! There is nothing for us, I should say, but to keep up a 'stern and unrelenting' front. Evidently Mrs.

McClure is not to be counted on for that. Letters under her convoy! He can persuade her to anything and if in the end we see a *ménage d trois*, I shall not be greatly surprised. But that wouldn't last. He would soon want another!"[1]

McClure apparently had tried to explain himself to Miss Tarbell and now in this letter Ida asked Phillips if perhaps they should pass some home truths on to Miss Wilkinson: "Would it not be wise to put his condition still more forcibly to her—to tell her of the other affairs, to make her feel that far from being the first and only one, there have been others, several of them—and the only reason they have not gone so far is that the other women have refused to travel and sky-lark with him? Why he told me himself, not a month before the break-up [a temporary lull in the romance] that it would have probably been the same with any woman that he cared for *'if she had been as yielding as Miss W.'* It may be cruel to tell her this but we seem to be the only ones to use the knife and somebody must do it."[2]

Just as Ida had appointed herself to chaperone her roommates in Paris, so she itched to take charge now. She continued:

> If you wish it and Miss W. will consent, I will go and see her and make an appeal for courage, etc. I fear I would be hard with her. I do not mind her romantic vein so much as I do the *graft*. I lost all my respect for her when I saw her wheedling money out of the Gen'l. I am not hard on those who love in defiance of the law—on the contrary—if it is a genuine thing. But this thing was too trivial and calculating to arouse sympathy at the start. But I will honestly try to put that out of my mind and help the girl if she will let me. I have had no answer yet to the letter sent last week. It is quite natural she should feel resentment toward me, but if it can be brought about it would be better for me to go . . . than for you . . . This is, of course, the most vital thing we have on hand and our inexperience in dealing with lunatics makes extra attention necessary!

They had reached the point of treating the General as a nuisance. Lincoln Steffens, back from some shameful city, was amazed. "I realized that those who had to live and work every day with him were learning to hate him."[3] When McClure was around, he was treated as their "play" editor. He barked orders which everyone pretended to obey with punctilio. Then they went to Phillips to find out what they really should do.

Young Willa Cather, who was sincere when she called McClure by his nicknames—the General, the Chief—described in a short story titled "Ardessa" the hubris of the group. In this story, published in *The*

Century in May 1918, she wrote of an editor, Marcus O'Mally, who "had built up about him an organization of which he was somewhat afraid and with which he was vastly bored. On his staff there were five famous men, and he had made every one of them. At first it amused him to manufacture celebrities. He found he could take an average reporter from the daily press, give him a 'line' to follow, a trust to fight, a vice to expose—this was all in that good time when people were eager to read about their own wickedness—and in two years the reporter would be recognized as an authority. Other people—Napoleon, Disraeli, Sarah Bernhardt—had discovered that advertising would go a long way; but Marcus O'Mally discovered that in America it would go all the way—as far as you wished to pay its passage. Any human countenance plastered in three-sheet posters from sea to sea, would be revered by the American people. The strangest thing was that the owners of these grave countenances, staring at their own faces on newsstands and billboards, fell to venerating themselves; and even he, O'Mally, was more or less constrained by these reputations that he had created out of cheap paper and cheap ink."

Cather went on to describe this editor: "He left his dignified office to take care of itself for a good many months of the year while he played about on the outskirts of the social order."

If Phillips, Tarbell, and the others forgot their debts to the Chief, McClure also forgot what he owed the staff, especially to Phillips. McClure's marital problems must have had particular poignancy for Phillips since Phillips had helped McClure to win his wife over the protestations of Hattie's father, a Knox College professor. Later, Phillips's father had mortgaged the family home to keep *McClure's* going. But as friend and partner, Phillips was increasingly regarded by McClure as his lackey. His decisions were overruled, his layouts torn apart at the last minute. He had responsibility but no authority, and it grated upon him.

Phillips simply irritated McClure. Phillips had allowed Jaccaci, the art director, to interfere in editorial matters until McClure felt obliged to fire him. Ever afterward, McClure found Phillips less and less trustworthy; but as he valued Phillips less, he valued Tarbell more. He depended on her to look after both the magazine and his family while he pursued other interests. In the spring of 1903, a weekend "retreat" was prepared for Ida at the McClure house in Ardsley, New York. McClure wrote his wife: "In buying things for Miss Tarbell's room I want you to know that I told her that *you* were planning to make her a nice home there. Miss Tarbell did us great service in the past two or three years when Jac was planning to be the whole thing and Mr. Phillips was blind [as to how the office should be managed]. In case of my death she would be your mainstay as Mr. Phillips doesn't realize other people's unreliability & I shall be away a lot next year and you will enjoy having her out."[4]

As far as McClure was concerned, Ida Tarbell was still his most trusted ally, albeit a disappointed one. When business took him around the country, he wrote Ida from Kansas City that he bitterly regretted her change in feelings for him. He recalled how sad she had been at the end of their vacation with the Rices and said he thought he could stand the years of waiting until he regained her confidence.[5]

McClure was chagrined that he had wounded her; he did not realize he had killed her love. He still seemed to think he had her total loyalty and blithely described to her a future in which she would permanently take the "ailing" Phillips's place: "When your book [on Standard Oil] is finished Siddall will be able to do a lot in the Magazine and be of great service to you and Boyden," he assured her. Other letters followed outlining how Baker and Steffens were to proceed with their stories and how promotional advertising, which he thought "weak and tasteless" under Phillips, was henceforth to be written.[6]

McClure also wrote to Steffens and Baker directly so that Tarbell or Phillips sometimes found their suggestions countermanded. No one knew the General's wishes until he breezed in to rip the copy from the printer's hand or write from the Alps that nothing had been done according to his specifications. Ida saw Phillips grow thinner, more pinched.

Hattie was also writing to Ida, telling of McClure's progress and his trust in the guidance of his wife. Ida saw that she might be able to influence Hattie, at least, and wrote: "You are able to command him in a degree which amazes me. It is the triumph of the superior and moral nature and he doesn't recognize your authority."[7] Ida said it hurt her to have intemperate orders roared in the office when Phillips had all the burdens, plus concern about Mr. McClure. "We need the man Mr. McClure is bound to be in a few months," she assured Hattie. "But the wholesale criticism is taking the heart and enthusiasm out of Mr. Phillips." She concluded by saying that she feared the office and business could not endure indefinitely the strains which were being put upon them.

After receiving word from McClure telling her again how to administer the office, Tarbell gently but firmly let him know that he was accusing their friend of his own infirmities. She defended Phillips: "The trouble is that he has not the endurance to do, day in and day out, the kind of work he did yesterday and is doing to-day. But that is your trouble and my trouble, my dear Mr. McClure. . . . He has all the different branches of the work in hand, which I have not, and of course, I never could get hold of them as he and you do. I will do everything I can to relieve and assist him, and if I honestly think that he ought to get away from it all I shall insist with all the strength I have, just as I do, you know, when I see you failing. At present things look very well and I do not think you need to worry about Mr. Phillips any more than perhaps we shall always have to be anxious about him, a man of delicate physical organization and of a still more delicate nature. The fact that Mr. Phillips is to be here will explain to you why it does not seem to me advisable to spend an hour or two a week in conference with the whole staff. If I were here alone I would do that, but when Mr. Phillips is here such a move naturally must come from him, just as it must come from you when you are here."[8]

As she struggled under the strains of the magazine, she thought she might be able to write her problems away by confiding them to a journal. She opened her small leather diary, took up her pen, and wrote:

"May 5, 1905. Bought nearly two months ago and not a word written—bought as books of this kind have been before for a companion and so dead to life I could not use a companion. There has come a point where it is life or death-in-life—and I am not willing to give up life. If the innermost accesses are to be entered I must go there alone. I am conscious so much of myself is evading me. And this poor little book is a feeble prop in my effort to reach the land I've never explored."[9]

Her diary was a safety valve which allowed her to release her strongest emotions. Her first long entry there revealed a very flustered woman with a great reservoir of romantic love and no perspective when it came to a man who impressed her.

Proximity, the hair on the back of a man's neck, the touch of his hand or sleeve, were too palpable to kindle Tarbell's soul. The idea of the unachievable, the removed, the person so lofty he seemed safely in another realm allowed her to adore before an altar of her own making. She longed to be overpowered in the place most meaningful to her— her mind. Carl Schurz, probably without conscious intent, had achieved this. It is likely that John Burroughs, the naturalist and essayist, did as well. His reflections on nature, his emulation of Emerson and Thoreau and friendship with Whitman, gave him a mythical stature. Burroughs also seemed to Ida to be as simple, sweet, and honest as her father. She began to visit him and his wife in the Catskills around 1900 when he was sixty-three.[10]

No one, however, had the impact of Henry James. Some time early in 1905, she saw his portrait. She thought James's face showed great sensitivity and comprehension, conquest and gravity. She noted especially his eyes, which seemed to see into deep matters: "I had looked at it [the

portrait] many times and sighed he was unattainable. I have never read
him much but I knew here was something big and wise and sweet—a
soul to sit by as one does by a cathedral and let its power filter in."
James was at that time revisiting America after an absence of twenty
years. Enthusiastic reception to *The Golden Bowl* brought him the opportunity of a lecture tour. Having traveled through the South, the
Midwest, and California, he was at the end of his journey and back for a
last visit to New England. George W. Cable, then a prominent writer
of stories set in the South, hosted a dinner to precede James's lecture
and invited the Hazens, the writer Gerald Stanley Lee and his wife, and
Ida Tarbell.

She at first declined the honor. She wrote in her diary: "All the rude-
ness—the ignorance, the imbecility, and inarticulateness of my life
flared up in me and I blushed to think of sitting near. But they wanted
me and I wanted to go. I dared to do it. I lay awake nights thinking of it.
Afraid and *eager*. For I knew there was something there for me."

She so yearned for James's esteem, it seemed no one else's had ever
mattered. "It is a thirst for his particular formal assurance I'm on the
right road. I'm real as far as I go. I am not a sham—that the soul is not
dead or sleeping for the soul is there—the being one with its noble
walk, its wide vision knows that is something. I wanted to be assured.
How pitiful I am!"

James had a commanding presence, though he was sixty-two, portly,
and half a foot shorter than she. The dinner party was tense with admiration. Cable amazed James by his detailed knowledge of characters
he himself had forgotten, then slavishly threw himself on his knees
while Ida giggled with embarrassment. James let them know he thought
lecturing beneath his dignity, but Ida harkened to his speech, "The
Lesson of Balzac," as if it were an oracle. Struck by James's use of the
word "saturation" to describe Balzac's absorption of life, she decided
her challenge was "To comprehend all—to wade boldly into life and
yet never let the thing—the experience—injure you. To keep always to
the mastery of it that you may interpret life."[11]

James told her he hoped she would be in Northampton for a few
days, then stopped back for a last visit with her. They talked about
French writers they knew in common such as the Daudets. Surely she
told him she had met his brother William when he lectured at Chautauqua Lake. James told Cable privately, "Miss Tarbell has done a great
work, that is it seems to me she has done a real work. She has a shining
personality." America assailed him with an impression of graceless ma-
terialism. Here was the woman whose work certified the greed he detected everywhere. When she told him she was troubled by what she
had written, that she hated the cruelty and brutality of telling the truth,

especially in the profile of Rockefeller,˙he advised her, "Cheer up. If there's anything you should cherish it's your contempts. Cherish your contempt, young woman!"[12]

She wrote staccato fashion in her diary: "I might have done better, was sadly conscious all the time that was the end of HJ for us. Am in a funk of soul because there could be no more. We talked a little of Paris, its charm. I know what she says to him. She says it to me too well—that much in common! I told him how I missed him *chez Daudet* and when he left he said, 'I hope we shall not miss again.' " Still under the spell of James she wrote: "A great leap and then dull renunciation! *Que bon?* I am not equal to it. But I deliberately sought another chance to see him. He had asked when I went home. I said I went to Boston and he was— or did I fancy it—disappointed! *Ce qu'on veut il voit!*"

James was in New York in mid-June and she wrote to him, but her invitation was forwarded to England. He responded after some months: "Your kind note of so many weeks ago came to me today and in this far place with a ghostly affect. It has apparently had strange postal adventures and languished long in successive pairs of neglectful hands only to give me now a sad taste of lost opportunity . . . the American adventure is already rather far away and half romantic: that evening at Northampton really and fantastically so . . . I am sorry not to have had the pleasure of seeing you again and I wish all continued strength to your elbow and glory to your name. Believe me very truly, Henry James."[13]

James was for Ida an ambiguous experience, but Sam McClure and John Phillips continued to be quite real. While Boyden was in Europe, Ida wrote him a letter describing recent events. She was reasonably confident that McClure had tired of Wilkinson: "I know he is not seeing her much—with me too much! We're doing our best, Mr. P. and I. Poor Mr. P. He comes to dinner with me and we are really getting to be almost easy in each other's presence! He is certainly the rarest—most beautiful soul on earth . . . and he has to pay for his qualities in suffering and in loneliness!"[14]

Boyden, who knew all about the General's adulteries, responded, "I'm gladdest of all of course of you and Mr. Phillips warming up. Work on him will be more appreciated than on the chief and it's quite a necessity from a human standpoint and only a little less so from a business. No one can of course bring Mr. P. present happiness but he doesn't expect that and each little day of it brings such a beautiful light into that countenance—and you can do more than anyone else, love. I sometimes wish it weren't so—this always putting it up to you to do everything because you can do it best only piles more responsibility on you who should be freer. But it's your own fault!"[15]

At this point Ida took charge, also, of her niece Esther, just graduated from Wells College in Aurora, Nèw York, and come to New York to be Ida's social secretary. The young woman was high-spirited, entirely un-selfconscious, and the perfect outlet for Ida's maternal tendencies.

"Ever since I was a child I went to my aunt for everything. She always gave her strength, her time, her breast pin, anything large or small you asked for, she gave you,"[16] Esther said.

Ida included the girl in all her activities for the three years of her stay. "Social was right," admitted Esther. "I don't know about the secretary part." Jaccaci saw them as a team. "Where you take The General you have to take the Captain too to make her happy," he said, and invited both of them to share his box at the circus. Esther recalled that the loud guns which punctuated the stunts startled her so that she held her head. "Even through my covered ears I could hear Aunt Ida sternly whispering: 'Don't be an idiot.' "[17]

Ida "received" on Friday afternoons. As she battled an unreliable chafing dish in the kitchen, she dispatched Esther to entertain the guests. On these occasions, Ida's efforts to instill decorum proved fruitless. While chatting with the Finley Peter Dunnes, Esther blew a lock of hair away from her face, prompting Dunne to look at her quizzically and inquire: "Did you ever try a comb?" At another time, Ida asked Esther to serve a bottle of wine. "I brought it in by the neck, and my, she lit into me," said Esther. Formality was apparently not Ida's strong suit, however hard she tried. Nor was it a noticeable trait among her household. At an elegant dinner party Ida served a fish so delicious that a guest asked what kind it was. The maid Kate piped up, "Sure, Madame, it's a faymale, I seen the eggs."

Sam McClure was also part of their social life. Esther too learned to adapt to his pace. One evening Ida came home early to announce that they were dining with Sam McClure at The Holland House at seven, but she told Esther to be prepared to leave the house at six. McClure arrived at eight and carried them off to Delmonico's.

That was, of course, characteristic of McClure under the best of circumstances, but he had a special reason to be distracted at that time. His operation consisted of more than just the magazine, and all were experiencing difficulties. The syndicate was losing money under McClure's brother Tom, so Phillips and Oscar Brady of the business office had to take it over. McClure, Phillips & Co. books had just tied up a quarter of a million dollars for a printing plant in Long Island City. The magazine's circulation was seesawing. In 1904, it was down by fifteen hundred, then up five thousand in 1905 when it reached three hundred seventy-five thousand; but after that Ayers' Directory of circulation doubted their figures and sliced their larger claims.

Disturbed by the rise of other magazines and exasperated by various health cures calling alternately for rest, milk, and squab, McClure

gyrated between Europe and New York and between fits of health and
exhaustion. His pathologically mercurial moods determined Tarbell's
response. When he was broken and beaten, she was gentle. When he
was bravely trying to reform, she was forgiving; but when he was rampant, firing commands and criticism, she rebelled. Once she had seen
his peregrinations as quests for new material. Now when she watched
him leave the office she was sure he was on the trail of some skirt. She
disdained his insights and ignored his urgings that she profile the
United States Senate, the body he regarded as the most powerful ruling
force in the world and a company of thieves.[18]

In this, she made a serious error. Just as McClure had been right
about her studying Napoleon and Lincoln, so he was right about this. A
year later David Graham Phillips's series, "The Treason of the Senate,"
appeared in *Cosmopolitan*, raising its circulation and fueling the reform
movement for direct election of senators. Meanwhile, Tarbell addressed
herself to the task of finishing the saga of Standard Oil in Kansas; and
finally, after eight years of sporadic editing, completed work on Carl
Schurz's reminiscences. McClure did not get his own investigation of
the Senate, but he dispatched staff writer Burton J. Hendrick to go after
life insurance companies, a subject Steffens had pursued unsuccessfully
for five months.

At the very time when McClure seemed to have ended his escapades,
he was threatened with blackmail. He was away on one of his trips
when Hattie McClure appeared at the office and laid on Ida's desk
"The Shame of S. S. McClure, Illustrated by Letters and Original Documents." Edith Wherry, the latest discarded mistress, was taking her
revenge and terrorizing them all with her "memoirs." Somehow
Wherry was placated and McClure was left free to indulge in his redis-
covered pleasure in life insurance scandals, Baker's series on railroads,
and the upcoming Russian-Japanese Peace Conference hosted by President Roosevelt. It seemed as if everything would be all right.

McClure's indiscretions were kept as quiet as Tarbell and her colleagues wished. It was their work which garnered all the attention. *The
History of the Standard Oil Company*, at least the story behind it, was
adapted—quite freely—for the stage: the image of a woman lacking
even the right to vote tackling the world's largest monopoly inspired
The Lion and the Mouse. In it, the heroine, Shirley Rossmore, daughter of a disgraced judge, determines to save her father by exposing the
man who has defamed him. She presents herself as a would-be biographer to John S. Ryder, the world's richest man—the very one who has
ruined her father. Happily, Ryder's handsome son falls in love with her.
Most conveniently, he gives her access to his father's papers. Then, the
elder Ryder, at death's door, begs Shirley to restore her father's reputation and to marry his son as well. *The New York Times* noted on No-

vember 26, 1905: "Just as Caesar had his Brutus and George III his Patrick Henry, so Mr. Ryder has his—Ida Tarbell."

After seeing the play at the Park Theater in Boston, Ida told the press she found Shirley Rossmore "noble" and was offered the role herself. A few days later at the Wieting Opera House in Syracuse, it was announced that Ida Tarbell would *probably* star there—for a fee of twenty-five hundred dollars a week for twenty weeks. It was the highest offer ever made an actress, but Ida declined. Instead, she played the part of Lady Macbeth to John Phillips's Hamlet—she urged him to break away from McClure.

At the end of 1905, after her articles on Kansas concluded, Tarbell received a confidential letter from McClure. He was sharing with her his greatest plan—the outline for his *Universal Magazine*. He explained it would be printed on cheap paper and sold at five cents a copy. Furthermore, he decreed it should carry only pen-and-ink drawings as he had decided half-tone engravings were incompatible with type. She objected because it would detract their energies from *McClure's Magazine*.

A few days later, McClure told her he had generated a quarter million dollars in backing. He projected annual income at two million; but besides the magazine, there was to be a People's University correspondence course, a Universal Library of uncopyrighted classics, a People's Life Insurance Company, and a People's Bank. Tarbell would remember these as McClure's Bank, McClure's Life Insurance Company, McClure's School Book Publishing Company, and McClure's Ideal Settlement.

It was, of course, foolhardy, and Ida thought the whole notion tainted by greed. McClure's potential empire probably seemed to him only an honest alternative to evil trusts; to Tarbell it seemed he was trying to cash in on all the moneymaking schemes they had exposed as illegal.

The rest of the staff agreed with Tarbell. Lincoln Steffens wrote his father: "Mr. McClure has been away, playing and getting well. He came back to work last fall and he started on a big, fool scheme of founding a new magazine with a string of banks, insurance companies, etc. and a capitalization of $15,000,000. It was not only fool, it was not quite right, as we saw it. It was a speculative scheme, and we protested. He stuck to his idea. He took counsel from financiers who have been exploiting (which means robbing) railroads, and it looked as if he were willing to do the very things the rest of us had been 'exposing' . . . we did not propose to stand by and see it exploited and used, even by the owner."[19]

McClure's counselors were Victor Lawson, publisher of the *Chicago Daily News*, a man who worked for the establishment of savings accounts through the post office; and McClure's former Knox classmates Robert Mather and Edgar Bancroft. Bancroft and Mather were both railroad lawyers and directors of banks, a capitalistic mix that did not appeal to the reformers. Tarbell would have no part of them or of McClure's scheme.

To it was added the lingering hurt of his philandering and her need for a change. When she started her diary, it seemed she had no place to run. Now seven months later it seemed that if escape was needed, she could flee Sam McClure. Her rupture from *The Chautauquan* nearly fifteen years before lifted the dead weight of closed opportunities and approaching age. Might she have thought in her innermost self, her "land I've never explored," that the way to rejuvenate herself was to rebel? To give up security and opt, as she had done in her youth, for freedom?

As Phillips tried to dissuade McClure against the new enterprises, Tarbell rallied Phillips, Boyden, and Siddall more closely about her and cultivated the thought that if McClure prevailed, they could resign. By January 1906, the mutiny was well underway.

Tarbell approached Finley Peter Dunne about joining them: "I know you would be of great use to us editorially. What I don't see is just how to work the thing out to your advantage. I think the relations would have to grow; we fumble a lot here in our efforts to keep straight. We are pretty brutal and skeptical with one another but you know us well enough to know that all this is perhaps the unavoidable pain of producing a thing which will really be sane and worthwhile, and the disillusion resulting from nothing ever coming up to our hopes. I believe if we could get down to some kind of a working basis that you would like us and believe in us just as we do in you."[20] Dunne began to give it very serious consideration.

Soon after writing this letter, Tarbell went on a vacation in the West with John and Jennie Phillips and William Allen White. Rockefeller's copper interests in Colorado were then coming under scrutiny and reporters importuned them about it along the way. White interviewed himself for their benefit and, since Tarbell had no desire to meet the press, White told them to leave her alone—she had left her moral sense back in New York. One newspaper editor contented himself with head-lining an article: MISS TARBELL EMPHATICALLY DENIES SHE IS IN COLO-RADO TO INVESTIGATE COPPER SCANDAL. A Los Angeles reporter thought he saw deeper. To him she seemed like a rock-ribbed Yankee with a typically New England air of potential martyrdom: "She wouldn't like it, but she would bear her cross." White impressed him as a man of wide curiosity, but Ida Tarbell seemed "not concerned with a particular thing until she had it impaled on her specimen board."[21]

The vacationing quartet emerged from the bottom of the Grand

Canyon to learn that McClure did not take their objections to the *Universal Magazine* seriously. He was staffing his new corporation and planning to give them all gifts of stock. Stiff from seven hours on mule back and braced by two days of good company and enough spectacular geology to recall the enthusiasm of her student days, Ida poured out her fury in a letter to Boyden. She was wrathful not only over "the diabolical condition in New York," but at the notion that their errant chief had suggested he might join them in Arizona. She fumed: "These letters make me furious. If anything could prove the General's inability to found and carry out a new operation it is this. The vital points he does not touch." By this time the General had figured out a way to incorporate the name McClure into his new projects and Tarbell thought this was an infringement on the magazine she had worked so hard for. She told Boyden: "The use of the name McClure is all wrong—out of the question as I see it. This system of securing the consent of everybody by means of gifts of stock is humbug. I won't touch it and if he goes on insisting on using the name McC he can take my S. S. McC stock. You see I am not fit to write him. Mr. P. as usual is an angel and has written him a beautiful letter which *ought* to show him what an inferior creature [he] is but which probably he [McClure] will consider as someway a consent to the scheme. You insist on his coming out here. I have just written you a message saying it would kill us and that I prefer to return. We should simply go mad with him banging away in the face of nature. Besides we will not stay at all if he comes . . . Don't let him commit himself any more than possible and urge him to wait until Mr. P's return. I am sure it can be fixed right then—if not we can secede."[22]

Tarbell drafted a more temperate letter to McClure on her hotel stationery suggesting that if he sold them his stock he would be free to develop other business while they continued *McClure's* along the lines he had laid down. They would conserve the old while he perfected the new. If he were determined to leave, they would, of course, sell. She couldn't believe, she said, that after twenty years they couldn't settle their differences.[23]

As Tarbell took Boyden into her confidence, so Boyden told Siddall. The word passed to Viola Roseboro, Mollie Best, and the rest of the staff. Boyden wrote Baker; someone contacted Steffens; the staff broke into partisan camps.

By the time the travelers returned to New York, McClure had again gone to Europe, leaving Tarbell and Phillips alone to plan. Phillips was, if not a weak man, an indecisive one, whose strength lay in partnership rather than individual action. For years he had been second to McClure and had been subjected to scorn and abuse. Even Curtis Brady, a McClure supporter, complained of the General: "He never said 'our' magazine, he always said 'my' magazine."[24]

At long last, Phillips either had had enough, or had finally found someone more supportive to lean on in Ida Tarbell. Everything one knows about him indicates it was difficult for him to change his life at the age of forty-five, but once the decision was made, he was serene in his commitment. Indeed, after Phillips told his old chief that he and Ida were resigning, he left most of the frenzy to Tarbell and McClure. McClure frantically tried to discuss it with Ida, but she said Phillips would speak for her. She scribbled in her diary: "Persisted only that I didn't like the whole business [of the insurance company and so on]— the way it had been done—all the crazy features (he seems to acknowledge craziness now)." McClure was dumbstruck to learn that Tarbell preferred Phillips to him. Tumultuous days followed.

While the principals battled and wept in inner offices, the staff whispered and wept outside. Some vowed loyalty to McClure, others thought the place would be intolerable without Phillips. At first, Boyden was the only one who declared that he would leave. At one point, McClure heard that the entire staff was walking out.

Trying to understand what was happening, McClure sought out Tarbell. His eyes were red from weeping and she was so distraught that she had to hold his hand. He reminded her of Napoleon at Fontainebleau, although he sounded more like Julius Caesar, saying, "And you, too, Ida Tarbell." Ignoring her own role, she told him the struggle was not between himself and Phillips, but between Phillips and his own soul, and that to save his manhood Phillips had to leave.

She recorded all this in her journal: "Awful for me. Could not talk. He referred to his love for me—said I all while had loved him in *l'affaire Wilkinson*. Feel he is not wholly sincere yet he thinks he is—am not cured yet. I ache dreadfully." McClure sobbed that he had always loved her, flung his arms around her, kissed her, and left her crying. She wrote: "I sat down sobbing hysterically but am more convinced than ever that we are right."

In the middle of this chaotic period, the spring of 1906, two things happened. First, Ida Tarbell bought a house in the country, largely from her book royalties. It was as if she wanted to dispose of her money while she still knew where it was coming from.

One morning during the fracas, she announced she was off to Redding Ridge, Connecticut, to buy land she had optioned on a whim. Boyden banged his fist on the desk, declared her unfit to be trusted, and insisted on going along to protect her. Later, charmed by the matched oak trees in front of the farmhouse and the gurgling brook in the rear, he allowed her to proceed with her purchase of the property and thereafter was solicitous over its changes and improvements.

Ida bought the place thinking it would be a refuge of solitude on the weekends, but in the beginning it was like a wonderful toy to share with friends and family. Esther accompanied her to Macy's Department Store where they bought provisions with gusto. They purchased staples by the pound, including a supply of pepper which survived the long-lived Tarbell.

The other noteworthy event that occurred that spring was that Theodore Roosevelt denounced crusading journalists as "muckrakers," a development which caused a sensation everywhere but at *McClure's*, which was busy with pyrotechnics of its own.

It had been two years since the president and others read Sam McClure's editorial on "The American Contempt for Law." In the meantime, nearly every publication had zealously investigated something—often to good effect as in Samuel Hopkins Adams's revelation of poisonous patent medicines which appeared in *Collier's*.

Readers, at least those who had not been numbed by all these disclosures, had begun to feel they were being cheated or poisoned by someone somewhere every day. As Mr. Dooley noted in the December 16, 1905, *Collier's*, things weren't like the old days: "If anything, ivrybody was too good to ivrybody else ... but now whin I pick up me fav'rite magazine off th' flure, what do I find? Ivrything has gone wrong ..." Mr. Dooley especially singled our "Idarem on Jawn D" and in so doing provided Miss Tarbell with a nickname. Henceforth, the staff gaily called her Idarem.

But in Washington, President Teddy Roosevelt was not so jaunty. Well-born, however he might like to dress up and play the cowboy, he feared what the common man was capable of doing, especially since his predecessor had been assassinated by an anarchist. The president implored Sam McClure to have Steffens "put more sky in his landscapes," and thus have the dirt in perspective: "It is unfortunate," Roosevelt wrote the editor, "to encourage people to believe all crimes are connected with business and that the crime of graft is the only crime."[25] He thought they should show the hideous iniquities—such as the slaughter of the French Revolution—of which mobs could be guilty.

Roosevelt's disapproval continued to build until Hearst's *Cosmopolitan* published the well-documented "The Treason of the Senate" in March 1906. The president was irate over the attack on Senator Chauncey Depew, whom he called "poor old Chauncey." Others termed him "the railroad Senator" because he had been president of the New York Central and served its interests in his public post. Still, at a meeting of the Gridiron Club in Washington, D.C., shortly thereafter, Roosevelt lashed out. The club was an organization of reporters and sought to encourage candor and bonhomie between public officials and the press. In his speech, which by tradition was off the record, Roosevelt likened the authors of exposure to the man with the muckrake in Bunyan's *Pilgrim's Progress* who fixed his eyes on cleaning mire when he might have seen a celestial crown: "There are beautiful things above and around them; and if they gradually grow to feel that the whole world is nothing but muck, their power of usefulness is gone. If the whole picture is painted black there remains no hue whereby to single out the rascals for distinction from their fellows,"[26] Teddy declared.

Word of the attack spread rapidly through the publishing and political worlds, and TR, always one to capitalize on a trenchant catchphrase, decided to repeat the speech. This time he spoke for the record at the laying of the cornerstone for the new office building planned for the House of Representatives. Privately, Roosevelt wrote to Ray Stannard Baker and Senator Henry Cabot Lodge that he was talking only of the scandalmongering newspapers of William Randolph Hearst.[27] But he made no such distinction when he spoke on April 14, 1906, however. In the public mind, Lincoln Steffens, Ray Stannard Baker, and Ida M. Tarbell stood condemned by the popular Teddy.

Weary of three and a half years of exposés, the press backed Roosevelt. Ellery Sedgwick, former *McClure's* staffer and now editor of the *Atlantic Monthly*, warned: "Men are tried and found guilty in magazine counting rooms before investigation is begun." *Collier's* opined that true investigators were finding their authority diminished: "Why listen to facts when diatribes are at hand?"[28]

Tarbell was so preoccupied by other matters that she seemed not to have grasped the importance of the ruckus. As she thought about it in later years, she could never decide if in fact she had been a muckraker, journalist, or a historian. Just as in her college days when she avoided being a "Delta girl," or a "Gamma girl," by taking the pin of every boy who offered her one, she refused to accept any label.

The press, which by now was aware of the situation at *McClure's*, attributed the company's trouble to Roosevelt's speech. The *Chicago Journal* said it had prompted Sam McClure to set his staff of muckrakers adrift; the *Sentinel* of Milwaukee claimed that Steffens and his like had only been interested in money and would now abandon muckraking. McClure and Phillips both denied any disagreement over the magazine's policy, but Phillips confirmed publicly that some of the staff might be leaving.

When reporters asked Tarbell if the battle were over editorial policies, she was noncommittal. Unable to learn the issues involved and feeling that Tarbell and her colleagues were ganging up on one man, the press sided with McClure.

Sensing an opportunity for profit, J. Walter Thompson, founder of the advertising agency, and Senator John Dryden, a founder of the Prudential Life Insurance Company, offered to buy into the magazine. McClure, who probably realized that such associates would compromise him, declined.

At one point, McClure sought to buy out Phillips, but, unable to face a truncated staff, decided instead to sell to him. Then he begged Phillips and Tarbell to take him back and they agreed—if he gave them total control. Tarbell was ready. She instantly drafted a memo allotting 360 shares of the Samuel S. McClure Company in trust to Phillips, Steffens, Baker, and herself with the option of purchasing within 5 years 300 more shares at $2000 per person. This group was also to receive a total of 200 shares of the book publishing arm. But McClure never signed the agreement.

Tarbell's quick and canny action, meticulously calculated down to the decimal point, had stunned McClure. He realized that while he had thought they were working out their differences, Ida was telling his brother and longtime associates that separation was the only possible course. She had called a meeting at her apartment of Siddall, Phillips, and the rest to decide whether to try to buy or sell. In contrast to Phillips, who was so nervous that his leg shook violently every time he sat down, Tarbell was tranquil in her resolve. As soon as Phillips left New York to visit his family, McClure saw a chance to appeal to him. He dictated a five-page letter for Phillips to discuss with his parents who had know Sam McClure for a quarter of a century. By inference, he did not want Ida Tarbell to be immediately privy to it: "My dear John, I am sure that you and I, if we had confined this discussion to ourselves personally, calling in three or four of our best friends from the outside like Mather and Charlie Taylor, this matter would never have reached this pass. . . ."[29] He declared it was nonsense to think that more than one man was needed to manage the magazine.

Writing with more respect and affection than he had shown Phillips in years, McClure implored him to go to Europe to rest for a year as McClure had done and then to return to his post. "I judge from your hesitancy you are entirely at sea as to what to do," wrote McClure. Without mentioning Tarbell specifically, he urged: "If from now on in these discussions we limit ourselves to discussing the matter with our two lawyers and with two people like Robert McClure and Oscar Brady, who are comparatively calm, and not take in the entire office, which is overwrought and hysterical, we shall come to a better and safer decision."

But that was not to be. On a snowy late March day, another agreement was drawn up whereby Phillips and Tarbell were to receive unspecified cash or stock as severance, and reduced weekly salaries—two hundred fifty dollars for Phillips and two hundred dollars for Tarbell—as they wound up their duties, which included completion of several more Lincoln articles. A week later, seeing that the settlement would take an indefinite time, Tarbell tendered her resignation "to be free to go on with any work I may decide upon."[30]

McClure broke down under this blow and took himself to Clifton Springs Sanitarium—Ida's sanctuary. From there he wrote that in view of her "extraordinary" service, he would pass a resolution through the board of directors giving her three months' vacation at full salary of three hundred dollars. He added that she would sail to Europe about May 1, spend a month in Florence, and join the McClures in Milan for six weeks. "So you will have had that three month's vacation and one month's work and we will all be so happy, well and strong. God bless us all!"[31]

She was seriously alarmed. "Board of directors" was a new phrase in the McClure vocabulary and the rest was jibberish. She feared that he was so confused that he would not buy them out after all. In a tizzy she telephoned him and was so vituperative that he wrote her afterward that he was doing all he could to meet her wishes, but that he had divested himself of sole authority and was relying on others to see that he did nothing foolish.

The financial state of *McClure's* was so complicated and the principals so emotional that matters were not settled for a year. Boyden, Steffens, Baker, Siddall, Dunne, David McKinlay of the book company, and McClure's cousin Harry joined Tarbell and Phillips in their walkout. As for her diary, Ida Tarbell never felt the need to write in it again.

Nine

A Second Crusade

Ida Tarbell allowed herself no time to feel the aftershocks of the split from McClure. She went on the road to enlist backers in a new venture—*The American Magazine*. Started as *Leslie's Weekly* over thirty years before, it had skirted muckraking but regularly discussed public affairs as well as offering fiction and humor. It was now up for sale and the *McClure's* rebels decided to set up their own publication with Phillips as the deserving head.

In order to buy the magazine, they needed $460,000 of which $160,000 was required in a few months. Tarbell and Phillips expected to realize $100,000 from McClure in the early fall, but as Phillips noted, "One dollar of SS's in the hand is worth a million of SS's in the bush."[1] And $400,000 in 1906 is the equivalent of $4 million in the 1980s.

Tarbell was galvanized by a combination of bravado about the future, defiance of McClure, and a sense of *esprit de corps*. It was a new beginning. Together she, Phillips, Steffens, Baker, Boyden, and Siddall were plunging themselves in debt and pledging past success as security for the future. At *McClure's* she had earned eight thousand dollars a year. *The American* would pay five thousand. "Miss Tarbell," Baker recalled, "was one of the most dauntless of the adventurers."[2]

To raise capital, Tarbell canvassed right-thinking moneyed friends. Between May and the end of June she went to independent oil men in Pittsburgh and Philadelphia, to Thomas B. Wanamaker, son of the retailer and owner of the *North American* newspaper, and some of her brother's contacts in the oil business.

In Boston, her prospects were manufacturers E. N. Foss and W. L. Douglas, known foes of the protective tariff: she was preparing an exposé of that very subject and felt that they would be most supportive of her efforts. "Just put it up to him that she is going to write in our new magazine on the tariff. They have got to help,"[3] Siddall wrote Baker who was off to solicit funds from an exponent of free trade.

Steffens also approached potential backers including "reform" mayors Tom Johnson of Cleveland and D. Percy Jones of Minneapolis, and other heroes of his "shame" series such as Governor Lucius Garvin of Rhode Island, and Everett Colby of New Jersey. New Jersey judge James B. Dill, an expert on business law, Progressive retailer Edward Filene, and stockbroker Robert Goodbody were also on his list.

Tarbell, Steffens, and their friends touted their magazine as an out-and-out organ for reform. A dozen or so of their hoped-for backers responded favorably and William Allen White later described the investors as men "whose eyes saw the coming of the Lord." With hindsight, he called The American "an organ of propaganda wrapped in the tinfoil of a literary quality which at least reflected the temper of the times."[4]

From James Corrigan, featured in her earlier character sketch as Rockefeller's ill-treated boyhood friend, Tarbell raised five thousand dollars in cash. Plumbing industrialist Charles R. Crane contributed, as did Walter R. Stubbs, a future governor of Kansas, and William Kent, a Chicago millionaire and California congressman. These are cited in papers pertaining to The American. The names of the rest have not survived.

Except for Stubbs, the contributors were acquaintances of Ida Tarbell. Ida's niece Esther recalled in particular the time Ida invited Crane to tea. He discovered, to Ida's embarrassment, a crack in her teapot and the next day sent a magnificent replacement. Esther was practical about this development: "I advised enlarging the hole in the Oriental rug before his next visit and Aunt Ida tried to look scandalized."[5]

Although she was a driving force, Tarbell was not one of the officers of the Phillips Publishing Company which was formed in late June 1906. Phillips was president, Steffens, vice-president, Boyden, secretary, and David McKinlay, treasurer. She was, however, first to sign the letter soliciting subscriptions. Her signature was bolder and bigger than she had ever used on any letter before and about twice as high as those of her colleagues.

The press paid the journalists little attention, being at that time occupied by the sensational murder of architect and man-about-town Stanford White, but Phillips and friends proclaimed The American to be a magazine of writers by writers. The announcement trumpeted: "We shall not only make this new American Magazine interesting and important in a public way, but we shall make it the most stirring and delightful monthly book of fiction, humor, sentiment, and joyous reading that is anywhere published."

It intended to carry the best literature, to offer the most intelligent forum for ideas, and to be positive in outlook. In other words, it was to be *McClure's*, only kinder. The announcement was accompanied by Sunday-best photographs of the staff. Tarbell was shown in a light-colored gown, a bow at her waist, open book in her hand, looking with calm confidence into the camera.

That *The American* felt itself on a holy mission was exemplified by the diligence of the usually erratic Finley Peter Dunne. He took a desk in their cramped offices at 141 Fifth Avenue and appeared with what Tarbell considered to be, for him, amazing regularity.

Always in the air was the vendetta against their old chief. Tarbell and Phillips were especially rancorous as they waited for the settlements. Baker alone struggled with guilt. He had learned that he had cost McClure fifteen thousand in the one libel suit sustained against their muckraking.

Fund-raising, articles still due to McClure, and perennial travels occupied Tarbell and her colleagues so that they did not have much time to work on their inaugural issue of October. 1906, nor on the following one. Boyden sent Baker a pleading letter in late July asking him to contribute something. All they had to rely on, he said, was Steffens, "and he is not the surest proposition in the world as you know. JSP is in Duxbury 'knocked out' but due in tomorrow. Miss Tarbell is of course in the country. So Siddall and I, left to ourselves, are getting kind of nervous over this November number."[6]

They constantly had to encourage or revive each other. When Tarbell went to Washington in August to read every *Congressional Record* since 1888 for her tariff research, Boyden dispatched an affectionate note which prompted Ida to respond that she was not the entirely self-reliant person he thought her to be. She commented that Phillips, who had come down to help her get a perspective on the tariff, "looked ill," but she assured Boyden that they should not fret unduly over their pioneer days: "It is to the future of the magazine we must look. We are laying the foundation for a great magazine respected for its freshness and reasoned opinion."[7]

Tarbell had reason for optimism, for believing that the tide of opinion was sweeping toward the direction of the high-mindedness *The American* intended to rally. On July 22, Attorney General W. H. Moody announced that suits would be brought against the Standard Oil Company for accepting rebates. A few weeks later, Standard Oil was indicted in Chicago for the same offense. In late September, strikes by Standard workers in Whiting, Indiana, erupted in riots; and on November 15, 1906, the U.S. Government began its suit in St. Louis to dismantle the Standard Oil monopoly.

As events unfolded, Tarbell repaired to Redding Ridge to study the tariff. She had originally intended to preside over her aging farmhouse and forty acres with benign neglect while she wrote and gathered wild-flowers; but rainwater dripped through the roof onto her papers, butter-cups were obscured by growing grass, and underbrush and weeds defied her sense of order. The brambles of homeowning began to catch the hem of her gown. She decided that only extra income from royalties would go into the place. Of this, a third would be for the house, a third for the land, and a third for furnishings. Soon money she had set aside for a new evening dress had to be used to purchase fertilizer. She began to take on more free-lance work, often writing superficial essays to make "extra income" for the farm. Ida felt she had a home at last and she named it Twin Oaks like the Hubbard mansion. Allowing the soil to be unproductive began to bother her. She had the field plowed, corn planted, and an orchard put in. She acquired a cow, a pig, chickens, and a workhorse she named "Minerva," after her own middle name.

She had planned to furnish the house gradually from bargain base-ment sales, but soon she discovered that one of her neighbors had pur-chased the contents of many an attic and shed and had set himself up as an antiques dealer. She perused his wares—which he called "teeks"—and discovered an old melodeon, a sort of accordion, whose visual beauty charmed her. Convinced that she could repair the bellows, she put down ten dollars and took it home. Henceforth, she and Esther watched eagerly for days when his horse and loaded wagon pulled up to his shop; they loved to have first crack at his treasures. Tarbell often said she didn't care about "things," but her attic allowed her to indulge a repressed love of hoarding.

Tarbell had fun in the country. She saw a lot of Jeanette Gilder, sister of *The Century* editor, herself a writer, editor, and critic. A large, strong woman, well-suited to the stout mannish clothes then popular for women, Gilder was masculine enough in appearance that Esther thought it a great joke to see Miss Gilder startled by a mouse and pro-viding a glimpse of silk petticoats in her fright.

With Jeanette Gilder, Tarbell drove over to see Mark Twain at his villalike home in nearby Redding. He regaled them with stories like the time he had tacked up a note advising future burglars that the only valu-able item that had not already been stolen was "the brass thing" in the dining room.

Ida's country place became *The American* staff's weekend retreat. Bert Boyden participated in its maintenance. He took care that appro-priate French wallpaper was purchased for the entrance hall and that sufficient food and guest blankets were obtained for the winter. The young Jack Reed was one of her favorite visitors. After Reed graduated from Harvard in 1911, Steffens found him a job at *The American*. Reed later became a radical journalist and Soviet hero, but the Reed who visited Redding Ridge was a bright, disingenuous young man who thought himself a poet.

One afternoon, Reed insisted Tarbell come out and see what he had discovered. He sat her on a rock and showed how an adjacent field could be turned into a Greek amphitheater. Reed approached the owner, convinced him to sell, then set about raising funds for the project. Years later Tarbell met a woman who said she had wanted to contribute, but Reed forgot about it all before he could collect.

In life, Reed did not possess the movie-star aura that Hollywood would later accord him. His friend Max Eastman described his first impression of the man: "He had a knobby and too filled-out face that reminded me, both in form and color, of a potato. He was pressed up in a smooth brown suit with round pants' legs and a turned-over starched collar, and seemed rather small and rather distracted."[8]

Another frequent visitor to Twin Oaks was John Phillips who came by when he didn't feel up to making the trip to the Cape to see his family. He continued to voice his befuddlement to Tarbell, even in personal matters. Their camaraderie did not disguise the fact that they were not producing an outstanding magazine. Phillips stopped by to see her once when she was vacationing in Providence, Rhode Island, and she cheered him up while privately sharing his anxieties. She passed hers along to Boyden: "We always have lacked a certain hustle, ingenuity, a general energizing effort such as we used to get out of SS . . . it's latent—a genius, and we haven't it in the staff . . . JSP sees it. He frets because he is not that kind and that nobody else is. We ought each to be doing a little more—daring something—more experimenting with ourselves—or else have someone that can. We must be discontented, Bert. But I don't mean unhappy or irritable but not satisfied—eager, pushing, inventive."[9]

An outside writer, William James, provided *The American* with the attention-getting article Tarbell called for. The eminent psychologist wrote on the phenomenon of "second wind," the way some persons were able to work through fatigue to tap a hidden level of energy. Readers felt they had at last found the key to Teddy Roosevelt's amazing vitality and had learned to get more out of themselves as well. *The American* gave them what would later be called a self-help article.[10]

Dunne was writing Dooley pieces and a column of opinion called "The Interpreter's House." Baker was filing pastoral reflections called "Adventures in Contentment" under the pseudonym of David Grayson, but Steffens was slow to contribute at all. He was in fact becoming a major strain on Phillips. *The American* had a smaller purse than *McClure's* had had and was less able to tolerate foibles—less able to underwrite them too. Steffens scandalized the staff when his profile of William Randolph Hearst, expected to unmask the newspaper lord as a potential political demagogue, turned into an admiring profile of Hearst's complexities. After an explosive meeting where Dunne charged that the piece read as if it had been written by Hearst's own editors, Tarbell, tired of wrangling, gave in to Steffens and closed discussion simply by asking how they should title it.[11] *The American* had hoped to be a forum for ideas. Unfortunately, debate within the office was acrimonious.

Unlike Baker and Tarbell, Steffens wanted to draw conclusions from the corruption he exposed. The others believed in the American system and the triumph of law. Steffens thought business unsavory by nature and man by nature good. In "Do unto others as you would have them do unto you," Steffens found his political philosophy which he thought could be realized through socialism.

His idealism, along with the practical problems he was causing *The American*, irked Tarbell severely. She expressed her irritation the day he proposed that they transform *The American* into a "Socialist organ." She tartly told Steffens that the magazine had to resist specific ideologies. "The serene young mother," as Steffens had described the Tarbell who smoothed tempers at *McClure's*, was gone.

Steffens was allowed to investigate San Francisco several months before Phillips urged him to hand in copy. Steffens replied with exasperation; Phillips countered with reproach. Phillips said hard work had boosted the income of *The American*, but he charged that Steffens, who had put his wife and mother-in-law on his expense vouchers, received more than anyone in proportion to what he had contributed.

Steffens's articles on how San Francisco and the West were improving their governments or reforming themselves appeared regularly after September 1907, but Phillips was growing impatient with long-distance editing and with Steffens' poorly documented allegations.

He wanted Steffens to come back to New York and to verify all his facts. Everyone sided with Phillips, even Jaccaci who had been Steffens's mentor at *McClure's*. These days Jaccaci lived abroad, but when he came back for a visit, he saw a change in Phillips and wrote Tarbell: "Why he is a happy man, that poor old friend of ours who used to be so unhappy, kicked, insulted and worried in his heart as in his head . . . his view of the Steffens matter *is perfectly just* . . . I am so glad this single disturbing element is going to be eliminated—it's too unjust to all the rest and above all to John. What a lunatic that Stef is! Because he has

been my friend I trust he is going to get such rough experience as may
do him good and save him."[12] In early March 1908, Steffens left the
staff.

He claimed in his autobiography: "I noticed, with some pain, shame
and lying denials to myself, that I was going easy. All by myself, without
any outside influence, I was being bought off by my own money, by the
prospect of earning money. I resigned from *The American*."[13] He
added: "I promised never again to work where my money was." He was
righteous, but the staff thought him unprincipled. The whining, manip-
ulative side of Steffens that Phillips and Tarbell knew was quite different from the public personality who went about marveling over
Christianity and, in latter days, Communism.

When Steffens left, he told them he was in debt and would have to
sell his stock. At some inconvenience, four or five shareholders bought
Steffens's common stock for two thousand dollars so that he could survive until he found another job. They felt aggrieved when Steffens's
fortunes quickly picked up. He accepted Edward Filene's offer to
"muckrake" Boston for ten thousand dollars and sold his Connecticut
house to industrialist Owen Young at a handsome profit.[14]

Ida herself began to feel mounting money pressures. Her brother
Will was having trouble meeting his debts and frequently turned to her
for help, which she gladly provided without asking interest. Will also
began to display certain anger against his employer, the Pure Oil Company. In a February 1908 letter to Ida, he said he wanted to discredit
the "figurehead" he had "bolstered all these years." It is uncertain that
such vituperation was justified, but Will did continue to function professionally and he testified as an expert witness in the government's case
against the Standard in 1908.[15]

Ida Tarbell's love for her brother and the financial demands she often
had to meet gave her little patience for the radical Steffens. She believed he was simply tired of journalism and was leaving *The American*
because he wanted to play a more direct role in events.

She herself wanted to influence public opinion only through reportage. The upbeat style of *The American* was an attempt to reform the
country by pointing out what had been repaired rather than what
needed to be reformed. Impressed by the way the city of Chicago took
over its streetcar lines from private owners and upgraded service, Tarbell went to Chicago in the summer of 1908 to cover the story. Rather
than stay in a hotel, she boarded at Hull House, the seedy mansion Jane
Addams had transformed into a vigorous workshop of social change.
Tarbell lived as one of the Hull House family, sat in on Ellen Starr's
cultural program which encouraged traditional Old World crafts, and
watched Julia Lathrop handle the appeals of mothers who wanted their
sons rescued from jail.

Ida Tarbell did not take a sentimental view of Hull House. She saw that Addams had a unique way of harnessing strong personalities: "She's so kind. That's really what had made Hull House. Her gentleness with everybody. Of course she's got so much sense, and so *considerate*—the way she's held all that gang, selfish and inconsiderate and opinionated, and also some awfully nice people."[16]

Addams was the only woman of that time who equaled Tarbell in public stature. The writer may well have felt subtle competition with this round little woman who had accomplished so much by maximizing her nurturing qualities instead of denying them. Addams's inspiration had been Toynbee Hall in the slums of East London where humanitarian work was done for the poor. Tarbell had heard of it around the same time Addams did. She had read everything she could about it and as an editor brought it to the attention of *Chautauquan* readers, but Addams went out and founded Hull House.

Tarbell was struck by the way Addams, who was so militant in her fight against injustice, would go through the house tenderly straightening chairs and dusting knickknacks. Some months after her stay, Tarbell sent a belated thank-you present and a letter which described how she herself was trying to help immigrants who were farming Connecticut. She told Addams she had been writing at her country home: "Of course I've been working—that *maudit* traction [Chicago transportation] problem has been bothering me but I've got it off at last and am at other things. So far I have been able to do my work mainly here in the country—six miles from a locomotive and not from a beefsteak. I like it. I fear you wouldn't, and yet I don't know, there are plenty of opportunities for service even here. Within six days I've had one case of hysterics, two wounds, one bad cold, one moral overthrow and two sick horses to doctor and I've brought them all through! As for social problems, why I've got the most wonderful cases of the absorption of foreigners you ever saw . . . I am sending a sample of one of our chief products. We raise three things up here—rock, battered mahogany and stained pewter. I'm sending a specimen of the last and I shall be proud if you will include it in the Hull House collection."[17]

Tarbell so enjoyed her quip about distressed pewter that she repeated it to many correspondents. Characteristically tardy with personal correspondence, Tarbell was exceptionally slow to thank Addams because she was preoccupied by her mother's and sister's health. After leaving Hull House, Tarbell stopped off in Titusville and found Esther, aged seventy-eight, close to death from a sudden illness, and Sarah overcome with anxiety. Tarbell sent Esther to a sanitarium and brought Sarah home with her.

Sarah bore most of the responsibility for Esther, but Ida tried to help. Most summers she invited her mother to Redding Ridge. During these

visits Esther undoubtedly told Ida how to manage her garden, her animals, and most certainly her hens, for Ida had been fascinated by her
mother's talent for raising poultry. During her *Chautauquan* days it inspired a never-completed short story and was the subject of much correspondence when she was in Paris.

Ida tried to give Esther treats, especially after Franklin Tarbell's
death. Once when Esther was in New York, Ida told her to dress up,
and without telling her where they were going she took her to see *Shore
Acres*, James Herne's realistic drama about a homespun New England
philosopher. As Franklin had frowned on the theater, the performance
was a revelation to Esther. "My mother sat through it, enjoying it like a
child," Ida recalled. When Ida asked Esther if she'd like to go again,
the old lady replied, "I suppose it's wicked, but I would."

Later, as Esther convalesced, she passed time by playing solitaire.
Sheepishly, she told Ida that Franklin would not have approved. Ida
noticed that Esther not only played the game—she adroitly cheated at
it.[18]

Tarbell's preoccupations were her family and *The American Magazine*, but Sam McClure continued to seek a place in her affections. His
magazine had weathered the defections of his closest associates, but he
still felt abandoned. Tarbell's correspondence shows that McClure
called on her so late one night that she had declined to see him, but she
agreed to meet him for breakfast at the Waldorf. Then, in July 1907,
McClure wrote that he was "starved" for her: "I dreamed of you. I
thought I was telling you how I found out that by speaking slowly &
calmly & acting calmly I found I had much greater influence on people
(I am actually doing this) & I thought that I was standing by your chair
& you drew me down & kissed me to show your approval. When you
disapproved of me it nearly broke my heart . . ."[19]

Their break was irrevocable, although in time Tarbell could again
think of him with affection. She concentrated on current projects and
The American. She would do two significant series for the magazine.
Her work on the protective tariff was so important in clarifying the
issue, arraigning its profiteers and tracing its cost to consumers
that she was invited to sit on the Tariff Commission. The second, on
the American woman, opened her to ridicule and the repudiation of
all she herself had become.

The tariff was, like the trust, a key issue of the day. One question was
whether free trade between nations made goods more affordable to the
consumer or jeopardized American business. Western Republicans and
reformers of both parties, those who were establishing themselves into a
force called Progressivism, insisted that the tariff fostered monopoly.

The controversy was a maze of rhetoric, greed, and statecraft be-
fogged by myth. It was certain that before income tax was levied in

1913, the tariff was the greatest source of federal revenue, but dissension arose over who should pay it. In the early days of the nation, the tax had been promulgated to nourish fledgling native industries centered in New England and to discourage an influx of British goods. The manufacturing North and agricultural South were in such disagreement over the tariff that the debate, with a push from the question of slavery, split the Union. Afterward, manufacturers wanted to keep out cheap foreign machinery, whereas farmers, who wanted economical equipment, suggested a tax on raw cotton from abroad. Around 1905, largely because of what they read and heard, people began to believe that duties on beef, sugar, tin, and iron protected big firms such as Armour & Company, Havemeyer's sugar refineries, U.S. Steel, and Standard Oil and not young industries. Moreover, they realized the public paid the price. That which had been intended to raise revenue for the Republic was now seen as the pelf of a few and an obstacle to competitive capitalism. Tarbell was eager to tackle the issue.

"What had particularly aroused me was the way tariff schedules were made, the strength of what we now call pressure groups—the powerful lobbies in wool and cotton and iron and sugar which for twenty-five years I had watched mowing Congress down like a high wind ... but it looked in 1906 as if the Day of Judgment was near, and I asked nothing better than to be on the jury."[20]

The series opened in December 1906 with a history of the tariff during the Civil War. Thereafter "The Tariff in Our Times" alternated with Tarbell's articles summing up Roosevelt's battle with the Standard Oil Company and short stories based on legends she had heard in her girlhood or during her biographical research.

Tarbell often remarked that her research habits reminded her of the white actor who, before he could play Othello, had to blacken himself all over. So it was with the tariff. She checked every rate schedule and read every *Congressional Record*, pamphlet of reform, and relevant book, particularly classic texts by F. W. Taussig and Edward Stanwood. Then she wrote or interviewed congressmen, attorneys, trade spokesmen, and manufacturers who had worked on tariffs. Congress emerged from her investigation as the tool of special interests.

When she interviewed Joseph Wharton—iron magnate, steel master, nickel king, and benefactor of the Wharton School of Business— Wharton coolly confirmed that he controlled certain legislators and that tariffs were decided not so much by Congress as by those who would profit by them. "I wrote the bill of 1870,"[21] he told her.

Before publication, Tarbell asked former president Grover Cleveland to review her manuscript. Cleveland had done the unprecedented twenty years before—he had sought to lower the tariff. This cost him so much support in his own Democratic party that he was defeated in

1888. Reelected president in 1892, he again strove—unsuccessfully—to lower the tariff.

Cleveland, living in happy retirement in Princeton, New Jersey, was delighted to help Tarbell. He exacted a price, however. When he saw that she had characterized his writing style as ponderous, he asked her to delete the offending adjective and she did.[22]

For two years her tariff articles dutifully recounted history. Then they caught fire with "Every Penny Counts" in which Tarbell reduced the intricacies of tariff codes to a single theme—the abuse of the average American—showing what the duty actually cost the consumer buying shoes, wool, and thread.[23] She charged:

"The last man to be heard from at tariff hearings in this country is the man who buys the goods . . . at a time when wealth is rolling up as never before—(this country increased its wealth between 1900 and 1904 by about twenty billions of dollars)—a vast number of hard-working people in this country are really having a more difficult time making ends meet than they have ever had before . . . "

Tarbell noted that the price of shoes had increased by about twenty-five percent in ten years. By that day's statistics, this meant that a family of four with forty dollars a year to spend for clothes spent eleven dollars and eighty-one cents on shoes. "This hardship comes largely from the tariff laid on hides in 1897 by the Dingley Bill. And why a tariff on hides? Simply to compel the American shoemaker to pay more for his leather."

She asked in conclusion: "Is this fair? Are the ones to consider first in this matter of hides the Beef Trust, the Leather Trust—the Upper Leather Trust—the 85,000 cattlemen and the 300,000 or so workers in leather, or are the ones to consider first the toiling millions living on a wage where every penny counts?"

Though she resisted the title of reformer, insisting she was purely a journalist or actually a historian, Tarbell crusaded against the tariff with great indignation. When the Charities Publication Committee showed that Pittsburgh laborers commonly worked twelve hours a day seven days a week for a substandard wage, Tarbell lashed out at their employers whom she called "Pittsburgh millionaires who fill the glittering places of pleasure in the great cities of Europe and this country, who figure in divorce and murder trials, who are writing their names on foundations and bequests and institutions." She called Pittsburgh a "tariff-made city" and made a point of the crime's cost to its perpetrators as well as its victims: "Justice takes a terrible revenge on those who thrive by privilege. She blinds their eyes until they no longer see human misery. She dulls their hearts until they no longer beat with humanity. She benumbs their senses until they respond only to the narrow horizon of what they can individually possess, touch, feel."[24]

Her censure was aptly timed. In 1909, from spring through summer, the House and Senate debated which raw materials would be taxed. It had some of the flavor of a casino, and the odds were that tariffs would be lowered. In April 1909, the House of Representatives passed the Payne Tariff Bill which removed the tax from coal, iron ore, hide, flax, and wood pulp, reduced other duties, and approved inheritance tax. In the Senate, a bastion of privilege, Senator Nelson W. Aldrich of Rhode Island was aghast. He drafted a bill which restored and increased much of what the Payne measure had taken away. By the time Congress passed the compromise Payne-Aldrich Tariff Act in August 1909, the public was outraged by the tariff and the tactics used. Much of the ire was directed at President William Howard Taft, President Roosevelt's personally anointed successor. He had promised the electorate that he would have the tariff revised and led people to expect that it would be lowered, not just readjusted. Taft never regained the popularity he had previously enjoyed.

Tarbell's series addressed a key concern, but *The American* featured other public issues as well. Besides politics, it ran articles on the strange personality of Germany's Kaiser Wilhelm. Baker was producing a series on race relations called "Following the Color Line." He found that American justice did not extend to the black man and he pleaded for enlightened action.

In contrast, Tarbell was determined to be impartial on the Woman question. It was a time for women, for the genteel poor to go to the office, the wretched to go to the sweatshop, and the wealthy to go to the club. Since girlhood, Tarbell had puzzled over woman's nature, much like the blind men of the parable who encountered an elephant for the first time. One held his trunk and said, "It's a snake." Another felt his leg and said, "It's a tree." Another fingered his ear and said, "This is a huge leaf." Tarbell knew that she had never resolved her questions about the nature of woman or about how she could lead a fruitful life. Now that women were emerging into public life and the working world, *The American* wanted to devote a series to them and Tarbell obliged.

She interrupted her tariff series to do so. As was her style, she began with a historical perspective and featured such heroines as Abigail Adams, Catharine Beecher, and the astronomer Maria Mitchell. However, the seven "American Women" features were biographical listings lacking bite. Tarbell's friend Mrs. Schuyler Van Rensselaer thought Ida would do better to examine the present. "What are you bothering with such unmeaning stuff for?" she asked. Tarbell was fascinated by the women she had uncovered and she felt she must understand them in order to be able to comprehend the new "emancipated" woman, but in Van Rensselaer's view, the past was much less interesting than the present. She was against suffrage, but totally for social reform.

The movement for social reform and settlement houses was active. Tarbell, partly through Van Rensselaer but largely through her journalistic contacts, became acquainted with such women as Lillian Wald who had instituted public-health nursing; and Florence Kelley, founder of the National Consumers League.

The settlement movement was by now at full strength. It was largely a response to the growth of cities and of industry, and to the influx of immigrants. The idea was that concerned people would live or work among those in poor neighborhoods. It was a way to help the underprivileged, particularly the foreign-born, but there was a recognition that those who helped the poor were enriching their own lives. Jane Addams said in her autobiography that she started Hull House because she was desperate for a constructive outlet for her energy.

Tarbell spent some time in New York's settlement houses to fill the gap left by the endless sociability of Sam McClure—but she sought to aid the disadvantaged chiefly through her pen.

Even as she clung to traditional roles for middle-class women, Tarbell spoke out vigorously on behalf of women who had to work in mills and factories. In a rare signed editorial titled "Man's Inhumanity to Women," she called on her sisters to urge the state of Illinois to preserve a ten-hour workday for women, rather than allowing employers to work those with child-bearing and -raising duties as long as they chose.[25]

In a letter published in the *New York Times*, Tarbell expressed sympathy for the Shirtwaist Workers Strike, a cause which inspired society women to join shopgirls in a fight for women's rights. The strike, sometimes called "The Uprising of the Twenty Thousand," began at the Triangle Shirtwaist Company after those trying to organize a union were fired. Tarbell's encouraging letter to the organizers said: "What you are doing not only helps me and other women in the struggle for life as we know it today but it is going to help the cause for all women workers who are to come. I am glad you do not have to struggle single-handed and unaided, and I wish you a great success in this our common cause."[26]

After she concluded the historical sketches of women, she resumed work on the tariff, but women, especially poor ones, were still very much on her mind. She saw that the tariff issue had special relevance to women, the managers of household budgets. She earnestly sought to demonstrate its personal effects. As she wrote to Viola Roseboro, "I am very unhappy about the tariff and I am trying to prepare the American woman for a raid on it!"[27]

Taking her crusade to the podium, Tarbell addressed the predominantly female League for Political Education. With passionate conviction, she told them that the consumer was paying double the fair price for cotton thread in order to support the thread trust, and that prices were rising without a corresponding increase in the wages of the poor. The *American Economist,* organ of the American Protective Tariff League, belittled her and her audience, yet clearly felt it prudent to make a formal reply. The paper sneered that Tarbell's hearers rode in automobiles and wore furs, yet worried over the cost of their stockings. Tarbell herself they dismissed as a woman with a "talent" for half-truths."[28]

Undaunted, Tarbell pressed on. She examined the cost and shortage of quality goods, particularly warm, durable wool which until the 1870s had been generally affordable. She asked friends—probably Lillian Wald and Florence Kelley—to interview indigent New York housewives. Tarbell learned that wool in the tenements was as scarce as diamonds.

Tarbell went to New York's tenement neighborhoods, the Lower East Side which housed the immigrant Jews, and the East Seventies where Slavs had settled. She found that some merchants were advertising "all wool" baby clothes at very low prices and she immediately detected fraud. She bought these "fine goods" and took them home to make closer examination. Remembering that wool was destroyed by boiling solutions of caustic alkali, she cut the items in half and submitted one part to bubbling solvent and the other half to boiling water. The clothes, she discovered, were cotton, not wool, and she told her readers so. Tarbell maintained that the high tariff in America made wool unaffordable and thus cheated the unsuspecting poor, forcing them to buy inferior goods at exorbitant prices.

After explaining all this in the November 1910 *American,* Tarbell called for a pure textile law similar to the pure food law. She said, "Personally, I am of the opinion that here is a valuable work for the women's clubs of the country. Women are necessarily more concerned in this matter than anybody else. They are the buyers. They should know." Then she showed some condescension, probably without meaning to. She added: "The study and analysis of cloth is not difficult and it is entertaining. It is admirably adapted to club work."

Having seen Ida Tarbell attack the Standard Oil Company with some success, the president of the American Woolen Company thought it wise to respond. He announced that the wool tariff had yielded sixty million dollars in government revenue and he said that he didn't believe it cost the people a cent more for clothing. Newspapers across the nation carried his statement and scoffed. The *Boston Post* asked who paid the tariff if the public did not: "Not foreign exporters, not wholesalers who passed the cost to retailers, and not retailers . . . " Wool clothes, the *Post* reminded readers, cost consumers much more than they had ten years before.

Not all response echoed Tarbell's view, of course. The *Philadelphia Evening Telegraph* insisted that tariff protection made the country prosperous and allowed it to build up productive mills, but the newspaper did allow that cotton and wool schedules had been framed for the benefit of "certain interests." In December 1910, Tarbell named, for the first time, the champion of these "interests."

A truly gripping drama needs a villain, but the tariff had too long a history to be the work of one man. She solved her technical problem when she discovered that Senator Nelson W. Aldrich, the Rhode Island Republican, was the architect of thirty years of tariffs. Ironically, his daughter Abby had married John D. Rockefeller's son and together they were raising a brood that would include the governors of New York and Arkansas, a chairman of Chase Manhattan Bank, major financiers, philanthropists, and art patrons.

Tarbell said of the senator: "I think it is entirely fair to Mr. Aldrich to say that from his first connection with Congress he saw that the tariff properly worked was the surest road to power and to wealth that this country offered to a politician."[29] She found him blameworthy enough to merit two separate articles—one on his career and the other on egregious industrial conditions in his native Rhode Island.

Soon after the Payne-Aldrich Bill was signed into law in August 1909, Tarbell traveled to Aldrich's state where infant graves, marked by numbers rather than names, exceeded four thousand. In outraged sympathy for the women who lived there she wrote: "After her ten hours at spindle or loom the woman hurries to a cold, unkempt house, which she must make comfortable and cheerful if it is to be so. Is it strange that the homes of the factory mothers are generally untidy, the food poor, the children neglected? How can it be otherwise. Her limit of endurance, of ambition, of joy, even of desire in life, has been passed. More appalling, she sees her ability to work falling off . . . the surprise is not that many drink but that more do not."[30]

In Pawtucket, Providence, and Woonsocket, she stood in workplaces sweltering at ninety degrees, breathed air that was soupy with lint, stood in the picker rooms where "machinery bellowed like a thousand angry bulls," by "shrieking spinning machines and the banging looms" which continuously shook her body.

She observed the lack of sanitary conditions—lint-topped buckets of water which were supposed to quench parched throats; dry, fetid closets for toilets; and men and women forced to change and wash side by side at the end of a ten-hour day. She found wages for a fifty-eight-hour week varied from $7.80 to $15.35, but even "top" pay was not enough to offset the tragic results of such squalid conditions. Health records showed that epidemics of bronchitis, pneumonia, tuberculosis, and industrial accidents due to fatigue rendered workers unfit by age fifty-five.

Homelife hardly existed. Children, often eight to a family, were placed in the care of nurseries and schools until age fourteen, when they themselves were old enough to go to work.

Unable to believe her own eyes, Tarbell verified conditions by reviewing social workers' reports. The resulting article took direct aim at protectionists who claimed the tariff benefited the American workers. *The American* sprinkled the piece with photographs of the mansions of mill owners and Senator Aldrich himself, who grew acres of apples, pears, and melons under glass in wintertime.

Tarbell wrote passionately of collusion between big business and politics, the exploitation of the worker and the consumer: "This, then, is high protection's most perfect work—a state of a half million people turning out an annual product worth $187,000,000, the laborers in the chief industry underpaid, unstable and bent with disease, the average employers rich, self-satisfied and as indifferent to social obligations as so many robber barons."[31]

This indictment marked the conclusion of her tariff series. As it reached magazine racks in January 1911, Tarbell asked Addams, who was visiting New York, and Lillian Wald to lunch with her at The Colony. Her letter of invitation showed she thought her efforts inferior to those who actually worked among the poor: "I feel a good deal of the time like an antiquated blunderblus [*sic*] firing at a modern fort but I suppose even a blunderblus might accidentally pick off something. You who work with living material and the young particularly are the real formers and re-formers of men and you dear Lillian Wald stand among the few at the top in my experience."[32]

In her own crusading, Tarbell had galvanized newspaper editors around the country, exposed an important senator to public scorn, and aroused the American consumer to the injustices of big business practices, but she did not see the impact she had had. This is especially sad because the tariff investigation throbbed with human feeling. She had pierced the nexus of trust and tariff, vested interests and the states' representatives, and revealed human misery and those who profiteered from it. Whatever the tariff's value to the country, she had found the cost.

Synthesizing rates and schedules and following the string of pay-offs as it stitched the legislative process had exhausted her and left her aching for rest. She had functioned as a single-minded writing machine, and now she wanted only to drop the topic of the tariff.

She thought its lobby too strong to fight. Industrialists insisted they had to have foreign markets, but they still wanted protection from competition. Organized labor, seeking to protect American jobs, backed them. "I felt after the bill of 1909 that there was nothing for an outsider like me to do but [wait for] revolution,"[33] she said years later.

Revolution was of course the last thing Tarbell would actually have wanted. One of her hopes was that abuses could be discovered and corrected before a violent protest: ". . . the only chance of peace and of permanency in this country lies in securing for the laboring classes an increasing share of increasing wealth," she warned in *The American* of March 1909.

Seeing the destitution of the mill towns, remembering the hellish steel plants she had seen with Dot Walker outside Poland, Ohio, Tarbell was unable to believe that such a situation could continue. She was convinced that agriculture and natural resources, not manufacturing, were the true bases of America's economy. Confident that manufacturing would be relegated to countries where labor was cheap, she did not concern herself in the dilemma of how women should fit into the industrial world. She wrote in a 1911 preface to a collection called *The Book of Woman's Power:* "The industrial woman as we see her today will pass as this country regains the industrial balance it has lost, as the present unhealthy and abnormal attention given to manufacturing ceases, and commerce and agriculture are restored to their proper place."

She was sanguine about woman's finding her appropriate niche and her preface said so in a way that did not speak well for women like herself who chose careers: "The best that can be done for her is to see to it that this brief industrial period does not impair her physically or morally for her high functions, and above all that it does not lead her to believe even dimly that there are happier or more useful things than those to which she instinctively turns."

The American Magazine was also trying to depict the world in a favorable light in most of its articles, although it continued to muckrake for a time. Besides Tarbell's tariff series and Baker's study of the decline of religion in American life, there was "Barbarous Mexico," which protrayed the conditions of peons in Mexico and the dubious role played by American business. But such articles were like the sudden rages of an otherwise sunny individual. *"The American Magazine,"* said Tarbell unapologetically, "had little muckraking spirit. It did have a large and fighting interest in fair play; it sought to present things as they were, not as somebody thought they should be."[34] The theater, the latest play, and the most interesting actresses were constant topics. Baseball stories appeared in season.

The editors were practical. They might have taken "Money is the root of all evil" as the text of their discussions, for it tainted if not entirely corrupted them. In early 1911, as the tariff series concluded, Tarbell, Phillips, and their partners sold control to Crowell publishing. Gossips whispered that a trust had purchased muckraking's most outstanding collection of journalists because a major Crowell stockholder was Thomas W. Lamont, partner of J. P. Morgan. A spokesman for

The American said that they were simply following the current trend of many enterprises and allying themselves with a "larger unit" which would provide them with greater resources. Still, Crowell must have been responsible for the inclusion of one uncharacteristic article—an affectionate memoir of JDR complete with his charge that "Miss Tarbell's exposé was just commercialism. . . . Not one word about that misguided woman."[35] Rockefeller cautioned his sympathizers on the pages of Tarbell's own magazine.

Tarbell had been out of New York during most of the Crowell negotiations, but she worried about them. Pain in her arm, probably recurring neuralgia, drove her back to Clifton Springs. While basking in four-hundred-degree ovens, she reflected on the magazine's policies and worried about Baker's upcoming article on Progressive Republicans, which would criticize the popular Teddy Roosevelt. She wrote to Boyden: "Give Teddy another chance. It will be a long time before people believe in a man as good. Of course you know I don't think he'll come up to scratch but I hope he will." She was concerned about the many critical issues that lay ahead and she warned Baker about Crowell's takeover: "We shouldn't amalgamate unless we are in control." She was against turning over the magazine to anyone who would compromise their editorial integrity, but she wanted them to temper their positions so they would not offend readers.[36]

After the merger with Crowell was concluded, she traveled to Stanford University in California to sit in on its six-week seminar on war and peace with such fellow students as Maxwell Anderson, a future Pulitzer Prize-winning playwright. She arrived low in spirits and besieged by a case of influenza, and then stage fright compounded her illness. She was startled to learn she was expected to speak at a Los Angeles peace rally and without preparation was afraid to appear. "When I refused to get out of my bed they took it as proof of indifference to the cause. The truth was that the idea of speaking extemporaneously was at that time terrifying to me; ill too, I could not, or perhaps would not, rally my forces. I would rather be regarded as a sneak than attempt it."[37]

The change of scene did fire her with several ideas for the magazine. She held lengthy, lively interviews with Progressives in California and was eager to do their story; she also planned to collaborate with Stanford president David Starr Jordan on "The Case Against War," thinking that they might take aim at Teddy Roosevelt after all. Under Crowell, none of these articles saw print. Characteristically, Roosevelt, who was also at Stanford, neither agreed nor completely disagreed with her tariff articles. She saw him in the middle of a group explaining that his job now was to keep the Eastern conservative and Western Progressive wings of the Republican party "flapping in unison."

To Baker she confessed to feeling more forceful in print than in Roosevelt's presence. "I waffle terribly whenever I see him face to face. He seems so amazing, and yet he is less amazing personally than he was. The fact of the matter is that his emphasis is not so great in important matters. He has come to where he doubts and explains, and men, like women, are lost when they get there."[38]

Nonetheless, she knew he was a man to watch. In February 1912, Teddy Roosevelt announced he was prepared to lead insurgent Republicans, the so-called Progressives, against the renomination of his old friend President Taft. Thus Teddy lopped off the head of the Progressive movement, Senator Robert La Follette, and placed himself in the leadership position instead. La Follette had been the engine of the Progressive movement, but Teddy seemed to them like a rocket who could dramatically effect their goals. Progressives eagerly switched their support from the broken-hearted La Follette to Teddy. Some key points were lost in the transfer. La Follette and his followers had espoused the regulation of trusts and reform of the tariff. Teddy preferred constitutional reforms such as referendum and recall whereby elected officials and judges could be removed from office in midterm if citizens disapproved of the work. Tarbell smelled trouble and quickly organized a private luncheon where she and some political allies could test Roosevelt's interest in reform. Among others, she invited William Allen White and Ray Stannard Baker, a loyal La Follette supporter. To Baker she explained her motives: "I think we may get a line on TR, at least we ought to be using every opportunity to get our minds clear as to what is to be done in the magazine. Do you realize that the shifting of the question to one of new government machinery [issues of referendum and recall] is going to do for the trust and tariff questions what the Panic of '93 and the Spanish-American War did—turn attention from them? While we are fighting over the kind of vote with which to dislodge the enemy, the enemy will do as he did in '93-4-5 and your '97-98—build his entrenchments tougher."[39]

She wanted Baker to console La Follette. "Don't let him think he's ended. He is not. If he were only willing to fight and not be president! There's going to be a sweep to him—believe me, to him,—La F—the fighter, not the presidential candidate."

Tarbell held her luncheon at The Colony Club, which fashionable women had modeled after the men's club of Pall Mall. "The Colonel," as TR titled himself, must have seen that the situation was a political San Juan Hill. Baker was a La Follette supporter, White was the senator's friend, and Tarbell was always ready to bait the ex-president on the tariff. Saying only that he thought La Follette insincere, too radical, and incapable of leading Progressives, TR deftly played to his audience, placing himself where the light shone around him like a halo. He had aged only slightly; his mustache was turning white but his hair was the straw color of youth.

Baker noted in his journal: "Again he impressed me with his wonderful social command of himself. He knows so well the right thing to say, to do: he was keenly sensitive to everyone in the party and during the two hours of the conversation he brought out something that was calculated to interest and please each of those present."[40] One doubts Tarbell was equally charmed.

Other guests at the Roosevelt luncheon were Elizabeth Marbury and Anne Morgan, daughter of the great J.P. Marbury, after Boyden and Phillips, was probably Tarbell's closest friend. Tarbell's earlier confidantes, Ada Vincent and Alice Hegan Rice, were both married, and now Tarbell was finding friends who, like herself, were single professional women.

Corsets could not control the two hundred pounds of Elizabeth Marbury, nor polite society her speech. A year older than Tarbell and born to a wealthy New York family, she had met Darwin, Huxley, and Spencer in her well-traveled girlhood. She later created the career of theatrical agent and thereby made her own fortune.

In 1903, Marbury and her housemate Elsie de Wolfe purchased the Villa Trianon at Versailles, once Marie Antoinette's favorite residence. One of their first visitors was Anne Morgan. They found her young for her thirty years; Marbury especially thought Morgan should train herself for an active role in the world. By 1912, Morgan had become a prominent advocate of trade unions and better working conditions for women, and de Wolfe, Marbury, and Morgan had become a triumvirate with private complexities no one can be sure of. As de Wolfe occupied herself more with decorating, Morgan and Marbury shared an interest in public affairs. Probably Tarbell found them to be the first women as engrossed as she in world events. From these two incessant smokers, Tarbell picked up her late-life habit of occasional and solitary puffing on cigarettes. Only at Marbury's home did she smoke in public.

Viola Roseboro, whose own language and demeanor were anything but genteel, disapproved of Marbury. "If she chewed tobacco she would be complete . . . It seems IMT is amused to hear her swear and storm around like a Tammany Chief; she is certainly entertained with E.M.'s large varied contacts with people and movements of some significance." But the acid test of Tarbell's affection was an invitation to Redding Ridge. "She would pass out before she would have E.M. up to the farm . . . ,"[41] Roseboro wrote with some asperity.

Indeed, Marbury was never a guest at Redding Ridge, so Twin Oaks was never allowed to suffer by comparison with the Villa Trianon. Together, Tarbell, Morgan, and Marbury were professional women *des affaires*. When the British author and journalist Arnold Bennett met them at a luncheon hosted by Phillips, he was amazed by their independence and their intelligence. He made note in his journal: "These three women all extremely interesting, all different, yet intimate, calling each other by Christian names, coming together on a personal basis just like men." He found Ida Tarbell "the most wistful and inviting of these three spinsters. A very nice kind face of a woman aged by hard work, by various sympathies, and by human experiences. A soft appealing face, and yet firm and wise. When asked to go down to Washington with Anne and Bessie, she said, 'I've only just come back . . . and I haven't been at my desk for four or five days.' Just like a man. One imagined her desk."[42]

Bennett was condescending, but Tarbell probably would have agreed with his description. Now in her fifties, Tarbell felt her loneliness acutely and filled her time with several women's clubs—The Colony, The Cosmopolitan, and The Pen and Brush. For all her involvement, Tarbell was not an avid clubwoman, claiming that women's groups were more concerned with the machinery of organization than actual accomplishment. Yet these activities often absorbed her.

She nicknamed The Colony her "swell club"and worked diligently to attract speakers of Progressive/Reformist stripe. Though she scorned the radical pronouncements of the social elite, she told William Allen White: "Over at my swell club, a couple of influential sisters have converted to radicalism . . . I think there is a real chance to do something here towards the conversion of The Four Hundred and their friends."[43] However she mocked or tried to justify her membership, Tarbell had been uncomfortable at The Colony Club since her very first meeting when a young woman tried to discuss the work of sexologist Havelock Ellis with her. Possibly as part of her study of women, Tarbell had read four volumes of Ellis's *Studies in the Psychology of Sex* which offered matter-of-fact discussions of masturbation, homosexuality, and sexual drives. Remarking that she had found Ellis's theories hard to take, Tarbell stood up and walked away from her questioner, leaving the girl gazing after her in surprise.[44]

Tarbell was initially indifferent to The Pen and Brush, a club composed of female artists and writers which she had joined in the 1890s, but in 1913 its president implored Tarbell to take over as president in order to solve an unspecified problem. The challenge appealed to Tarbell whose pet theory was that if a problem was not discussed, analyzed, or argued, it solved itself. She agreed to accept for a twelve-month term, provided no one ever tell her the difficulty she was to resolve. She served as president for thirty years—and never did learn what the initial crisis had been.

After she became embroiled in her executive responsibilities at The Pen and Brush, she reassessed her activities. Her niece Clara, who became Ida's social secretary after Esther married, recalled: "She had to protect herself against her warm-hearted instinct to do any and everything people asked her to do. Every so often a cleaning-out campaign would take place . . . One evening I saw her take a long list of clubs to which she belonged and cut it in two. [She said,] 'This group is too wealthy for me.' 'This is entirely social and not for me.' 'I never use this one.' And so on. The following morning a number of resignations were mailed out. Those which remained on her list were mostly groups of serious-minded women struggling for an ideal and for these she was willing to sacrifice time and energy." At the same time Ida was willing to see Clara's girlfriends who were ambitious to be writers. "Though I tried to protect her, she rarely refused an interview."[45]

Clara, who lived at a settlement house on Jones Street, was far more eager for experience than Esther had been. Clara's daughter Caroline told the author that for a time Clara roomed with a girl named Bessie Brewer who had a brief (and undocumented) affair with Marcel Duchamp. Clara recalled parties given by Mabel Dodge attended by, among others, Dodge's lover John Reed and Isadora Duncan who in Clara's words "lay on the couch asking for seduction."

In her memoir, Clara wrote of her aunt during these days: "I wonder at Aunt Ida's tolerance and patience with me for I was fertile ground for every idea—very young, very stupid, and very eager to 'taste life.' Yet she never criticized, dictated or even suggested . . . I learned more from her method of silent treatment than thousands of words could have taught me . . . I remember one day saying to her that I was going to join the Suffrage Party and march in the big parade being held in New York. She looked at me in a non-committal way and said, 'Clara, what is the platform of the Suffrage Party?' " Clara could not answer. "What she did with that simple question was to make me realize how little I really knew about what I was marching for."

Tarbell apparently felt that few women understood the world's realities. She thought of few women as her peers. Roseboro once observed, "I never saw IMT talk to any woman except most unconsciously *de haut en bas*. It is so natural, simple and gracious, it seems people do not get onto its subtleties, but it amused me much. Now this is a thing it would be cruel to bring before her by any suggestion for it would be such an odious revulsion of all she is conscious of in her social ideals."[46]

Tarbell's correspondence shows that through the years she was helpful to women whenever she could be, especially to those who had proved their ability and seriousness. But the specter of a revolution in woman's role unsettled her. After a quarter century of working in the world, she herself no longer needed to be defiant in order to remain independent. She had made her life, but her writings on women showed she did not like her handiwork. She tried to maneuver herself away from woman's traditional place, but the new women she found around her wanted to change society. Tarbell thought that was a mistake.

Tarbell was not the only successful professional woman who urged aspiring sisters to reconsider. Often female physicians advised women to be homemakers. One said that the outside world where "the mightiest forces of the universe and evolution are concerned" was not woman's "noble sphere." Another, Minerva Palmer of Rochester, warned in 1890 that whenever woman left home for education and opportunities, they were met "by disagreement from one of the best informed and most philanthropic class of citizens—the doctors."[47]

Even Elizabeth Marbury, writing her memoirs, cautioned as late as 1923: "If a woman through her own conceit registers against marriage in favor of some problematical career she will find, provided she lives long enough, that all through life she is at best only a misfit. She may live creditably and even accomplish infinite good . . . nevertheless she has missed the normal expression of all these things clamoring within her for utterance."[48]

Motives for such statements were tangled. First, many were probably jealous of their status as the first or only woman ever to achieve a certain place. Second, women who had experienced the working world wanted to say that it was not wholly as glorious as homemakers supposed. Perhaps they feared that their sisters were not up to the rigors of the larger world or perhaps they were simply tired. Certainly Ida Tarbell was. As she approached the age of sixty, she found the past hollow and the future bleak. Hope waned. Her sense of urgency ebbed. She had seen thirty years of editorial battles and thought very little had been accomplished. She was beginning to grow old.

Ten

A Bad Woman

Ida Tarbell, who had thought herself radical and bohemian in her college days, now found that she was one of the most conservative women speaking out. She had achieved economic independence, but she was still limited by expectations of what women were to be. Not having accepted woman's destiny for herself, she approved it for others. Her ambition had spun her out into the world; her preconceptions hurled her back to where she had come from, and her mind wheeled round, pulled by two opposing forces.

The Woman Question of the early twentieth century was composed of two parts. The first concerned woman's nature—could she, should she, take a role in the world outside the home? The second question was more concrete—should women be allowed to vote?

These issues were too emotionally laden for Tarbell personally for her to be able to assess them clearly. In articles later collected as *The Business of Being a Woman*, Tarbell passionately upheld the value and power of the homemaker. It seemed to her that woman, not man, was head of the household. Her rambling articles stopped just short of saying she had misspent her own life. Writing of young girls confused by the militancy of the 1870s, she was clearly referring to her young self. She observed that the central fact of a woman's life was child bearing and rearing, but lamented that a child, especially a young girl, was steered away from the facts of life as if they were something evil.

Tarbell went so far as to blame poor sex education for three social ills: woman's revolt against marriage, her difficulty in choosing a proper mate, and her lack of respect for homemaking. Unhappiness oozed from her pen, outlining the shadow of her mother, Esther Tarbell. Esther had always had the ability to unsettle her daughter and Ida had a constellation of worries concerning her mother's health or disposition, Sarah's sacrifice, or Ida's own inadequacies. One of Esther's visits to New York left Ida so agitated that Lillian Wald was seriously alarmed. Despite Tarbell's lifelong circumlocutions, her articles make it obvious that she resented her mother for instilling in her a negative feeling toward marriage.

In her article "Making a Man of Herself," Tarbell conceded that the dissatisfied woman had some just complaints—she should be allowed to feel she was paying her own way, and she should develop outside interests so as not to feel useless when her children were grown. Tarbell further opined that woman lacked the vision necessary to achieve greatness; thus young girls must be made to understand "the essential barrenness of the achieving woman's triumph, its lack of the savor and tang of life, the multitude of makeshifts she must practice to recompense her for the lack of the great adventure of natural living."[1]

That was enough to rouse feminists. On April 15, 1912, suffragists called a rally at the Metropolitan Temple in New York, specifically to respond to Tarbell's papers. Charlotte Perkins-Gilman, the feminist writer, told the assembly they were making the unusual effort because of "the ability and dignity and power of the woman who writes them and not because of the ability, dignity or power of the papers themselves."

Methodist preacher Anna Howard Shaw ridiculed Tarbell for saying that women could have defeated the Beef Trust by patronizing independent butchers. Shaw ventured to say, "I wonder where the railways, the packers and the alien landlords and the government-protected cattle come in."[2]

Tarbell was taken to task in private by women she respected. Florence Kelley, whom Tarbell admired as an "old war horse—straight out and out," accused her of betraying the cause of women. After this encounter, Tarbell reiterated her convictions and her doubts in a letter to Kelley: "We seem to me in our effort to enlarge our lives and to serve society better to look too much to the way men try to do these things. That's what I mean by my ugly and unsatisfactory phrase 'Making a Man of Herself.' I have done it myself and I have watched hundreds of other women do it. Somewhere in there something is wrong, my dear Mrs. Kelley. I don't know that I am going to be able to get it out. I am afraid not . . . I don't believe you know how hard it is really for me to feel that I am not altogether with you and Jane Addams and a lot of other women, every one of them worth vastly more to society than I am."[3]

Soon afterward, Addams and Lillian Wald, cofounder with Kelley of the National Child Labor Committee, asked Tarbell to lunch. Knowing they wanted to take her to task, Ida parried every conversational opening, passing the salt whenever the talk turned serious. The meal was amiable and inconclusive. "I was a regular devil. I wouldn't let them come to a head and they didn't bring it to an issue," Tarbell recalled. But she was hurt by Addams's remark which was thoughtlessly conveyed by a mutual friend: "There is some limitation to Ida Tarbell's mind."[4]

Indeed, the most active women of her time all ridiculed Tarbell, if not to her face, then behind her back. Helen Keller, whose mastery over multiple handicaps astonished the world, was a militant suffragist, though her revered teacher, Anne Sullivan Macy, was not. Learning that the great Ida Tarbell was an "anti," Keller, impatient at age thirty, exclaimed that Tarbell was growing too old to understand the changing world. Her words, passed along, stung Tarbell sharply.

Many of Tarbell's closest friends had applauded her defense of the home. Ray Stannard Baker, who went to hear Tarbell give the annual Phi Beta Kappa address at Mount Holyoke College, wrote about her in his diary: "She covered herself with glory: and the essence of her message was quite contrary to the modern propaganda of the advanced woman. She said the present restiveness was the result of self-consciousness [selfishness] and that the true new woman would turn to the development of the duties of her sex rather than to attempt to invade the activities of men. She thought, so I gathered, that the duty of woman to the state was as sort of state housekeeper or home-keeper—a larger vision of domestic management."[5]

Tarbell intended to rouse women to do their duty. It was a cold-shower world she urged them to and she did not confine her whistle blasts to The American. For Woman's Home Companion she wrote an article in May 1915 called "Twenty Cent Dinners." Using the example of a Chicago girl who attempted to kill herself because she said she could no longer bear a world where she had only cheap food, Tarbell replied that spirited people were often willing to go without food and to make the most of the little they had.

Intending to hearten her readers, Tarbell said of the near suicide: "The wrong society did her was not in giving her so little money but in depriving her of the moral and mental training necessary to use effectively what she had. Somehow, out of the medley of unrelated ideas which had found their way into her brain to be brooded over in hours of fatigue and disappointment, she had developed overwhelming self-pity, a detestation of a life which was meager and struggling."

Most readers were shocked by her callousness, but Tarbell did not defend herself unil the 1930s when she insisted she had been right and predicted that even in the Great Depression, some people would have extraordinary success because they dared to take risks and sacrifice cheerfully.

Of the stacks of mail she received, one letter so impressed Tarbell that she had it typed for her confidential files. A woman named Juliet V. Straner, an anonymous contributor to *Ladies' Home Journal,* wrote Tarbell that her husband had gambled away her money and that she had raised her two daughters only with the help of her mother. Each girl married a man who failed in business and one died under her burdens, leaving Straner with her little boy. The woman lamented that they had worked hard and had nothing while those who did little were prosperous: "Oh, honey," she told Tarbell, "when you write about home—well, of course, it's all true and we've got to keep on saying it— but if you ever fancy you've missed a whole lot missing motherhood— just don't think so anymore. With the knowledge I have of life no power could tempt me to bring a child into the world or undertake to raise it."[6]

Although she might have seemed to be a successful spinster lecturing to other women on the merits of sacrifice, Tarbell was in fact meeting heavy obligations to her own family. In her sermonlike articles, Tarbell asked no more of her readers than she was willing to do herself. She was the most successful Tarbell and thus she felt obliged to help the rest. Will's son Scott, a graduate of Haverford and Princeton, was trying his luck in Kentucky oil fields and hitting dry wells. His father had already invested in his ventures, so increasingly, Scott turned to his Aunt Ida for small loans to bail him out.[7]

Will had left the Pure Oil Company, traded in various oil stocks, and even at one point tried to buy the Drake Hotel in Titusville. By 1913, a concerned Ida tried to discover the state of the family finances, but Will wrote her that he wouldn't dream of harassing her with details of the debts: "You're not so used to them as I am." He assured her that their mother and Sarah would have enough to get along on. "I'm sorry I'm not in as good a position as they are. My worry is for Ella [Will's wife] and myself but when I run out of insurance premium funds probably Providence will drop me dead and that will fix Ella."[8]

Will lacked financial acumen, but his expertise in the oil business was unquestioned. One burgeoning Oklahoma oil company sent him to Brazil and Argentina to scout Latin properties which were being bought up by Europeans.

Meanwhile, despite the antagonism she aroused, Tarbell fearlessly continued to comment on women in widely differing situations. She stated that economic status, dictated by luck, marriage, or birth, determined where a woman fit in society, and she accused the privileged of not living up to their obligations, especially their responsibility to poor girls who turned to prostitution to support themselves. For instance, Tarbell maintained that domestic service was preferable to the factory as a career for the poor.

In many articles she stressed that affluent women should make the effort to train domestic help properly and so keep young girls from taking up unsavory professions as their livelihood. Her own innocence and trust backfired on her in the matter of her own maids, however. The first one had to be fired after several years' employment for drinking and disturbing others in the building. The next was let go at the superintendent's request; she had made Tarbell's kitchen a "place of assignation." Another, a girl from Redding Ridge, roused Tarbell from bed with piercing shrieks that she was dying. Tarbell applied the usual remedies for cramps until she realized the girl had been giving herself an abortion. At one in the morning ambulance orderlies removed the girl from Tarbell's home. Shortly thereafter, Tarbell moved from West Ninth Street to 120 East Nineteenth on Gramercy Park—quarters too small for nieces, nephews, siblings, or live-in maids. When she wished to entertain, she simply took guests to the nearby National Arts Club.[9]

To write from personal experience, one needs experience and insight, yet Tarbell tried hard to uphold a tradition she herself had carefully avoided. Not surprisingly, the result was confused. Editorializing was not her forte. Finley Peter Dunne rarely accepted her contributions to "The Interpreter's House," a monthly column of editors' observations. "You sputter like a woman,"[10] he told her.

Despite her oft-repeated convictions on woman's place, when it came to the question of suffrage, Tarbell insisted she sat on the fence. "While I am not willing to work for the ballot, I am not willing to work against it," she would write to Jane Addams. But in fact she had been a member of the New York State Association Opposed to the Extension of Suffrage to Woman since 1903, joined its executive board in 1908, and in 1911 was named an executive of the national group, although the title was largely honorary.

Tarbell tried to enjoy the exercise of debate. She wrote Jane Addams after her stay at Hull House in 1908: "I think we're going to have a lively *woman's* winter. Society in New York has determined to intellectualize itself! Of course the women must do it. The first efforts may be amusing but it's a good thing and something will come of it. I believe woman's suffrage is going to get a substantial lift from efforts that are now under way. Mrs. Mackay is planning like a statesman for a campaign of education and though I'm so lukewarm on suffrage, I am rejoicing over the effort."[11]

She secretly thought socialites campaigning for the vote absurd and scoffed: "Catherine Mackay and Mrs. O. P. Belmont wanted everything and suffrage was something they didn't have."[12]

She insisted that before she could take a position she had to understand the fundamental problem. She herself asked what effect the woman's vote would have on society. Suffragists said women with the franchise could cure all ills. Tarbell didn't believe that, so she argued against the vote. It was the proverbial problem of not seeing the forest because she was studying spruce and pine trees. Like other "antis," she philosophized on the abstract notion of woman's nature while avoiding the basic question—were women citizens? Did not all citizens have the right to vote? Ray Stannard Baker cut through obfuscations when he wrote in the June 1912 *American:* "Are women people? In a few places Negroes are people in a political sense, but in the South there are 9,000,000 of them [women] who are not people. In a few places women are people, to be trusted with democratic instrumentalities, but in most places they are not. If we could really agree on who are the people, we should have all our troubles settled in a twinkling!"[13]

John Phillips could not understand Tarbell. He told her she seemed illiberal and contradictory and suggested she was too proud to say she'd been wrong to go with the antisuffragists. At one point, he invited her to explain her position. She said she couldn't do it in a conversation, so in response she wrote him a fourteen-page, triple-spaced sometimes-defensive reply: "You seem to be coming to the conclusion that what Hellen Keller is reported to have said of me not long ago is true—that is, that I am getting too old to understand and sympathize with the aspirations of a growing world! It is quite probable that there is at least a suspicion of truth in all you say. I have always found it difficult to explain myself, even to myself, and I do not often try." Here she noted on her own copy in pencil: "And I feared partisanship—inferiority." She seemed to be afraid she would find herself somehow lacking if she looked too deeply within. Her ambivalence was clear throughout the letter. She said she doubted that women would use their ballot any more wisely than men had or that it would educate her any more than it had him. But she hinted that women might be superior after all: "I confess I've always pitied men a little that they could not know the death struggle for a new life and I always had a feeling of superiority over them . . ." She quoted George Bernard Shaw's scrubwoman: "If three-quarters of you was killed we could replace you with the help of the other quarter . . ." Thus wrote Tarbell, mother of none, to Phillips, father of five.

"Women may discover women in this operation," she continued. "It is a discovery many of us need to make. The ballot, perhaps, would help reconcile us to one another. But I don't know that it has done so much for men in this particular." She went on to say that she was in sympathy with those who wanted to vote and to be in the full current of things, but concluded: "When you come down to it, I suspect the reason I feel as I do about suffrage is a kind of instinct. It is no logic or argument. I mistrust it—do not want it."

In her next sentence, she indicated she thought having the vote would alter women's role: "I feel so sure of woman's place, so clear in my mind about her part in things. It is really worth being 'old,' dear Mr. Phillips, even worth being twitted in public on that fact by my younger sisters, to be so proud and so sure of anything as I am of the place and the value of women in the world—without the ballot."[14]

It was not only her younger sisters who "twitted" her. Back home in Titusville, Esther Tarbell, approaching eighty, was astounded by her daughter's position. "Ida's mother thought she missed the boat on suffrage,"[15] recalled childhood friend Annette Grumbine. Many other women agreed with Esther. On August 26, 1920, when the Nineteenth Amendment extended the vote to women, a suffragist told Ida: "The millennium has come. You'll see what a world we will make." To this Tarbell replied with some perceptivenesss: "Women will not find themselves in the political field in less than fifty years." "You are a bad woman,"[16] she was told.

She was still a good worker. After finishing her essays on women, she abruptly returned to economics. Tarbell contributed a mild three-part analysis of the investigations made by the Pujo Committee, the House Committee on Banking and Finance. She called it "The Hunt for a Money Trust," but possibly because of the influence of the magazine's new management, the piece lacked verve. Tarbell diversified from economic topics to a first-person adventure story describing her trip in a "flying boat" or airplane. In a silk hood, cork jacket, and goggles, she resembled a fly in a bonnet, but she soon lost herself in the amazement of being in midair. She was thrilled to see a man in a sailboat respond when she managed a feeble wave. "I wanted to laugh and shout," she wrote. "The sense of exhilaration is one that I have never known before. You seem to have gotten so far above all physical fears as you are above the earth, and you have a curious sense of being a part of the whole thing."[17] Euphoric, she wanted to stand up in the plane, but just then the pilot abruptly swept down and landed the plane with its pontoons in the water. When the men on the dock demanded to see if she was shaking, Tarbell proudly presented two steady hands.

She experienced another twentieth-century phenomenon when the Authors League, which she had helped found, asked her and a few other writers to appear in a motion picture to benefit the organization. Each writer was to choose for dramatization a favorite scene of his or her own composition. Tarbell selected a Lincoln piece. She presented herself at the Vitagraph studio in Brooklyn, annoyed with herself for having consented to such a project. It had occurred to her too late that she would be forced to see herself on the screen, a prospect that intimidated her. Someone led her into what she called the "movie factory" where men were rummaging through a disorderly mess of scenery and erecting a set. Various people, painted strangely with cosmetics, took their places and began to act before the cameras. Ida watched simultaneous scenes of college girls being frightened by a mouse and people at a card party. Discovering the efficiency with which all this was accomplished, she began to see moviemaking as a complicated business in which she must perform her small part as professionally as possible. As the director requested, she took her place at "her desk," scribbled with great melodrama, paused, looked up at a portrait of Lincoln, pantomimed inspiration, and resumed writing furiously.

Her feelings of foolishness as an actress were submerged in her awe at the whole process. "The only emotions I have to record," she told a *New York Times* reporter, "are the haughtiness with which I went in and the meekness with which I came out."[18]

She was not one to deny the improvements and innovations in the world. The subjects she worked on now were uplifting. She seemed to have finished with scandal and corruption. In "The Golden Rule in Business" for *The American,* she featured benign business leaders and idealized men's work as she had formerly done women's. She thought she was striking a balance: "My conscience began to trouble me. Was it not as much my business as a reporter to present [the positive] side of the picture as to present the other?"[19]

Even the radical Lincoln Steffens thought he saw a better day dawning, and was beguiled by the innovative principles of scientific management which went into production of the Model T. "Henry Ford," he wrote, "was a prophet without words, a reformer without politics, a legislator, statesman, a radical."[20] Ford did care about his workers, but often what passed for humanitarianism was simply modernization. The coming of the electric light, which replaced the smoky torch, and studies by efficiency engineer Frederick Taylor proving that decent working conditions increased productivity encouraged more humane conditions in factories. Tarbell spent four years visiting tanneries, steel mills, and laundries around the country. Having nearly choked on cotton fibers in Rhode Island years before, she was delighted now to emerge from a twine factory without a speck of lint on her dark suit. "I never saw a machine I did not want to run," she once commented. Thus she readily absorbed details of varied manufacturing and in her articles extolled firms where labor and management cooperated, where conditions were sanitary, and where shorter hours increased output.

She doubtlessly believed industrialists were policing themselves, though some steel plants were later shown not to be as enlightened as she thought. Praise of big business was not, however, the kind of work readers expected from Ida Tarbell.

Tarbell was aware that she was not taking a popular tack. "It has taken more courage for me personally and for my magazine to try to gather up and present as a real movement the constructive work which we believe is being done in this country, and which means enormous benefit to the workers, than it ever did to carry on . . . a history of Standard Oil," she wrote to John Finch, associate editor of *The Survey*, a magazine of social conditions. Finch was studying labor and welfare practices at the time and told her she should be harder on industry. She observed wryly that readers applauded when she described people being chopped up in machinery; but when she wrote about firms that proved this sort of tragedy unnecessary, she was accused of having sold her soul to the corporation.[21]

Skeptics had an additional reason to doubt her: the Crowell interests were tightening their hold on *The American*. Publicly, Tarbell and her old colleagues avowed that nothing was changing, but privately they were troubled. As early as 1912, Baker was enraged over the way his Progressive-leaning stories were toned down. Ida, hoping their vision of the magazine would yet survive, implored him to be patient: "I cannot bear the idea of another break-up," she wrote. "We shall be able to do far less if we are scattered and our work scattered. After all, it isn't much worse than some of the interferences of SSMcC. . . If they had refused to publish your article I should have walked out and I think the rest would, *but* the article is in."[22]

Finally, in 1915, Crowell bought out Phillips's remaining interest in the magazine and the old staff, knowing they would now only be employees and not partners, disbanded. Siddall stayed on as the new editor with Phillips listed as consultant.

At last Tarbell was what she had wanted to be in her Paris days twenty years before—an independent free-lance writer. But this burning desire had flickered away over the years. Her first reaction now was to realize how much she had depended on daily contact with her friends: the boisterous luncheons, the gossip, the action. She was appalled to realize she would have to pay her secretary from her own pocket, as well as carry the cost of stationery, postage, and telephones. To keep up her apartment and her Connecticut house, she wrote free-lance articles on two subjects—woman's life and factory work.

She was regarded as sufficiently informed on industrial matters that she was summoned before the Federal Commission on Industrial Relations which met in New York in January 1915. Before an audience which included mine organizers Mother Jones and John L. Brown, Tarbell urged worker and employer to cooperate in mechanizing the workplace. She was greeted with derision. Suffragist Florence J. Harriman tried to goad Tarbell into admitting she was against female suffrage but failed. All Tarbell would say was that women, not men, kept women from the vote, but she did not explain herself. Another commissioner intimated that she was an enemy of labor. She retorted that she regarded herself as a laborer and that she thought their leaders had a lot to learn but added, "It is a great mistake for the employers not to foster unions and for the unions not to understand new methods."

The press expressed surprise at the attempt to heckle her. "She proved repeatedly that she was more than able to hold her own against batteries of interrogatory and to give cogent reasons for every opinion she expressed,"[23] said the *New York Herald.*

Her status as an expert brought her an invitation from the American Federation of Labor to participate in the first Industrial Conference, held in October 1919. She did not find it a happy experience. For one thing, President Woodrow Wilson wanted the conference to set guidelines for cooperation between labor and management, but inevitably, the ongoing strikes became the focus of discussion. Second, she was in constant contact with John D. Rockefeller, Jr., who was so resolutely polite that he hailed a cab for her. Finally, Samuel Gompers, president of the AFL, repeatedly thwarted her. She and Lillian Wald tried to introduce a resolution, advocated by the Women's Bureau of the Labor Department, which would have limited woman's work day to eight hours. It also stated that wages should be established on the basis of occupation and dependents, not sex. Gompers wanted no diversion from the specific issue of daily wages to more generalized social reform. What made Tarbell especially furious was his intervention on the issue of collective bargaining. The conference was divided into three groups representing labor, management, and the public. As a member of the last, she was in favor of the formation of individual company unions. Gompers, who had a vision of one national body to represent workers, said company unions were inadequate. This question of who could represent labor in collective bargaining shattered the Industrial Conference.

Tarbell neither liked nor trusted the wily Gompers, a sensibility she shared with others. Yet, when a committee member wanted to submit evidence to the conference proving that Gompers had lied when he said the American Federation of Labor had never antagonized shop unions, Tarbell blocked it, insisting they deal with issues, not personalities. To Phillips she poured out her frustrations: "I am not concerned with how it puts us before the public, but what disheartens me is that when we fought so hard to get a liberal interpretation of collective bargaining; when we fought so hard to get them [labor] the right to bargain through representatives of their own choosing, that they should have been the ones to have tried to block the new spirit in industry."[24]

In Tarbell's lifetime, factories had superseded farms, women began to work in them, and the small entrepreneur became the salaried man. The good and the bad were not easy to label, though many tried. In this new world, neither her private nor her professional life was as she expected it to be.

PART IV

VALOR

Eleven

Workhorse

Ida Tarbell was wrong in thinking she had avoided "entangling alliances." She had been ensnared from birth in the mesh of her family. In the late 1910s, family ties tightened and knotted her fate for the rest of her life—her brother Will suffered a mental breakdown. According to personal letters, it was soon clear to Sarah and Ida that he had unwittingly done the Tarbell fortunes as much damage as John D. Rockefeller had.

Because the bankers of Titusville knew Will, they had allowed him to overborrow on his share of Franklin Tarbell's estate. When his loans were due he found he was insolvent, so Ida was forced to take charge: "I said I'd pay it but that if we could bring the property through I should keep that amount I'd paid with interest. I'd never done that before when I paid his debts. But it would be madness not to. Ten thousand dollars when you have to earn it all yourself is not a trifling sum and he would just throw it away."[1]

To help make money to clear the debt, Sarah laid aside her paintbrushes for the last time and learned bookkeeping.

Adding to Ida's gloom was the catastrophe of general war throughout Europe. In August 1914, she and some colleagues sat in a Hungarian restaurant on New York's Houston Street discussing the latest news. The others' sense of America's isolation was strong but Tarbell murmured that before the battles ended it would be America's war too. Wanting peace, but thinking war inexorable, she declined an invitation to join Henry Ford's Peace Ship. Ford planned to have respected figures sail across the Atlantic with him to plead with combatants to end the fighting, but he received few acceptances from the notables he invited (though Sam McClure was one of the passengers). Few seemed to take the mission seriously, but the invitation was another cause of private debate between Ida Tarbell and Jane Addams. During a telephone conversation, Addams tried to convince Ida to go. Tarbell finally said, "If you see it, you must go, Miss Addams. I don't see it and I can't. It is possible [that] standing on a street corner and crying, 'Peace, Peace' may do good. I do not say that it will not, but I cannot see it for myself."[2]

The war continued but temporary deliverance from personal financial concerns came in late 1915 when the head of a lecture bureau asked Tarbell to embark on a forty-nine-day tour of forty-nine towns in Ohio and Pennsylvania for the munificent sum of twenty-five hundred dollars. Ida's friends cautioned she would be wandering in the hinterlands of the United States with no more dignity than a Swiss yodeler or a spoon player, but for twenty-five hundred dollars, she was ready to do it. In a curious coincidence, these itinerant mixtures of education and entertainment were called Chautauquas.

Determined to give people their money's worth, Ida took voice lessons at the American Academy of Dramatic Arts in New York and dutifully went home to do her exercises. She roamed her apartment vocalizing "Ma, me, mi, no, ba, be, bi, bo." To strengthen her diaphragm she lay on her back, placed books on her stomach and breathed deeply until her diaphragm was strong enough to lift five books. From the time she signed her contract until she set forth in mid-June 1916, her lecture on the "Ideals of Business" filled her head and hampered her writing, but that seemed not to matter. She described herself as mired in a rut, unable to write anything but six-thousand-word articles—a book or a thousand-word squib would have been impossible. The lectures offered her the chance to earn her living and, she hoped, to contribute to people's lives.

Roseboro was horrified when Tarbell vowed to talk to the people in their own language. "No one ever wrote valuable stuff with that kind of aim,"[3] Roseboro wrote to a friend but dared not tell Tarbell.

Life on the road in searing summer heat was not easy physically or emotionally. Her first audience was the citizens of Niles, Ohio, a steel town not far from Poland. She stood outside the khaki circus tent blazing with lights and watched scores of men, women, and children leave their dingy unpainted houses and flock to hear her lecture. As nearby furnaces panted heavily, she mounted the podium, looked down into their work-lined faces, and tried to speak on ethics. "All my pretty tales seemed now terribly flimsy. They were so serious, they listened so intently to get something; and the tragedy was that I had not more to give them."[4]

Lecturing was physically demanding but lucrative, and she decided to continue it. Twice a year for five to six weeks in 1916 and 1917, she went on the road. She liked seeing the country—the people who were so eager to make more of their lives intellectually and materially—and she got a kick out of the new Model T's puttering along the roads. Before beginning each lecture she would scan her audience to guess which ones wouldn't believe a word she had to say, which would ask her about the single tax, and to decide which woman had the loveliest hat.

She respected the other hardworking "talent" and admitted to disliking only one other person on her circuit—William Jennings Bryan. After the Armistice, she spoke out in favor of giving certain guarantees to France; he was against them. She was told to cut her talk. As for Bryan, "The Great Commoner," famous for his Cross of Gold speech advocating unlimited coinage of silver, Tarbell said: "He in no way tried to influence my opinion, only to shut it off."[5]

Some nights she slept on the train as it carried her to her next city. She would awaken realizing she was on a crowded sleeper car indecently packed with dozens of people and would become nearly nauseous with the thought of it. She dealt with changes in schedules and missed connections and with being passed from the jurisdiction of one Chautauqua bureau to another. Ida had always prided herself on being superior to her physical surroundings; now she craved information about where she would lay her head. When she asked about the next town, her question was framed in terms of the hotel, its bathrooms, and whether she was to have one. On a little calendar she X-ed off each day, happy to have it over with.

Night noises, drafts, and beds preoccupied her. At the end of the tour she found she could draw a diagram of any room in which she had slept, placing the bed exactly in relation to the windows, doors, and bathroom.

She could have done otherwise with her life. In late 1916, after his narrow reelection, President Wilson asked her to sit on his Tariff Commission. This would have been the first such appointment of a woman. Wilson chose Tarbell, newspapers speculated, because she was a woman (and by then women were chaining themselves to the White House fence in agitation for the vote) and a Pennsylvanian. But in Wilson's opinion she had also written more good common sense about the tariff than any man he knew. Grateful as she was for the honor, Ida declined. "I might have done it out of curiosity if I had been alone in the world, but I didn't think a commission could be much help in making a bill,"[6] she told Baker.

Lecturing and free-lance articles—several on woman's life and one, for *Collier's*, on President Wilson—paid her money she needed to keep up her apartment, her farm, and to pay off her brother's debts; but her neat if demanding arrangements were knocked askew first by outside events and then by her own ill health.

As America threw itself into the Great War, Ida Tarbell was felled by a series of events. President Wilson had called her to Washington to work on the Women's Defense Committee. It was composed of a dozen women, mostly suffragists, who were expected to be only window dressing for the war effort. Tarbell said in her memoirs that her own greatest achievement on the committee was to loot adjacent offices for chairs, and that the most pleasant meeting was when they discussed potential food shortages and ended up reminiscing about how their grandmothers strung apples. Tarbell also served as honorary president for the American Chocolate Fund for the U.S. Expeditionary Forces in France, and other straw-clutching, morale-boosting efforts.

Ida had barely begun work with the Women's Defense Committee when word came that her mother had died. She calmly phoned her maid and told her to pack, continued on as planned to a wedding, telling none of the guests what had happened, and then took the train to Titusville.[7] She went calmly through the funeral and preliminary arrangements to sell her childhood home, then returned to Washington and collapsed.

Ida was taken to Johns Hopkins Hospital delirious and disastrously underweight. The expected diagnosis was overwork and stress compounded by an ulcerated tooth, but instead doctors discovered a spot on her lung. Apparently, Tarbell's customary ability to throw herself into work after periods of rest had masked telltale symptoms. Tuberculosis is a frantic disease of deadly pallor followed by flushed cheeks, hyperactivity alternating with languor, coughing, and progressive emaciation. This wasting away once had the romantic name of "consumption," but even before the development of streptomycin, it had a no-nonsense treatment—rest, fresh air, healthy food, and isolation from family and stress.

Ida remained at Johns Hopkins three months. Under supervision, she was forced to eat three meals a day, to swallow six raw eggs and five glasses of milk. She wept with frustration at being made to eat so much and sometimes she nearly choked. Only her family and closest friends knew her malady. Bert Boyden sent fresh flowers every day and arranged to have the practice continued after he went overseas. The youngest of her old associates, Boyden was now forty-two. He had been roused by the preaching of the charismatic evangelist Billy Sunday, and after the war began, he thought he could help serve the effort by going to Paris with the YMCA.

Being in the hospital when there was war work to be done, however tangential, pained Ida. She wrote to the chairman of the National Woman's Defense Committee, Anna Shaw (her old critic on the issue of suffrage), that her hospital stay was being extended and she hinted she had had some operation: "I have been putting off the matter for several years now and I am afraid I cannot do it any longer,"[8] she said. She told Shaw she had had to cancel her lectures, the reliable source of her income; but since the doctors were finally allowing her to do some dictating each day, she hoped that she might be able to help with the committee. The outcome was "Patriotic Shopping," written for the *Woman's Home Companion*, which became part of a stream of advice to the housewife on the minutiae of life in wartime.

Once her hospital stay ended, Ida visited her own doctor, Harlow Brooks, and complained her illness had left her with a trembling, and weak right leg and a tongue which still stiffened. She had had trouble swallowing all the food on her hospital regimen and still sometimes came close to choking. Dr. Brooks recognized the symptoms of Parkinson's disease, a progressive shaking palsy that would spread from her right side to her left and set her hands to quivering with a defiant unreachable life of their own. There was no treatment; there was no cure, so Brooks simply told her not to worry and to go about her life.

The onetime group of colleagues found different ways of involving themselves with the war. Steffens went to Russia and returned home to tout its revolution; Baker wrote articles in support of the Allies which were syndicated in pro-German areas of the country; McClure, who had visited Germany before America entered the war and had found its people fitter than Allied propaganda suggested, was suspected of being a German agent; and Phillips took a job as editor of *The Red Cross Magazine*.

Phillips had a small apartment in New York not far from Ida Tarbell and they met faithfully for relaxed conversations each Sunday evening. Although their correspondence indicates this standing date meant a good deal to both of them, John Phillips's wife was untroubled. Their friendship was ardent but apparently not romantic, even though relatives and mutual friends, such as Roseboro, were aware of their devotion. Tarbell still looked to him as editor and advisor, especially in matters of her career. Her publisher was eager to have her write on natural monopolies—specifically the theory that some industries, such as oil, tend to consolidate competition rather than promote it—but Tarbell had another idea. In three years of lecture tours around the United States she had seen small towns slowly gear up for involvement in the European conflagration and she wanted to tell the story as a novel.

Phillips encouraged her and helped her shape the book. The result was *The Rising of the Tide*, written in less than a year for a one-thousand-dollar advance. It was her claim to the title of novelist, and one she did not stress.

Tarbell's novel featured the love stories of two couples: the young muckraking newspaper editor who falls in love with the daughter of the town's richest man, a girl who matures when she is caught in the German invasion of Belgium; and the idealistic young minister and the town's "career woman," a schoolteacher. This girl, Patsy McCullon, was a composite drawn partly from Ida's friend from Poland days, Clara Walker, and partly from Ida herself. Left a widow and a new mother at the end of the novel, she valiantly faces a life alone.

Although the book had many potentially exciting elements, including a German saboteur, *The Rising of the Tide* was flat. Tarbell's characters were one-dimensional, predictable types representing various traits of public opinion. They were products of Tarbell's adult reason and much duller than the characters she created in her fanciful Paris days.

Critics tended to be kind, but their benevolent attempts were reluctantly honest. Ida accepted her novel's fate stoically: "It seems like one of those million things which were dropped into the vortex of the war, and like most of them, would never come to the surface."[9]

Tarbell had missed the war, but her health—and assignments from Phillips's *Red Cross Magazine*—permitted her to travel to Europe to see what passed for peace. In January 1919, she was sent to Paris to observe the Armistice and the Versailles Conference.

She was also determined to aid old friends from her earlier days in Paris, Madame Marillier and Charles Seignobos. Unsure of their safety and hearing stories of terrible shortages, she prepared herself to rescue them from any emergency. Into her trunk she wedged saddlebags loaded with high boots, blankets, woolen tights, and hose. Then she obtained an enormous ham with which to feed her starving friends.

Postwar traveling was as tedious as the first steps of an invalid. With all her eccentric luggage, her difficulties sometimes bordered on the absurd. When at length she landed in Bordeaux, at docks built by American Expeditionary Forces, Ida had the ham loaded onto the Paris train where it fell from an overhead rack and nearly crushed two young Quakers who were intending to help with reconstruction. Finally, when she tearfully and triumphantly presented the ham to the healthy but worn French couple, Cécile Marillier and Charles Seignobos were grateful, but also astonished by her stunt.

The France Ida encountered was damaged and weary from trying to reassemble pieces that would never fit together perfectly again. The Red Cross installed her in the Hôtel Vouillement, but at every opportunity she returned to her old Latin Quarter. The *laiterie* where she bought milk in her student days and several other buildings and people she had known were gone—victims of Big Berthas and German air raids against Paris. "Abri"—"shelter"—signs were still posted and many still took care to shutter their windows at night as they had when light attracted danger. Repairs had been postponed for five years—smashed windows were jagged, broken heaters still cold, and once-gay Parisians dressed in black. Tarbell, shaken by the changes, nearly broke down in tears when she saw that the meticulous Mme Marillier had allowed a bedroom door to go unhinged.

Paris in 1919 was a kaleidoscope with bits of her life reassembling in new patterns. Members of the old Seignobos circle had achieved enough recognition to be called to Paris for the conference. Charles Borgeaud was there to present the Swiss plan for the confederation of nations, and H. W. Steed was now foreign editor of *The Times* of London and about to be named editor. Tarbell held a reunion luncheon, but time had dulled the once-keen friendship and diffused their once-common interests.

The McClure's/American group was more compatible. They gathered across the Seine, along the Rue de Rivoli near Red Cross headquarters where Paris had the cast of characters of Washington in wartime, complete with doughboys wanting to go home. Ray Stannard Baker, press liaison to the American delegation, William Allen White, August Jaccaci, and Lincoln Steffens were all in attendance. So was one of Ida's old Sunday-school students from Meadville—Frederic Howe, a writer and lawyer, pretending to be a newspaperman so he could be at the conference. While many writers wangled free-lance credentials with Baker's help, Tarbell and White roamed the town freely in their Red Cross uniforms.

Tarbell also carried, for times when a press pass would not do, a letter from Woodrow Wilson. Unbeknownst to Tarbell, he had tried to do still more on her behalf, listing her as part of the official legation. She remained ignorant of his intercessions until amazed friends told her about it soon after the conference began. She investigated and found that Secretary of State Robert Lansing, objecting to having a woman serve in the legation in any capacity, had forestalled Tarbell's inclusion by neglecting to inform her of it. She accepted Lansing's veto, probably because she did not want to force herself on him, by telling herself she was untrained as an internationalist, a humility which had not deterred other American officials in Paris. Just as she had once passed up the opportunity to be the first woman on a federal commission, Ida Tarbell now declined to be the first to represent her country in a diplomatic legation.[10]

Even if she had pressed her claim, her role would have been mostly honorary. The four Allied leaders framed the terms of the peace behind doors firmly closed to subordinates. Woodrow Wilson, whose country had been protected from devastation by the Atlantic Ocean, took an idealistic stance and lobbied for a League of Nations and a merciful peace. David Lloyd George, Georges Clemenceau, and Vittorio Orlando, heirs to a thousand years of embattled history and fifty-two months of destruction, wanted reparations, protection, and booty.

All the negotiations took place away from the sensitive ears and nimble pencils of the press. In cafés and thoroughfares, journalists were left to justify their presence. Some five hundred special correspondents had been sent to Paris at great expense and they needed to produce copy. From the outset, they protested the secret diplomacy and clamored that they, as the conduits to the common people who were to benefit from the peace, should be included in the conferences.

Tarbell's assignment was to write about how people had come through the war, so she headed toward the industrial north of France which had been most heavily damaged. She left Paris in a Red Cross car with a doughboy chauffeur as soon as highways opened. Years of continual attack had made the land a rubble of abandoned tanks, artillery shells, and hand grenades. The earth was so shattered that the lime beneath its surface had been exposed.

Ida saw nothing alive, neither cat nor dog nor hen. The only sound was that of the cold rain. She traveled to Albert, Lens, Rheims, and Laon. Beyond Armentières, she attempted to enter closed Belgian territory, but her car fell into a shell hole. Twenty colonial soldiers from Annam, which was later to become part of Vietnam, carried the vehicle a quarter mile to safety while the English officer responsible for cleaning up the area berated her loudly.

Ida filled her notebook with stories of people she met along the way, such as the group of orphans raised in the trenches. They were ignorant of social niceties like proper nose-blowing, but they judged her Red Cross uniform, with its four-in-hand tie and sensible shoes, *"pas chic."* At Cambrai, she met with the directress of the hospital, whom the Germans had condemned to solitary confinement for concealing soldiers. Just freed, the woman was delighted to find that her old job had been held open for her. Especially touching to Tarbell were the peasant women at Vic-sur-Aine who came from miles around to weep as they beheld the first egg laid after the war.

In Lens, once an industrial city of twenty-three thousand inhabitants, now reduced to two hundred, Tarbell found citizens rebuilding their homes with the aid of the one available handsaw which was lent out by the hour. She soon learned to distinguish signs of habitation—a break in high-piled debris, tracks in brick dust, a shell hole stuffed with straw or tin over a shattered tile roof. The American was so shaken by what she was seeing that when she visited a woman in a hovel and found her darning socks, the simple sign of sanity transfixed her.[11]

Thus she was in no mood to be overawed by Jane Addams whom she found awaiting her in Paris. Addams had been touring damaged areas for the Red Cross and visiting the grave of a beloved nephew killed by the war. When Tarbell told her how disturbed she had been by the children of Lille who had lived like ferrets during the war and were now plagued by dysentery, Addams seemed indifferent and suggested she think about the German children. Tarbell retorted: "Miss Addams, I do think of them, but why not think of these children, too?"

Addams countered, "Think of the German prisoners in France!"

Tarbell grew irritated and snapped: "The German prisoners in the devastated regions are getting the same rations that the refugees are; they are getting the same rations of the English soldiers, and that is more I fear than the French and English prisoners are getting."[12]

The Peace Conference had a way of exacerbating differences and strengthening bonds. At the very time when old friends were especially precious, Tarbell and William Allen White feared that August Jaccaci was dying. He lay at the Hôtel Vouillement stricken with the influenza that had killed so many in 1919. Tarbell and White took turns sitting up with him until he recovered enough to be moved, and his friend, the painter Tavanier, invited him to stay at his house in Barbizon. As Tarbell helped Jaccaci down the hall, she grew convinced that it was their final good-bye. She embraced Jaccaci with such fervor that they scandalized White and Baker.[13]

But Jaccaci, as usual, had a surprise in store for his old friends. He recovered fully and in a few weeks invited them all out to lunch near the forest of Fontainebleau. Tarbell, White, and Baker commandeered a Red Cross car for the occasion and had a glorious day. On the way back, they allowed the chauffeur to show off his skills. Trees and road seemed to blend in a haze of dust, and they took mischievous delight in driving from the road a limousine in which huddled a terrified American couple. As they passed the car, the trio gaily waved and discovered they had blithely terrorized no less than Thomas Woodrow Wilson, president of the United States.[14]

Soon after this, the conference ended. Tarbell disputed what so many professed—that the Allies had made an end to war, that this had been "the war to end all wars." She felt strongly that the vindictive reparations demanded of Germany almost guaranteed another conflict. The night Wilson, Clemenceau, Lloyd George, and Orlando approved the treaty to be presented to the Germans, she went to bed and wept.[15]

Colonel Edward House, Wilson's adviser, informed Tarbell that the president wanted her to go to Geneva where the League of Nations would be headquartered, but she declined. "I thought there was enough to do at home," she wrote in a draft of her autobiography, "but I would have given a great deal to be there as an observer." She needed to give only her consent, but that Tarbell never gave. All her life she had wondered what woman could do and to her was presented the opportunity to demonstrate that she could be a diplomat and policy maker, but she shrank back.

The closest Tarbell came to taking advantage of these opportunities was her participation in the International Labor Conference the following October and in the inconclusive Unemployment Conference of 1922. More satisfying to her was the Washington Conference on Arms Limitation which she covered for the McClure Syndicate in 1921. The conference was originally intended to discuss naval disarmament but became an attempt to solve rivalry over the Orient. Japan had entered World War I through its alliance with Great Britain and had seized the opportunity to take over German properties in China. It was the only nation besides the United States to emerge from the Great War strengthened. The hope was that the Arms Limitation Conference could head off conflict between these two new powers.

The assembly proved to be historic. Britain, the United States, and Japan agreed to balance naval strength at a 5-5-3 ratio for fifteen years and signed a Four Power Treaty with France. All promised respect for the rights of others and fairer treatment of China, but Tarbell wrote that everything would depend on the Japanese.

She gathered her articles into a book called *Peacemakers—Blessed and Otherwise*. She took a personal approach to the state of the world and reviewers liked it, without knowing quite what to make of it. "Sane and worthwhile," said *The New Republic*, ". . . except that she wears too conspicuously on her sleeve the broken heart of the world." *The Review of Reviews* took note of her chatty style: "Some of her comments are caustic, while all are pointed and illuminating. If her account is in any degree inadequate as history, it largely makes up for such lack in vividness and intimacy as a narrative."[16]

About this time a man began to pester her about her magazine career. He insisted he could do her good by acting as her literary agent. Now in his mid-fifties, a former representative of a London publishing house, Paul Reynolds had come up with the novel idea of representing authors for a commission. He approached Tarbell with the idea that she could expand her income by writing more frequently for women's magazines. She declined to give him her phone number or any idea of her fees; as a test, she then sent him an article written by an aged and not too literary man who needed financial help. She told Reynolds to get a thousand dollars for it. Reynolds made his customary figure-eight doodles on the manuscript, then passed it along to his assistant, Harold Ober, who apparently decided the project wasn't worth taking. He simply noted: "This is too much for me."[17]

Only after Reynolds sent Tarbell a $675 check for "The New

Woman Power of France," a spin-off of her *Red Cross* pieces, did she take him seriously. Reynolds generated assignments, placed her work, and handled financial details so that she earned more than she expected. "You will be the salvation of my old age!" she exulted. Happily for her, the dean of literary agents had overcome her reluctance with his persistence.[18]

She resumed her grueling lecture schedule in 1920, setting out for a month or so around Lincoln's birthday, a time when she was always very much in demand. The lecture tour was more rigorous than her prewar trips. The once-impeccable Ida Tarbell traveled the country in torn stockings and droopy hemlines, an older lady obliged to raise her hems to contemporary midcalf length.

She wrote in her autobiography: "Frequently I occupied two different beds a night, and now and then three. It was a brutal, exhaustive business, but I learned to climb into an upper berth without a fuss, to sleep on a bench if there was no berth, to rejoice over a cup of hot coffee at an all-night workmen's lunch counter, to warm my feet by walking a platform while waiting for a train. By the end of the first season I had developed a stoical acceptance of whatever came. This, I argued, saved nervous wear and tear. I think now a certain amount of indignant protest, useless as it would have been, might have put more zest into my travel, as well as into my talking."[19]

Before the war, lecture podiums had been rudimentary but the platforms of the 1920s were arranged to heighten drama and importance. It was apparent that few in the audience knew who she was. Sometimes she was introduced as the author of books on Siberia which had actually been written by George Kennan, or of stories penned by Edna Ferber, but these indignities were minor. One master of ceremonies explained why she had never married, while another called her a "notorious woman." Sometimes she would be arranged in tableaux with begowned local ladies so that while Tarbell was speaking, the audience was pointing to the other women onstage and criticizing their dresses.

Her refuge, as ever, was Redding Ridge, Connecticut, where she would work every morning in her sun-flooded library on the unpolished mahogany desk littered with manuscript drafts and mail-order catalogs offering insect sprayers. Seed catalogs drove her to extravagant orgies of selection. She considered the relative merits of the "mammoth" versus "abundant producer" varieties. She paid close attention to bulletins from the Agricultural Department and the Bureau of Plant Industry's interest in how the Chilean willow and the Japanese cherry tree would acclimate to Connecticut.

Once a year she gave an old-fashioned dinner party for fifty or so local people. She learned how to use the Dutch oven in the living room and cooked a suckling pig with an apple in its mouth, and vegetables and fruits from her garden. After the meal she would take her place at the piano for a community sing.

Tarbell extolled her Czech caretaker Paul Trup as the personification of Rousseau's Natural Man, the repository of all folk wisdom, but she defied him in two things. He wanted to modernize her stone fence by encasing it in cement, which she refused to do. He also insisted that she devote her garden to fruits and vegetables but each season it was vivid with red, yellow, and purple flowers. Peonies and roses were arranged before a low, ivy-covered wall. Poppies, descendants of those given her by J. P. Mahaffy at Chautauqua, bloomed everywhere, and the Oriental varieties had appropriated the strawberry bed and much of the ground that was intended for beets and onions.

Her friends had no trouble thinking of presents to buy her. One gave her an aristocratic black Orpington rooster. Tarbell admired the sight of him in her yard, but Trup and the hens hated the multicolored English bird. He died suddenly and Tarbell attributed his death to homesickness. Her mare Minerva was a faithful servant and friend for years, as was the Jersey cow which she named Esther Anne.

The house was as tastefully furnished as Ida's frequent purchases of American country antiques—then not highly valued—could make it, with rush mats on the floors and delicate floral wallpaper in most rooms.

At her very own Twin Oaks, she felt close to life, especially when a new generation came to live there. Ida had given her niece Clara and Clara's husband Tristram Tupper a little cottage on the property after Tupper returned from the war. Here Tupper, who later went to Hollywood to write for the movies, began his writing career. One day while her grandniece Caroline was still tiny, Ida insisted Clara and Tris take the afternoon off while Aunt Ida babysat. The Tuppers returned three hours later to find Caroline barricaded with chairs and pillows on the horsehair davenport, wearing her triangular diaper backward. "The rear flank was dangerously exposed," Clara recalled. "I never did tell Aunt Ida. Her pleasure was too great, her exhaustion too apparent, and her sense of accomplishment too satisfying."[20]

At this time, Tarbell was also preparing to take up work in which she had more expertise—she was going to update her story of the oil business. The drama of the independents was being relived by her nephew Scott who was determined to make a fortune in oil. With his wife and family, he tried his luck in Kentucky, Oklahoma, Missouri, and Kansas. The discovery of Southwestern oil fields and rich reserves around the world had engendered new companies to challenge the Rockefeller empire at the same time that the automobile and the oil furnace ushered in the Oil Age. There was more money than ever to be made from petroleum and Ida Tarbell kept up with the competition over it, especially when the government got involved.

In May 1921, the Harding administration transferred control of certain naval oil land reserves at Elk Hills and Buena Vista, California, and Teapot Dome, Wyoming, from control of Secretary of the Navy Edwin Denby to that of the Secretary of the Interior, Albert B. Fall. The following April, Fall leased Teapot Dome to Harry Sinclair, president of Sinclair Oil, who formed Mammoth Oil Company specifically to handle the leases. The lessee of Elk Hills was Edward Doheny, chairman of Pan American Petroleum. All this was done without competitive bidding. Fall would later tell a Senate committee that he wanted government lands tapped so the oil could not be drawn off by those who were drilling on adjacent fields.

In June, speaking freely at a dinner party given by Bert Boyden's brother William, Tarbell launched into a discussion of the impropriety of Mammoth Oil's taking over the drilling of public lands, and charged that Standard Oil of New Jersey held more than fifty-one percent of Sinclair Oil stock. One young guest, who proved to be the secretary of a Rockefeller associate, protested that the Standard did not control Sinclair stock—only its oil lands and pipe lines. He insisted that Standard Oil companies were not involved in Teapot Dome, only private individuals. He further told her that the Standard Oil companies were irritated that the Indiana operation had been allowed to "swallow" the Midwest and promised interesting developments as the Standard Oil companies fought things out.[21]

In any event, Tarbell noted that the principals of the Mammoth Oil Company were Standard men. Besides Harry Sinclair, there were James E. O'Neil, president of Prairie Oil and Gas Company, purveyor of crude oil to Standard Oil of Indiana; Walter Teagle, president of Standard Oil of New York; Robert W. Stewart, chairman of Standard Oil of Indiana; James W. Van Dyke, president of Atlantic Refining Company; and Henry W. Blackmer, president of Midwest Refining Company, a subsidiary of Standard Oil of Indiana.

Prairie and Atlantic were part of the Standard Oil monopoly cited by the Supreme Court in 1911. As far as Tarbell was concerned, this group had continued the old system of interlocking directorates, whereby the Standard Oil Company controlled and owned "competitors" by virtue of having key officers "invest" or assume directorships in rival companies. She continued to follow developments as best she could.

In August 1923, popular President Warren G. Harding died. Within a few months, the grieving country learned that under his administration, officials had made vast private fortunes from their public duties. For his secret efforts on behalf of the oilmen, Secretary of Interior Fall had received over a quarter million dollars in Liberty Bonds from Sinclair, and an interest-free "loan" from Doheny for a hundred thousand dollars. This scandal broke in early 1924.

When *The New York Times* asked her opinion, Tarbell summed it up this way: "Excessive amiability on the part of President Harding and stupidity on the part of Secretary [of the Navy] Denby who didn't seem to know what he was signing. Mr. Fall seemed to know very well what he was about."[22] That was to be her only public contribution to the debate—a pity because she ran across tantalizing clues she never followed up.

Senate investigations revealed that early in 1924 Sinclair had given Fall bonds from the holdings of an obscure firm called the Continental Trading Company Ltd. of Canada, whose officers, Tarbell would later note with glee, were all connected to Standard Oil—Henry W. Blackmer, James E. O'Neil, Robert W. Stewart, Harry Sinclair, and Colonel Albert Humphreys, who sold Continental oil which Continental then resold to Sinclair. In these transactions the investors made personal profits totaling three million dollars.

All this was revealed later during protracted Senate investigations. Sinclair, Stewart, O'Neil, and Blackmer decamped for foreign shores and were repudiated by John D. Rockefeller, Jr., who had assumed the leadership role his father had once held.

As the Teapot Dome scandal unfolded, Tarbell had hopes of proving ongoing malfeasance by the Standard Oil Company, but one major effort went into protecting someone she believed in. This was a man she had known since her days on the Woman's Defense Committee, a diffident man in his fiftieth year who had won the respect of the world for relieving the famine in Europe after the Great War. His name was Herbert Hoover.

Few men in the world enjoyed as much esteem. An orphan, self-made millionaire, and accomplished engineer, Hoover seemed so noble to both political parties that in 1920, before Hoover declared himself a Republican, Assistant Secretary of the Navy Franklin Delano Roosevelt wrote of Hoover: "He certainly is a wonder and I wish we could make him President of the United States. There could not be a better one."[23]

Tarbell shared this sentiment; but like most, she was never able to relax with the reticent Hoover who was too shy to look a person in the eye and who spoke with awkward terseness.

Hoover continued in public service and joined Warren Harding's cabinet in 1920. In May 1922, when Tarbell was in Washington to interview Woodrow Wilson, she told Hoover, now Secretary of Commerce, that she was appalled by the transfer of naval oil land to private drillers. Hoover answered with a laugh: "I wrote the contract." Tarbell told this to Phillips, who told a cartoonist for the *New York World*, who told his managing editor. In the midst of the Teapot Dome revelations in 1924, when Hoover was touted as a possible vice-presidential nominee, a *World* reporter came back to Tarbell and asked her to confirm the story. She told him she regarded the honorable Hoover as too great a national asset to be implicated in such a debacle.

Her conscience troubled her, however, and she called the managing editor of the *World*, William P. Beazell, a fellow graduate of Allegheny College. Tarbell told Beazell she would speak to Hoover, but that the story should not be published without notifying her. When Hoover's name did not appear on the 1924 ticket, the *World* dropped the matter. Tarbell, still anxious, sought to warn Hoover and set up a meeting with him. At the appointed time—on Friday morning, September 5, 1924—she found Hoover at her apartment door. Guests usually signaled their arrival by whistling near her window, but the Secretary of Commerce reached her doorstep without such formal preliminaries. Hoover earnestly assured her he had no knowledge of Teapot Dome contracts before they were signed. He said that when she had mentioned oil contracts in Washington two years before, he had not realized she was talking about Teapot Dome. He thought she must be referring to the leases that he had been working on for the Honolulu Oil Company involving Buena Vista, California.

Hoover maintained that the Teapot Dome contracts were drawn up under Fall's orders by officials in the Interior and Navy departments, probably in consultation with the oilmen who were to profit by them. Hoover told her: "I can easily get statements from both departments saying that they were never submitted to the Department of Commerce."[24] Of course, such letters, which he did provide, are not conclusive proof that he was not unofficially asked for his opinion as a man who had recently written other oil leases.

One wonders why Hoover, the Secretary of Commerce, negotiated a Honolulu oil lease which should have been the affair of the Department of the Interior. It may have been because Hoover had directed mining companies, and Honolulu operated its first claim under mining law. Tarbell, who dictated a seven-page memorandum of the talk, seems to have been willing to trust his word.

These leases, as Hoover told Tarbell, had been a source of contention since the Wilson administration, when the Honolulu Company took a claim on Naval Reserve #2 in Buena Vista and developed it with great profit. When the lands were withdrawn for the use of the Navy, Wilson refused to give Honolulu a patent or right to the land. Secretary of the Interior Franklin K. Lane complained to Hoover that this seemed unfair. Hoover told Tarbell that Wilson's refusal had been politically motivated.[25] When the Republicans were back in power in 1920, they attempted to right what they regarded as this injustice. The lease the administration drew up for them, apparently written by Hoover, was dated February 11, 1922.

Tarbell dictated the ollowing for her files after Hoover's visit: "H says that when he came to office the Honolulu people came to him and he negotiated a lease—I suppose through the Departments of the Interior and the Navy—giving them a right to develop their territory on the basis of a royalty to the government of 35 to 40 per cent of the oil. He said he thought he had done a fine thing for the government as well as acting justly by the oil company. Says that this Honolulu claim will come up in the next investigation and that probably the fact that he negotiated the lease will be know[n], that it is the only lease he ever had anything to do with, and that is what he had in mind when he talked with me . . ."[26]

The Honolulu claim did not come up again, but the Honolulu Consolidated Oil Company had come before Senate investigators the previous October when the committee heard that Secretary Fall had authorized the lease of public oil lands to the Honolulu Company with the verbal approval of President Harding.[27]

However Hoover downplayed his involvement with oil companies, Tarbell's memorandum indicated that Hoover wanted one of his dealings known: "H says 'There is one oil matter in which I took a part which nobody has noticed, which I should think is something you might like to work out.' He said that in 1921 he had told oil men that there was danger of production falling below the country's needs and he suggested they get into foreign fields in Venezuela, Peru and Bolivia to preserve America's supply." Tarbell commented, "His opinion seems to be that if our supply gets very low the prices will rise enormously, and that then the companies like the Standard that control the big supplies will make such enormous profits that it will be necessary to do something drastic. It is an interesting view. It might force on the government the taking over of the oil land though he doesn't say so." She did not need to note that North American companies, especially Standard Oil of New Jersey, were already involved in Latin America. Her brother himself had worked down there.

Tarbell described the end of their interview: "I say that I hope he doesn't feel that I have troubled him unnecessarily. He says, 'I think it was fine of you to tell me all this and I am very grateful.' I told him that it all came up in the way of editorial talk and it was not mere gossip, or any intent to gossip, and that everybody, so far as I knew that knows anything of this was loath to say anything about it lest they might injure a man that they felt was of great value to the country."[28]

Hoover apparently satisfied Tarbell, but one discrepancy throws Hoover's story into doubt. The Teapot Dome and California leases given to Sinclair and Doheny were a subject of wide controversy when

Tarbell and Hoover discussed them in May 1922. On April 22, 1922, newspapers announced that Senator Miles Poindexter called for an investigation of the leases. On May 5, Tarbell talked to Hoover in Washington and told him she disapproved of the contracts. One would have to have had to be much further removed from public opinion than was the Secretary of Commerce to doubt that Tarbell meant Teapot Dome, Sinclair, and Doheny when she brought up naval oil contracts.

In any event, at that point the contracts were merely questionable. They became a national disgrace after it was learned that Secretary of the Interior Albert B. Fall and the Republican party coffers had profited directly from Sinclair and Doheny who held these leases. If Hoover was not perfectly candid with Tarbell—and it cannot be proved that he was not—he may simply have wanted to distance himself from the scandal.

Hoover was, after all, recognized everywhere as a possible presidential candidate. By the time he talked to Tarbell he had already seen numerous political careers ruined by the exposé. The Republican party had by then been discredited for accepting seventy-five thousand shares of stock from Sinclair Oil, the implication being that this gift was a payoff for past and future favors. As for the Democrats, their leading candidate, William McAdoo, son-in-law to former President Woodrow Wilson, was found to have done unrelated but profitable legal work for Edward Doheny, a prominent beneficiary of the Elk Hills-Teapot Dome leases. *The Springfield Republican* best summed up how the guilt by association damaged the Democratic front-runner. It nicknamed him "McAdieu."[29]

Until the Watergate disclosures of the 1970s, Teapot Dome was the country's greatest scandal and it reeked with the corruption of the oil business. It was a story tailor-made for Tarbell, who was always avid for news of the business and who kept up with her old oil sources. Oddly enough, she never entered into the controversy. The closest she came to discussing it was a short article she wrote for *The New Republic* on November 14, 1923. She pointed out that finally, more than a decade after the Supreme Court's paper dissolution of the Standard Oil Company, the divisions were starting to compete with each other. Possibly alerted by what she had heard at William Boyden's dinner party, she wrote that the Midwest arms of Standard Oil—Standard Oil of Indiana and the Prairie Oil and Gas Company which both produced and refined oil—were trying to undersell the Easterners—Standard Oils of New York and New Jersey—which only refined. At last, she said, competition was rearing its head. Tarbell asked hopefully, "Is the Standard Oil Company crumbling within?"

Despite the fact that she peppered away at Standard Oil, John D. Rockefeller's son sought her advice on a matter of importance to him. In the late 1910s, he hired a man named William Inglis to help his father evaluate both Tarbell's and Lloyd's books and to reply to their charges. Transcripts of these interviews show that the elder Rockefeller, still vigorous and alert, sidestepped all criticism. His son was at first satisfied. He wrote Inglis: "To be able to take the words out of her own mouth and prove the case against [Tarbell] is of the utmost value, and I am so glad that father is pursuing this study with you with his customary patience and thoroughness."[30]

In 1924, intending to prepare a book, John D., Jr., whom Tarbell met at the Industrial Conference in 1919, asked her to review his father's comments, and brought them to her apartment on Gramercy Park. Tarbell read the material carefully and was assured that Rockefeller had merely sidestepped all charges and in no way exonerated himself. Apparently she convinced his son on this point, for he wrote to George Vincent, president of the Rockefeller Foundation and son of that Bishop Vincent who cofounded the Chautauqua Institute: "Miss Tarbell has just read the biography manuscript and her suggestions are most valuable and quite in line with some of those which you had made. It seems clear that we should abandon any thought to the publication of the material in anything like its present incomplete and decidedly unbalanced form."[31]

Ida Tarbell was again captivated by the story of petroleum and planned a third volume of *The History of the Standard Oil Company* which would again attack Rockefeller. She even obtained financial backing from Samuel McClure who had lost, and was regaining, control of his magazine. Her old chief offered her seven hundred fifty dollars plus two hundred fifty dollars' worth of stock for each of some dozen planned articles, and Tarbell was ready to plunge in, to tell the story of the opening of the Southwestern oil fields, of Standard Oil's international war with Dutch Shell for mastery of the world's oil, and to delve into rumors that the real story behind Teapot Dome was Standard's inside war for control of the business.

In the meantime, interested people had long found it impossible to buy copies of *The History of the Standard Oil Company*. In frustration, a rising attorney in Louisiana named Huey Long, then beginning a career that would take him to the governorship and the annals of demagoguery, offered to tell her everything he knew about the Standard Oil Company and to pay her one hundred dollars if she would send the volumes to him. Many, Long among them, insisted that the Standard had bought up all the books to keep them away from the public. Whether or not this was true, it was certain that her books were caught in the break-up of the McClure group. The plates traveled to Moffat, Yard and Company, then went to Doubleday, where Tarbell would not allow them to remain because that company published Rockefeller. G. P. Putnam's Sons offered to publish her history but finally Macmillan acquired the rights. Macmillan held off reissuing her first two volumes in anticipation of the updating she planned, but she never actually began the job. Thus was lost whatever Tarbell might have contributed to the episode of Teapot Dome.

In 1924, rather than institutionalize her brother Will, she installed him and his wife at her Redding Ridge "retreat" near her niece Clara. Since Tarbell bore the financial responsibility for the entire family, she turned from oil to what would be more immediately profitable—a biography of Judge Elbert H. Gary, chairman of the U.S. Steel Corporation. She convinced McClure to accept these installments in lieu of her oil exposé.

Gary's was not a life she was eager to write and she at first declined. As she wrote to Rutger Bleeker Jewett, editor of Appleton-Century: "As I look at him he is one of the best types that the 'hard-boiled' big business period has produced, but the best of that period does not stir me to great enthusiasm or make me desire to hold him up as a model."[32] That was in January 1924.

Refusing to accept her answer, Judge Gary said he would open all his material to her. However, that would not have laid him open to an exposé, even if Tarbell had had the heart for it. Gary sent her a memo saying that if she found anything distasteful she would not have to go on—she would be paid for her time and her materials would be taken over by someone else. Her fee would be ten thousand dollars for the book and another ten thousand for serialization.

She temporized. She wrote her publisher in late February: "I have too much respect for my remaining vitality to use it up on the U.S. Steel Company and its head, even a great one." Then she went off for a lecture tour stretching from Bradford, Pennsylvania, to Pawhuska, Oklahoma, where she was stricken by near-pneumonia. By June she decided to work on the book, but without a contract; and by September she totally capitulated. She told Jewett on September 3 that she would start at once if he would send her weekly checks for one hundred fifty dollars or six hundred per month as he chose. Six days later Gary let it be known that he wanted her to start immediately.

Publicly, she insisted that she was glad to write about a good businessman for a change, that she felt honor-bound to balance the picture she had created of American businessmen; to put, as the late Teddy Roosevelt had asked so long before, "more sky in her landscapes" and less dirt. But her history with Gary indicates that she had to swallow hard and suffer much before she allowed herself to earn her money this way. She had never liked Gary. During the Industrial Conference in 1919, which Samuel Gompers had sabotaged by refusing to discuss anything but collective bargaining, she wrote Phillips that she was also disappointed by Gary's insistence on arbitration as the means of settling labor disputes. Tarbell would have liked each man to be more willing to compromise.

Moreover, she had interviewed Gary in 1911 for her series on the humanizing of factory conditions and she told him he would have to pay more attention to the problems of labor.[33]

Gary, who had been a right-hand man to J. P. Morgan, lacked the force of builders like Rockefeller, Carnegie, and Morgan. Gary was the prototypical corporation man, but he did have certain achievements to his credit. In a new age of regulation of corporations, he avoided the appearance of monopoly while preserving the reality. He was a master of public relations and a champion of the rights of stockholders. Gary insisted that they be informed about the state of U.S. Steel and he prevented its officers from profiting from inside information. He adopted a stock purchase plan for employees in 1903, but he held workers to a twelve-hour day and to grueling fortnightly twenty-four-hour shifts.

The major weakness in Tarbell's book, which was published in late 1925, was that it was so sympathetic. Once she wrote that consolidation of an industry served only to boost a commodity's cost to the consumer. In the Gary biography, she praised him for eliminating competitors and thereby forging a stronger steel industry.

Who knows if Tarbell did not intend the public to read between her sugared lines? A much-quoted passage on page eighty-one of her book showed how Gary helped Morgan get around the law by legal methods. The Tarbell of 1902 would not have approved of such finagling. The Tarbell of 1925 offered it as an example of Gary's acumen.

The response of *The Nation*, which was never consistent in evaluating Tarbell, was indicative of the way most reviewers greeted her effort. In an April 14, 1926, review titled "St. Elbert of the Heavenly Trust," Benjamin Stolberg charged that Tarbell had never really been critical of business practices, she had simply been personally angry that Rockefeller "squeezed the Tarbell fortunes dry." He said, "This book is receiving wide notice, certainly not on its own merits for it is a rather shoddy performance which ordinarily would command no more than a stick or two. It has, to be sure, the subtly worked attraction of being somewhat pathetic: for Miss Tarbell to have sunk to the reduction of complicated facts into simple falsehoods is a bit sad . . ."[34]

The partisans of Standard Oil were delighted. William Inglis, who had interviewed John D. Rockefeller, Sr., about *The History of the Standard Oil Company*, was gleeful. He wrote to the son's secretary, "What do these reviews show? Do they not declare that the author has—perhaps unconsciously, certainly unintentionally—destroyed herself? If she was right in denouncing the Standard Oil men, how can she be right in praising the steel men, who followed in the path the Standard Oil men made?"[35]

In the midst of this criticism, her preeminence as a Lincoln biographer was assailed. In 1923, she had published *In the Footsteps of the Lincolns*, tracing the history of the family in America; it was the fruit of her meditations on Lincoln and her years of research. Critics acknowledged her work, while complaining that she was more than ever the biased devotée. Some eighteen months later, Carl Sandburg, whose poetry had won a special Pulitzer award in 1919, produced *Abraham Lincoln: The Prairie Years*, which won glowing praise for its literary and biographical merit. Sandburg had done herculean library research and had sought Tarbell's advice. To show his thanks, he sent page proofs to her and one other Lincoln scholar. "Yourself and Oliver R. Barrett [collector of Lincolniana] are the only persons receiving advance sheets as you are the two who have helped me most," he said. Her reaction was generous and enthusiastic: "Your method is so like you and gives a quality of freshness to material which delights me. I believe you've done a new kind of book."[36]

There are signs she was daunted by Sandburg's achievement and by his power as a writer. In her memoirs she observed: "We all come to rest our case on the work to which we have given our best years, frequently come to live on that, so to speak. When the time comes that our field is invaded by new workers, enlarged, reshaped, made to yield new fruit, we suffer shock. We may put up a 'No trespassing' sign, but all to no use." Benjamin Thomas quoted her as musing: "I am such a slave to facts, dates and things I mean, that I fail to see the great facts often."[37]

She had come to an age of reflection. Now in her late sixties, Ida Tarbell observed that the world simply repeated itself and that events mattered far less than individuals. She kept her friends for life, but death deprived her of the two she least expected to lose. John Siddall died of cancer in 1923 at the age of forty-eight, having become prey to a bitterness that mocked all his former optimism. In 1925, fifty-year-old Bert Boyden was felled by pernicious anemia which he had contracted in Poland during the war. Near the end, he struggled up the stairs to Ida's apartment for one last visit while she watched him, smiling brightly and pretending she saw nothing amiss.

And by now the gay atmosphere of Ida's Twin Oaks was gone. Will's arrival meant the end of real entertaining. As she observed to a correspondent: "My little farm turned out to be a family sanitarium where keeping people in health instead of raising things from the land became the main object."[38] Ida gave her bedroom to her brother and an adjacent one to Ella. For herself she took a narrow downstairs room with a single window. Her plain iron bedstead was softened by a coverlet made by her mother from scraps of a quarter century of Tarbell gowns.

Ida forgave Will everything, even episodes when he held them at gunpoint or threatened to kill Ella and himself so that they would not have to freeze to death during the winter. Sarah alone took Will to task. In turn, he charged Sarah, who had bought five acres from Ida in 1920, with embezzling Ida's funds, and attempted to have Sarah jailed. Ida professed that her only consolation for these embarrassing scenes lay in finding Will's behavior terribly interesting. She once defended him: "Let me say that I consider my brother a remarkable person, great possibilities combined with irresponsibility, immense egotism, charm, gaiety, but in money matters incapable of holding on to anything, generous, indifferent to accumulation, quick to sacrifice if irritated or stirred to pity, an amazing creature."[39]

The periods when Will was subdued hurt her more than his rantings. Ida told Roseboro at one point that Will seemed to accept his situation: "It breaks my heart," she said, "but it is immeasurable relief to those who are with him constantly, to Ella. When he was so stormy and rebellious and intolerant; pouring himself out against every one all the time it was terrible for her [his wife]. It was never hard on me—I was too interested."[40]

During the peaceful days, the three old people—Ida, Will, and Ella—would sit before an open fire, preferring the soft flames of an old-fashioned lamp to harsh electric light as they listened to the radio. Occasionally, the name of Ida Tarbell came crackling over the air. Her story, "He Knew Lincoln," had been dramatized February 12, 1924, on *The Eveready Hour*, the first sponsored network broadcast. Sometimes she was interviewed because of her value as one of America's most interesting women or because of her merit as a relic of a long-gone America. Tarbell said that whenever the Redding Ridge group heard her name announced the others looked at her in astonishment and she would feel that she had done something criminal.

Aside from her family, Ida still allowed few people to intrude upon her time. Her preoccupation was work, as a woman named Ada Peirce McCormick, whom she met in 1923, soon found out.

McCormick, a round little woman in her thirties with hair perpetually escaping from her chignon, was better at activity than accomplishment. Her family had made a fortune in Maine timber and her brother Waldo was an accomplished painter. Wedded to an insurance man, Ada decided her expertise was marriage and she arranged to give a course on the subject to three hundred students at Bucknell University in Lewisburg, Pennsylvania. Her first lesson was how to make a notebook from brown paper where students could draw funny pictures about matrimony. Later in life, McCormick threw herself into such projects as the effect of television violence on children, the threat of the atomic bomb, and the force of Gandhi. In these years, however, she was the typical poor little rich girl.

Her own mother had not been very affectionate, and Ada ever after looked for a substitute. She thought she found one in her godfather's wife, in the mother superior of an Episcopal convent, and finally in Ida Tarbell. To her, Ida Tarbell seemed a "tall, stalwart-looking woman in white so wholesome looking and suggesting the picket fences of New England and cookie jars, and your favorite aunt, and Jo March grown up."[41]

The first stage of Ada's Tarbell campaign was to write letters which she hoped would provoke response—did Ida agree with Anita Loos that gentlemen marry brunettes? Finding such chat ignored, she sought advice on how to write. Eventually, Ida recommended that she apply to Viola Roseboro, who consulted for a fee.

Ada thought Viola a genius for suggesting she use strong verbs and substitute nouns for pronouns, but she did not give up on Ida Tarbell, a determination that would prove to be a mixed blessing to the beleaguered journalist.

Only two assignments, both undertaken for *McCall's Magazine*, promised to equal the importance of the work of Tarbell's earlier years, but she allowed deadline pressures to rush her.

In 1925, *McCall's* commissioned her to do a story on the deflating of the Florida land boom. It was the first journalistic work Tarbell had done since the Arms Limitation Conference, and she hoped that it might limber her up for serious writing again. She agreed to write three articles of ten to twenty thousand words each for sixteen thousand dollars less expenses. Her schedule was punishing. She arrived in Florida on February 20, 1926, and delivered the first article a week later, the second on March 15 and the third on April 15. It was more of a jump start than a limbering exercise.

She traveled the state for several months interviewing civic leaders, speculators, architects, natives, and hoboes. The Florida land boom was an emblem of the 1920s, the ultimate in boosterism and get-rich-quick hot air. Around 1922, promoters and entrepreneurs who had bought up Florida land sought to "subdivide" and sell it to winter-weary Northerners at a huge profit. After an initial rush, buyers became less plentiful. Fierce hurricanes and stories of those who had been hoodwinked slowed the rush and values dropped. Tarbell reached Florida at the crest of the frenzy. She wrote Phillips from Gainesville that Floridians now longed for slow, steady development: "The boom is flattening out unquestionably and all Florida is hoping for farmers to come and save them—and they've run out of land [to sell]." She foresaw a healthy future for the state once speculators left and thought Florida a good investment: "I'd love to buy twenty acres," she wrote Phillips, "but don't worry. I won't. I'll probably never see the place again."[42]

Tarbell had reason to be proud of her seventy thousand words titled

"Florida—And Then What?" which ran from May to August 1926. It was a wonderfully descriptive history of Florida with an explanation of its imbalanced economy. *McCall's* was sufficiently impressed that the editors sent her off on another great news story—the phenomenon of Benito Mussolini.

It was more investigation on the gallop—a four-part series on Mussolini's regime for twenty-five thousand dollars. The editors wanted her first article by August first, thinking the world situation so volatile that delays could evaporate the value of her report.

Tarbell said of the assignment: "Uneasy as I was over the way things were going in the United States, I vaguely felt that when I was asked to go look all this up that possibly there were lessons there . . . However," she added with characteristic honesty, "the real reason I went to Italy was because I was offered so large a sum that I though I could not afford to refuse."[43]

It was regarded as a dangerous undertaking. An undersecretary of state predicted she would be arrested. Others told her she dare not speak French while there. Her old friend August Jaccaci, now ensconced in Vence, France, and passionately attached to his young and beautiful Italian housekeeper, told her she would be searched and warned her not to carry any writing that could be construed as hostile to Mussolini.

Only what she called her "natural dislike of giving up an undertaking" kept her from refusing the assignment. At age sixty-nine, with a manic-depressive brother to support, she had no appetite for international intrigue. The one concession she made to fear was to practice the Fascist salute, just in case, in her Paris bedroom. The fact that none of the dire predictions came true disposed her even more favorably to Italy.

Tarbell made Rome her headquarters and she traveled to the agricultural south, to San Marino and Calabria where Mussolini was encouraging new methods of growing wheat more productively; to the industrialized north, to Milan, where the Pirelli firm was making underground cables for Chicago; and to Turin, with its hydroelectric and Fiat plants. She was as fascinated by these as she had been by America's modernized factories. Seeing her interest and adventurousness, young engineers took the aging Tarbell high up on girders and trestles to show her their work, much to her delight.

In Rome, in the early weeks of August, she was doing some research in the embassy and saw the ambassador, Henry P. Fletcher, a one-time Rough Rider, who urged her to interview Mussolini immediately. She tried to tell Fletcher that she was wholly unprepared, that she wanted to change from her morning dress into something more formal. He insisted she go immediately, so she went directly to Mussolini's headquarters in the Chigi Palace. For ninety minutes she waited in a room filled with petitioners ranging from peasants bearing a statue they had dug up on their property to an admiral who wanted to report on the fleet at Ostia. When at last she was led toward Mussolini's office, visions of the imperial despot's bulldog jaw and bulging eyes filled her head. Instead of organizing her thoughts, she pictured a very small Ida traversing an interminable room where a large dictator sat rigid at his desk, ready to bark orders and have her thrown out. When the door opened, however, she saw *Il Duce* a scant sixty feet away and he was smiling. Robust, forty-three, he shook hands and said, in English, "I'm so sorry to have kept you waiting. You must be very tired." Switching to French, which he spoke more fluently, he took control of the interview and asked her what had most interested her about Italy. He was delighted that she had noticed his housing projects and pontificated: "No nation can survive, no people can be happy, when the home life of the manufacturing and industrial classes is miserable and unfit."[44]

He ended the interview, which he extended from five minutes to thirty, by kissing her hand. She left, flustered and relieved, regretting she had not mentioned William James, whom Mussolini was said to have admired. Much as *Il Duce* charmed Tarbell, he extended to her only a minimum of the courtesies he often permitted the foreign press. He allowed other journalists besides Tarbell to sit in his presence if their countries were sufficiently important, and invited some to his home. Apparently, *McCall's* did not rate sufficiently high for him to meet her at the door of his office; yet he did allow her to walk, not run, the twenty yards to his desk.

Tarbell was not the only one of the old McClure crowd to appreciate Mussolini's forceful manner. Sam McClure also met him that year and wrote to his wife: "We had a beautiful talk . . . [Mussolini] is full of force & Charm and kindliness. It made my heart beat hard for a long time after I left him."[45]

Just thinking about *Il Duce* caused Steffens to wax bombastic: "God said, 'I will have a political thunderstorm, big enough for all men to notice and not too big for them to comprehend, and through it I will shoot a blazing thunderbolt that will strike down all their foolish old principles, burn up their dead ideas, and separate the new light I am creating from the darkness men have made.' And so He formed Mussolini out of a rib of Italy."[46]

Viola Roseboro was vacationing in Italy at that time and joined Ida in Rome and Siena. She described Ida's reaction to the despot: "Mussolini certainly did put the comehither on the statesman lady . . . The rascal knew what he was doing. . . . Ida was moved to great pleasure in the power combined with the winsomeness in the man as she found him. She found my distaste for his public self, his bombastic talk, his awesome poses, rather silly, not important enough to resent. She explained his Kaiser Wilhelmlike speeches by saying he was an Italian speaking to Italians; she who always hates with such an inborn hatred any loose tall talk."

Roseboro detected more eloquence than wordiness about great figures like Garibaldi and thought she knew why Ida was so tolerant of Mussolini's excesses: "Here was one of the males who in other days and circumstances would have filled little young Ida's dreams for a while . . . I heard her let go about that dimple (chuckling) several times. All those things that are at such a variance with the old work horse she calls herself and to the serious worker she is and is known for pleases me a lot."[47]

They reached Siena in time for its annual festival. The town was packed, but Roseboro managed to find them tiny rooms in a *pensione* with one far-off bathroom for twenty people. Roseboro described Tarbell's delight: "Her chief excitement was when we found out that the horse drawing us was the animal we had seen the day before dressed up in the most gorgeous finery all over himself and leading the grand procession. That was truly a thrill. I mean for her. I was more dully stupid and grown up about it."[48]

Guided by a female archeologist, Ida toured Pompeii, including areas closed to the public. She found Vesuvius less thrilling than Colton's *Common School Geography* had led her to expect, but enjoyed a wild ride over the mountains to see the Bay of Salerno and Ravello. The sight was so lovely she had to force herself to go to bed, then woke up at 4:30 A.M. to see the dawn.

Her soul thrilled to the beauty she was seeing, but sometimes Ida ached with loneliness and exhaustion. She finished her second article by the middle of August, rested in Genoa, then went to Turin to begin the third. Each day she worked until five and then went for a walk. Weekly she wrote home, wistfully asking if her pepper plants had come up, if the "mess flower" bed had turned out all right, and if the corn was as tasty as she imagined. She would sometimes catch herself on the brink of buying a postcard for her mother—who had loved to see all the places Ida went.

When she could think of nothing better to do with her free time, Tarbell joined the crowds going to the pictures. While working on the Standard series at the turn of the century, she had relaxed by going to the theater and hissing the villain. In the 1920s, she turned to movies. Turin offered Tom Mix, Charlie Chaplin, Mary Pickford, and Ida's favorite, Rin Tin Tin. She caught the end of an improbable Western and cheered with the audience when the dog saved the day.

Ida returned home at the beginning of November when her report, "The Greatest Story in the World Today," began in *McCall's*. The three-part series was generally favorable toward Mussolini, but cautioned that his autocratic methods required careful scrutiny. In the introduction to her third article, her editor revealed Tarbell's thoughts about the Fascist leader: " 'The Despot with a Dimple'—such might have been Ida Tarbell's description of the world-famous Mussolini after she had finally penetrated the labyrinths of Italian Officialdom and reached not a minotaur, but a very human personality with 'one of the loveliest smiles she ever saw!' The most noted of all America's women journalists found Italy's new dictator a man neither violent nor forbidding, and one who had reached his exalted position through actual ability and force of personality."

Twenty years before, Ida Tarbell had described John D. Rockefeller as a scaly amphibian, but now she seemed intrigued by animal magnetism. Tarbell had not intended to convey Mussolini's Latin charm to her readers, but her comment was widely quoted. It obscured her more prudent remarks. Tarbell wrote that Mussolini's political creed was not entirely convincing to an American disturbed by his private "army" and by censorship of the press, but that he had stirred the Italians, changed daily conditions, and converted thousands into the Fascist ranks.

She saw that he had improved the productivity and efficiency of Italy and opined that in Mussolini, the Italians had found their Moses, and so he would remain: but he had raised expectations so high that he would ultimately have to disappoint. She predicted that like Napoleon he might well overreach himself. Several times she expressed doubt that he would be allowed to live out his natural life. There had been three assassination attempts while she was in Italy. She told friends that she hoped he would survive until *McCall's* concluded her series.

As it turned out, Mussolini held power until 1943, then lived in the protective custody of the Nazis for two more years. But even they could not protect him. He was finally captured and killed by Italian anti-Fascists in 1945.

It was her work, not Mussolini, that Tarbell saw mutilated that year. *McCall's* cut back her articles to accommodate a late-arriving seventy-five-thousand dollars worth of advertising. Twelve years later, when John D. Andrews, secretary of the American Association for Labor Legislation, requested copies of her articles, she sent carbons of her originals and said of what was printed: "The cutting seemed to me to rather destroy the effort I had made to get something approaching a logical narrative. It was difficult for me . . ."[49] Roseboro urged her to write a book on Italy, but she never got around to it.

Instead she continued to write for magazines. Prohibition was the big topic now and Ida announced she was against it because it made lawbreakers of everyone.

She still wrote about Lincoln. *The Atlantic Monthly* claimed it had uncovered new Lincoln letters, including some to Ann Rutledge. Tarbell permitted herself to be convinced of their authenticity and lent her prestige to them. Within weeks they proved, to her embarrassment, to be bogus.

Then, in the election year of 1928, she wrote on politics. Her old hero Herbert Hoover was nominated for president, but she was unwilling to help him. She noted that Hoover was, after all, a Republican. Perhaps Ida Tarbell thought she should shield him during the Teapot Dome uproar because she wanted the public to have an opportunity to vote for the man, even if she felt she could not support his party. In the end, she endorsed Alfred E. Smith because of the tariff. She claimed that "something over fifty years ago the Republican party decided to make common cause with one class of citizens, the manufacturers . . . ,"[50] whereas Smith was for the common people.

When Smith lost, her fury was so great that her latent antipathy for women burst forth: "I have always known that you could depend upon my sex for a full measure of prejudice and conservatism, but I did not think it could be so bad,"[51] she wrote a correspondent.

By now, Lindbergh had landed in Paris instead of the Atlantic Ocean, young people thought of themselves as flaming youth, and Sigmund Freud's theories shocked moralists, but Ida Tarbell was unmoved. She held to her beliefs, even those that seemed antiquated prejudices. Almost a decade of writing was still ahead of her, but the most demanding work, and the most valorous, was the financial support of her family and the battle against her own physical deterioration.

Twelve

At Rest

Her body was willing enough to tell her she was getting old, but even if her legs had not begun to stiffen and her hand to tremble violently, the changed world around her would have testified to the passing of time. Headlines about John D. Rockefeller's latest philanthropies had replaced those of years before which questioned how he made his money, and the new generation admired and respected him. On the lecture circuit, she saw villages on railroad lines fade while those along highways flourished. Finally, "Chautauquas" gave way to the increasing popularity of radio and brought an end to Ida's days on the road.

Letters from Ada McCormick continued to fill Ida's mailbox, chastising her for her lack of response. Exasperated, Ida insisted she was far too busy earning her living to have time to attend to personal correspondence. At last, Ada found a way to be important. She offered Ida a loan to help ease her financial problems and sent presents—a necklace, an umbrella, and twenty handkerchiefs. Ida declined the loan and threatened to return future gifts. Sheets and towels appeared in response. Then Ida surrendered to pampering. In her thank-you note she said she was trying to feel "like a lady" in her fine linens, but she no longer knew how to feel grand: "So many ladies rubbed me the wrong way that I became a Barbarian, wearing homespun and ignorant of vanity. Now I'm off on the old lady-track again."[1]

Tarbell and McCormick did not meet again until October 1928 at the Cosmopolitan Club in New York. Ida approached the younger woman doubtfully, not sure she recognized her. Ada in turn was shocked by Ida's appearance. Instead of the strong, ruddy woman she had first encountered in 1923, Ada saw a slight, frail, worn person who looked her years and seemed to need protection. The worshipful Ada took detailed notes on their conversations until Ida started laughing, and brushed away her questions on religion and truth. Nonetheless, Ada resolved she would be both daughter and Boswell to the great Tarbell. Realizing that Ida valued work above all else, Ada claimed that she would turn her own writing abilities toward producing Ida's biography. Tarbell thought the whole idea ridiculous and asked what anyone could make of her life; but, perhaps as a way of repaying Ada for her presents, she answered eager questions. At this time McCormick began to pay Viola Roseboro five dollars for each letter she could provide about her old friend. Needing the money and loving to gossip, Roseboro complied.

Blankets and nightgowns poured in from Ada. Ida protested—weakly—that cheap cotton flannel pajamas were more her style. She noted, "I'm afraid these stamps mean 'Write Ada daily. Use us to send your message.' Well, my dear, I'm afraid you'll not get a daily message save by wireless."[2]

Next Ada proposed a joint savings account—Ida sent her five dollars. Then Ada wanted to hire Ida's investment counselor, a man who had worked on the business ends of both *McClure's* and *The American*. Ida told her to consult her husband and father instead.

Despite Ida's constant anxiety about money, the stock market crash of 1929 did not affect her unduly. She had some seventy thousand dollars invested in bonds and such stocks as American Telephone and Telegraph, Du Pont, the Baltimore and Ohio Railroad, Kennecott Copper, and International Harvester. On October 23, 1929, after stocks had slid downward for some time, she toted up the value of her securities and found she was ten percent poorer than she'd been sixteen days before. She wrote Sarah, "I'm glad I didn't have margins to keep up." On October 29, she read that terrified sellers dumped over sixteen million shares of stock on the market. Fortunes were lost around the country—her friends the Rices were financially pinched the rest of their lives—but Tarbell was confident that if one could hold on and look to the future (she was now seventy-two) everything would turn out all right.[3]

Tarbell was still inundated with assignments. She had agreed to write a book titled *The Nationalizing of Business* on the consolidation of big business for a series Arthur M. Schlesinger, Sr., was compiling. Its due date had been September 1923. She did considerable, though intermittent, research on it at great expense to herself. Completion would have helped her financially—if for no other reason than it would have prevented her from spending her time and money on research materials for it—but she plodded on. She was willing to abuse her talents to make money, but not her ethics. She did not submit her work to the frustrated Schlesinger until 1936.

In the meantime, she wrote a biography of Owen Young, chairman of the board of General Electric and co-author of a plan to readjust German reparation payments. It was published in 1932 and was greeted with the same skepticism that met her favorable biography of Gary. The closest she came to doing a third volume of her *History of the Standard Oil Company* was writing an introduction to *The Birth of the Oil Industry* by a young Allegheny College professor named Paul Giddens. Tarbell had committed herself to too many projects and felt gnawed by obligations. Steady royalties and investments should have allowed her to feel financially secure, but she did not know how long she would be able to work or how much Will and her own old age would cost her. Will's children, who had insufficient incomes and many children to raise, also sought her help occasionally, especially during the Depression. She tried to make sure that, barring her own breakdown, money would continue to flow in.

By 1931, Ada McCormick and her husband Fred had moved to Tucson where Ada arranged for Ida to lecture on biography at the University of Arizona. Ida accepted the invitation not so much because of the income, which she would have earned through magazine articles, but because she hoped Arizona's February sun would warm her wintry bones. In addition, she wanted to see her nephew Scott who with her help had purchased a ranch in Roswell, New Mexico. The train trip west was difficult but fascinating. From her window she saw roads filled with caravans of the unemployed, the Okies of the Depression with their household goods loaded onto trailers, going from state to state seeking jobs. As she neared Tucson, she was stunned by forests of saguaro cacti in the shapes of candelabra, standing as high as fifty feet. In *The Delineator* of March 1932, she wrote that they seemed like creatures, not plants: "Each saguaro is an individual—an individual protected from the touch of its own kind as from the touch of all that moves by an armor of strong slender daggers of its own making, sharp as stilettos, and as dangerous." The thought of such defense seemed a fitting prelude for her meeting with Ada McCormick.

Ada attempted to manage Tarbell's time and activities, but Ida stonily resisted manipulation. Their letters had been affectionate, but once they were together they fought. The tension drove Ida to smoke a cigarette. She told Ada: "One reason I came out here was that I thought after I was under the roof with you for five weeks that you would be more sensible about me. Over-fondness ruins a friendship because the other one can't respond and feels a fraud to take something that he can't pay back in kind."[4]

This and other protestations were recorded as McCormick's biographical interviews continued. Ida had arrived so ill with flu that she had to stay in bed for most of the time that she was not lecturing. As she recuperated, Ada asked about her Paris days, taking down each answer verbatim, even those that trailed off in exhaustion. Then she handed them over to her secretary for typing.

Ida requested that she have her own secretary. Patricia Paylore, twenty-one, had just earned a master's degree and was to be Ida's instrument for circumventing Ada's will. Paylore told the author: "Miss Tarbell had me smuggle in two guest-sized cakes of Ivory soap under Ada's watchful eye. She didn't like the fancy soaps Ada used. Also, she had me take her laundry downtown because she didn't want Mrs. McCormick's maid to bother with it."

Ada frequently complained that Ida was more interested in Patricia and in her hairdresser—to whom Ida gave an extremely generous tip of fifty cents—than in Ada's dinner guests. It was largely true. Patricia only worked for Ida a few weeks before she was felled by chicken pox, but in that time she confided that she was torn between staying at home as her mother desired or going out on her own. Before she left Tucson, Ida told Ada to let her and the girl have a private lunch. Of that meal, Paylore recalled: "Miss Tarbell said to stick by my mother no matter what sacrifices had to be made and she told me to call upon her anytime I needed her."[5]

Ida shared one of her own traumas with the young girl. Paylore arrived one day to find Ida weeping—the *New York World* had shut down. The paper had featured Walter Lippmann, her favorite editorial writer, a man liberal in politics and conservative in morality. "How can I start the day without Walter Lippmann?" she cried, blowing her nose.

Such private moments were few in number. Besides work, there were social demands on Tarbell. Tucson drew Easterners in winter time, among them Jane Addams who faithfully attended Tarbell's lectures. Ada thought Addams and her friends were like schoolgirls, especially after the founder of Hull House impishly took a banana from a table arrangement, then put the peel back in the bowl where she had found it.

That happened before Ida came home. When Ida arrived, vanity prevented her from being as unguarded as the others, who removed their hats to show how careless of convention they had become. Tarbell, who felt she needed a wave, primly kept hers in place.

Ada saw great social possibilities in inviting them all to lunch. "I'm such a heart-to-heart person that I should think that would be much more fun," she told Ida who retorted: "Well, neither Miss Addams nor I are. She'd take her hat and go home if one started any probing . . . She is interested in national issues and that is what we would talk about," Ida insisted. Ada confessed she thought her headstrong, inquisitive manner did alarm Miss Addams.

Also in town were the John D. Rockefellers, Jr., whom Ida saw in the dining room of the Arizona Inn. When the Rockefellers left, Dr. Henry Osborn Taylor, a noted philosopher of history, came over and told Tarbell: "No matter who tells me you're a bad woman, I tell them you're not." By now, Ida's character was getting a low rating from Ada McCormick who was letting friends, including Viola Roseboro, know that Ida was not the guest she had hoped for. When Ida was ill, Ada had the cook serve them dinner on trays in Ida's room and was forced to reschedule engagements she had planned for Ida. Such attentions—which Ida certainly would have preferred to forego—prompted Ada to think she had turned her house into a convalescent home; and when Ida was not suitably grateful, Ada sulked.

Ada showed signs of being jealous of Ida's niece and nephew. One of Ida's main reasons for going to Tucson was that it would be relatively easy for her to see Scott's new home. This visit cut into Ida's hours with Ada, and when the time came for Ida to go, Ada protested that the trip would be much too strenuous. There was some truth to this, of course. On her three-hundred-mile bus journey back from Scott's ranch, however, Ida was thrilled by a sandstorm and blizzard which terrified the other bus passengers; but she later confessed that the trip had brought on a recurrence of hemorrhoids and she took aspirin with a little whiskey to sweat away a cold. She said with some pride: "The proof of the pudding is in the eating, and I am much stronger than other women my age." Ada wrote Phillips, of whom she had heard through Ida and Viola, complaining that Ida was overtaxing her strength.

Ida had barely recovered from her exertions on behalf of Scott when her niece Clara Tarbell Tupper arrived. Clara was now living in the Hollywood area where her husband had taken a job as a screenwriter, and her visit to her aunt was undertaken partly to tell her gently that she was getting a divorce. After Ada heard the news, she chattered about how she herself had worked for stronger divorce bills. Ida wept bitterly over Clara's news and grew enraged over Ada's intrusions, later warning Ada: "I wasn't as mad as I could be. I was outraged at the indignity. I will not be bossed by anyone. I'd given you plenty of hints before. You drove me simply wild fussing over me. I will not stand it."[6]

Aggrieved by Ida's independence, Ada said, in Clara's presence, that Ida kept promises to everyone except herself. Ida shouted, "Never again will I mix business and friendship . . . the longer I stay here the harder it is for me when I get back to New York. I have to keep in with my editors. There are young women pressing in on me all the time." She added that her brother was always terrified that she would never come back whenever she stayed away too long.[7]

After Ida left for home, Ada wrote in her notes: "It wouldn't have killed her to mother me that last morning, meaning baby that I am that if I could have tumbled into bed beside her and put my head against her warmth, that it would have comforted all this soreness out of my heart. I didn't mean that I never got into bed with her when she was having breakfast but it was always as remote as a street parade and twice I did early when she was half awake, but unwelcoming . . ." McCormick recorded their dialogue thus:

Ida: "I'm not used to a bedfellow. You ought to learn to sleep."

Ada: "I never sleep much without Fred."

Ida (*rather irritably*): "Well, you ought to be with Fred."[8]

Finally, accepting that what mattered to Ida was Ida's family, Ada took Ida's grandniece Ella, who was in college in Tucson, under her wing. Starting in 1933, when her magazine income began to dwindle, Ida allowed Ada to lend her money. Tarbell wrote a promissory note stating that she would repay a thousand dollars a year at six percent interest, but when she fell behind, she said Ada would be repaid from her estate after she died.

Ada sent checks to Scott's children; then, as a counterweight to her generosity, she kept all the cancelled checks and headed a ledger sheet on the matter "Finances and gratitude."[9]

Ada McCormick was buying attention, helping a friend, and assuring indebtedness both emotional and financial. But she was also a real help to Ida who once said that Ada had been the first security she'd experienced since she left her job at *The American Magazine*. "You've cushioned my life a little, which isn't always easy materially, and given me the feeling of someone who cares man to man. I'm not one for hero worship."[10] The quotation is from Ada's papers, but they have the sound of Tarbell.

Once Ida was back in New York, she spent her strength as carefully as she spent her money and she made some adjustments. Instead of popping out of bed at seven as she once had, she luxuriated until seven-thirty, musing about the day. As she made her breakfast—a single cup of coffee—she flexed her ankles, touched her toes, did a little limbering dance. Around eleven, her secretary, Thelma Wolfe, arrived to type, handle mail, make the little black bands which held Ida's eyeglasses, and see that Ida's sash was properly tied if she was going out to lunch. At the beginning of each season, Ida asked Thelma Wolfe's opinion of her hats. She tried each on, asked if it were fashionable, sorted her stockings, and straightened her dresser drawers.

Ida's evenings were quiet. She had a low opinion of the cheap fantasy of most movies, but she loved Disney cartoons. She devoured two or three detective stories a week—*Trent's Last Case* by E. C. Bentley and Dorothy Sayers' *Gaudy Night* were two of her favorites—but she often read and reread Virginia Woolf's essay, "A Room of One's Own" which was a testimony to woman's struggle.

Distress over money surpassed her natural reticence. Paul Reynolds had urged her for several years to write her life's story before she finally signed Macmillan's contract in October 1935. She begged Viola Rose-boro to protect her from herself: "It nauseates me to take off my clothes—just the upper garments—in public. Please take on the job, dear Rosie, and don't let me saying anything that is silly."[11]

Tarbell, who shrank from self-examination, decided that hers would be an "external" biography, disclosing as little as possible of her inner life. But as she began reminiscing, idealized memories of her childhood flowed into her dictaphone. By now a mistress of armchair research, she wrote to the New York Public Library and the Library of Congress to find out when *The Police Gazette* was reduced to a smaller format so she could figure out the date (it was October 19, 1867) when she and Laura Seaver had indulged their innocent orgies of pubescent curiosity. While in Meadville attending a trustees' meeting of Allegheny College, she looked around for her old landmarks. The Chautauqua building had been turned into an auto dealership and Flood's house had been torn down.

Writing her autobiography was like cleaning some closet of her heart, discovering deep recesses that yielded both treasure and debris. She was surprised to realize how different she was from the Ida of 1880 or 1910. Whole years seem to have disappeared: "The strangest thing to me as I attempt to review my past is the long strips of my life through which I passed of which there is apparently no memory in my mind, nothing that I see, nothing that I hear, nothing that I felt . . ." she observed in her notes.

She remembered her debt to Robert Walker of Poland, Ohio, and devoted several pages to defending him against charges that he had ever duped William McKinley. By now, her old friend Clara was in a nursing home in Ohio. Tarbell was anguished that her brother's presence at Redding Ridge made it impossible for her to help Clara.

However much it cost her to dredge up her past, according to her correspondence, her publisher was not pleased with her mellow memories. "Macmillan wants more sensationalism," Tarbell wrote Roseboro, "but even though I'm in debt I won't do it. I'll send it elsewhere." Phillips agreed with this stance, but Roseboro noted that Ida's first draft had not even disclosed such harmless intimacies as the fact that she had played with dolls or that she had had any siblings. In response, Tarbell wrote: "I had a brother who died, but I fear that mentioning him cuts too deep."[12] Under Viola's prodding, one doll, Frankie, Jr., Sarah (to whom the book was dedicated), and Will were added to the story of her life.

Possibly because she was reserved about personal relations, she at first omitted John Phillips. When he read her draft and discovered this, he was quite hurt and said so. Her letter of apology was abject. She said she had lain awake all night fretting that he had lain awake worrying over it. "Why did I ever get into this?" she asked him. "Money of course. Money I couldn't refuse when I found out what the price was like." She indicated one of her chapters would be "How I Discovered JSP." That chapter did not appear, but he was given credit and praise whenever possible.

Ada McCormick was not mentioned at all. Tarbell assured her that this book would be the story of a working woman's outside life, and said that if she did not live to finish it she wanted Ada to have the notes and outlines—with the hope that her royalties would cancel all debts.

Ada McCormick caught wind that a book of recollections was in the offing. She wrote to a Macmillan editor that Ida was the support of her brother, nieces, and grandnieces (which was somewhat an exaggeration), and said she hoped her letter might be the introduction to Ida's book. Later, McCormick wrote the same news to Dorothy Canfield Fisher, a popular writer who was a member of the Pen & Brush Club which Ida still headed; and so news of her financial straits reached new ears.[13]

Tarbell had hoped to serialize her book, but few offers came. Edward Weeks of *The Atlantic Monthly* had asked for an early look at her manuscript, but declined it in a letter as brutal as it was honest. He explained that *All in the Day's Work* lacked humor; that her characterizations, because they were uncritical, were bland; and he said that he found she was not a nimble writer. Tarbell took this in good spirit. She answered that she had not sent him a finished manuscript and hoped she would profit from his criticism.[14] She did enliven her memoirs, but it was by no means a spicy tale. It was a straightforward, unassuming book in which modesty shadowed the real achievements of her life. In it she professed to believe that however beleaguered the world might be, a good night's sleep was the antidote to cynicism.

Time had rendered the past benign, but the present still proved to be treacherous. From Viola Roseboro, Ada learned the names of Ida's friends. In November 1936, Ada decided to inform Anne Morgan about Ida's finances, and suggested they take up a collection. Morgan replied that she doubted that Ida would apply their money to her personal needs. Ada rejoined with a sordid description of Ida's situation. That was enough for Morgan, who responded angrily that Ida was "fine and sensitive" and that contributions on a group basis would shame her deeply.

Privately, Morgan then set about to help Ida in a manner that would allow her dignity. Two months later Tarbell was thrilled to receive a contract from Pathé Film Company which asked her to serve as historical consultant for a film they were doing on the history of the oil business. Anne Morgan, who had proposed the idea, acted as Tarbell's agent.

In these days, Ida Tarbell's hand often shook so violently that it rendered her dictaphone useless. She could no longer hold the microphone steady. Once she was able to control her shaking hands in public by clasping them. Now she sat on them. Not satisfied with the explanation that such infirmities were the result of old age, she began to research palsy and found out about Dr. Henry Parkinson and the disease to which he had given his name. When she confronted her doctor, who had kept her ailment a secret from her in an attempt to be kind, he confirmed her diagnosis, but predicted that she would probably live a hundred years. Far from feeling reassured, she wondered how she would ever be able to support herself.

Soon after that her ramrod posture failed and she would find herself pitching forward. Instead of walking, she jerked herself along with crab-like movements. Other Parkinsonian symptoms—restlessness, fatigue, depression—just blended with the typical condition of old age.

Family illnesses threw the Tarbell siblings into panic. Will was deeply wounded when he learned Ida had Parkinson's disease. When he tried to express his gratitude for her help, she cut him off, unwilling to let him acknowledge that she supported him.

As much of a burden as he was, Will was very dear to Ida. When he suffered a heart attack in early 1934 and snow-packed roads hampered efforts to get him to a Bridgeport hospital, Ida was so overwrought that she had to stay with Sarah for several weeks until word came that Will would recover. Of them all Sarah, who had always been the sickliest, was the most matter-of-fact about illness, although she too experienced the breaks and strains of old age.

On November 5, 1937, Ida Tarbell was eighty years old. The outpouring of affection in response to her birthday totally amazed her. It took her and her secretary two days to open all the letters and arrange all the flowers. A milestone-loving media hailed her as if she were a rare and valuable piece of folk art whose beauty lay in its age and usefulness. The Pen & Brush Club, which since 1913 had refused to elect anyone else its president, gave her a tea; Tarbell read paeans to herself on editorial pages and attended *The New York Times* Book Fair in the newly opened Rockefeller Center built by the fortune she had worked to discredit.

In interviews she took the opportunity to speak out against Hitler and to caution that the New Deal was promising more than it would be able to deliver. An interviewer for radio's *Heinz Magazine of the Air* asked her what it was like to be the dean of American letters. She replied that her claim to fame was working into her eightieth year. After a *New York Times* reporter asked if she would ever quit working, she quipped: "I can't. I don't come under Social Security."

Her birthday dinner reunited her with the John Finleys, the Bakers, and Sam McClure who dominated the evening with tales of his marriage, courtship, and the creation of the magazine. "We all listened as if we'd never heard the stories before,"[15] Tarbell wrote Roseboro gaily. Now when her old friends met they scrutinized each other's health and appearances closely, partly out of concern and partly from a competitive spirit.

Titusville also honored her in these last years of her life. In January 1939, when she was eighty-one, the tall, frail woman wrapped in a black lamb-trimmed coat, slowed by age and Parkinson's disease, revisited the old Tarbell house on Main Street, where a photographer asked her to pose for The Associated Press. She did, with her glasses slightly askew on her nose. Her car drove down the snow-covered hill where she and Will used to slide on his sled, "The Red Devil," to the place where Monsieur Claude tried to help her speak French, and the Benson Library which she had encouraged local women's groups to build but which had not carried *The American* because of its anti-Standard leanings.

Titusville gave her a Recognition Dinner in the high-school gymnasium catered by the cafeteria staff of the YMCA. After her old friend Annette Farwell Grumbine introduced her, Ida rose and three hundred people stood with her. During their long and enthusiastic ovation, she could not hide her tears. She tried to be humorous: "I have been writing for forty or more years," she said, "but never before has anything like this occurred." She recalled her friendships, not trusting herself to mention the name of Josephine Henderson who had died a decade before, and said: "It was lucky for me that my family came to Titusville. I received the best instruction in life in this city and the good things given to me in those early years have remained with me. I got a good start here and I shall always consider Titusville my home and later I shall rest in beautiful Woodlawn [Cemetery], no more beautiful spot in the world."[16]

The blessing of long life is debatable. In her last years, Ida Tarbell shouldered more responsibilities even as her shoulders hunched with age. She seemed to soften; her capacity for kindness seemed only to grow. Once when she required hospitalization in New York for heart trouble, she insisted that the doctor not admit her to St. Luke's because her secretary's husband had died there and she didn't want Mrs. Wolfe to have to return to the place that had brought her pain.

As Viola Roseboro wrote McCormick: "She seems to me to . . . get warmer as she grows older. There is a marvelous warm good will that emanates from her; that is the word; it is not announced, it radiates. All sorts of people I find feeling it, along with her intrinsic importance."[17] Her own fatigue increased her empathy for others. Increasingly, Tarbell found herself thinking of a puppy that she had found in 1906 after she left McClure. She had rented a house in Nantucket and the collie that was there gave birth. The weakest of the litter kept crawling away to die, but Tarbell would bring it back to the sun. Over and over the puppy kept struggling away, trying to find a place to die in peace. She thought she understood that puppy now.[18]

She started work on a new book—*Life After Eighty*—so that old age would provide her with material, if nothing else. She asked Dr. John H. Kellogg for literature on his Human Betterment Institute at Battle Creek, Michigan. He responded by sending her samples of his many products. Apparently in the interests of science, the once-decorous Tarbell made a full report on her bodily functions: "That LD-Lax of yours has been especially effective. I followed directions in taking it and think it has been particularly welcome to my colin [*sic*]." After thanking him for helping her "digestive apparatus," she admitted: "I would like to join your Autocracy of Health, but I am afraid I am not militant enough in that regard to tea, coffee, alcohol and tobacco and all that clan for your ranks. I like a glass of sherry now and then and when I have a cold a bit of whisky. And I do drink a cup of coffee, though I like Postum. I hope this confession will not cast me into the outer darkness of your opinion."[19]

Her charm was deceptive. She wrote Viola Roseboro that she was suspicious of health products, having tried Kellogg's without enthusiasm. Often the two old ladies exchanged letters consisting of nothing but wild and wavy lines. No one will ever know if the correspondents could comprehend each other.

Death notices intrigued her. Scanning the headlines, she saw that heart attacks claimed many. "If I didn't do as [the doctors] told me I saw I was headed for the obituary column," she gamely wrote in her manuscript. "Mr. P.," as she called her disease, had rendered her hand useless, so at eighty she taught herself to type. Her heart allowed her to sit up only an hour a day, and she was firmly limited to this by nurses and a vigilant Sarah. Often she used the time to write to Phillips. Margins and shift keys defied her, as did the spacing bar; and for some time she made exclamation points by combining a period with a capital *I*. In a letter which displayed these technical difficulties, she told Phillips: "What disturbs me is that I am so slow. If I could write quickly I believe I could have a lot of fun, for to my surprise I can compose on the machine quite as well as with my pen."[20]

Her New York apartment had been her working studio but was now a great expense. In 1940, she closed it with much regret; it was a visible

sign that her working life in the world had ended. Worried about finances, Ida rented out the Little House that she had once lent Clara,
and sold forty of her fifty acres. She wrote Alice Hegan Rice of her life:
"I am not allowed to step up or down, so we have rigged up . . . a little
apartment especially for me—a study, a bathroom, a bedroom and
dressing room. My friends in New York who live in steam-heated places
(and I suppose in Louisville too) fear that I'll freeze to death. Indeed,
my only trouble is being too warm, and when the thermometer falls to
zero, which it has on several occasions, it's so exciting to take care of all
the cold spots—there are plenty of them in such an old house as this. I
always had an idea weather was one of the most interesting things in the
world and I know I am right now. The beauty of the view from my
windows gives me unending joy . . ."[21]

She seems never to have acknowledged any self-pity. Income tax in-
furiated her, but she did not resent family demands. She arranged for
her nieces to inherit a larger share of her estate than Scott to offset her
aid to him through the years; only to protect Sarah from having to
watch over Ella as well as herself did she ask Will's children to allow
their mother to live with them.

During Will's last illness, his wife Ella went to stay with their daughter Esther. After he died in March 1941, Esther wanted Ella to return
to Redding Ridge. Ida wrote Phillips of the prospective meeting: "It's
going to be a rather messy gathering, I fear. I thought I had things fixed
up for the rest of my life, but I seem to have upset not only my own but
the family apple cart. Now if Hitler comes over he will finish the job
and in that case I shall go about shouting HEIL PHILLIPS . . ." Her
exclamation point was an asterisk and a dash.[22]

There was much fear that the Germans would attack America's
coast, and the people of Connecticut prepared for it. Tarbell wrote to
her old *McClure's* colleague, Mollie Best: "Sara[h] and I will stay here
unless we are ordered out, but I don't look for bombing along the coast
at the moment. It's too obvious, and the blow will come at some unexpected spot if they follow their usual strategy. But we are getting
ready—this Town of 1500 is prepared to take over 600 evacuees from
Bridgeport. I hope they'll do as well when the 600 come as they do in
rehearsing for them."[23]

Sarah, nearing eighty herself and tired by the tasks of finding food in
wartime and coping with ration books, was vigilant about keeping people away from Ida. Few slipped past her—her grandniece Caroline
managed to get in and found Ida expecting to recover and go back to
work. Ada arrived at the house, pushed her way in to Ida's room, and
was allowed to stay exactly one minute.

Sometimes Ida could be querulous, usually over small things. Once
she wanted a loose button sewn on and her nurse asked her to wait.

Wanting the task done at once, she began to cry and recognized then that she had become an old lady. "There was Mr. P. shaking like an aspen at the idea," she later wrote, pecking the words out on her type-writer. "You wanted to be attended to at once. You were old and sick and feeble and 'They' wouldn't sew on a button. It was not the injustice of this babyishness that brought me to terms. It was the comicality of it. 80 years old and ready to cry because a nurse or a guardian burdened with things to be done didn't stop and do something which could wait. Was that what made old age a nuisance for the world—one of the things. I made a resolve I would tabulate, chart, my nuisance symp-toms."[24]

She thought of developing a Montessori system for the aged—a method whereby old and trembling fingers could learn again to thread needles and loop buttons and negotiate the treachery of a bathtub. She and JSP, who had cracked his head when he slipped in the tub, shared these ideas, which were now as significant to them as the trust had ever been, through war-slowed mails.

Of course, Ida Tarbell never finished *Life After Eighty*. Pneumonia, shingles, and the determined ministrations of her sister would not allow her to overtax her strength. Just before Christmas 1943, Ida Tarbell sank into a coma. One newspaper later said that she had a moment of consciousness and requested that carolers sing "Hark the Herald Angels Sing," but that, according to those who were there, was apocryphal. On January 6, 1944, Ida Tarbell died of pneumonia at the Bridgeport hos-pital. As she wished, her body was taken to Titusville, and there the woman who struggled to be both a lady and a success was finally laid to rest.

In life she had never found repose. As a woman in a male world, she felt herself so inferior, especially when glimpsed from the height of her dreams, that she dared not face many aspects of herself. Ida Tarbell was not the flinty stuff of which the cutting edge of any revolution is made. She was a reasonable woman who thought she tried to accommodate herself to circumstances, not to change them. Yet she was called to achievement in a day when women were called only to exist. Her tri-umph was that she succeeded. Her tragedy was never to know it.

Acknowledgments

This is a happy task, shadowed only by the need to omit many names because of lack of space. My thanks go first to Stella Edwards, the librarian of special collections at Pelletier Library of Allegheny College where most of Tarbell's papers are housed. Besides her help, I appreciate her friendship, and that of her husband Sam. I also thank everyone at Pelletier Library, particularly Margaret Moser, the head librarian, and the people at Drake Well Museum. I would like to express my gratitude to Bonnie Smith and Vance Packard, Jr.; Ferdinand Lundberg; Linda Showalter; Rolf Kaltenborn of the Kaltenborn Foundation which gave me a grant; Ellen Steese of *The Christian Science Monitor* whose assignments enabled me to research Tarbell's Paris haunts and The Lincoln Trail; and all the librarians around the country whom I encountered in person and through the miracle of photocopying.

Extra special thanks go to Ida Tarbell's grandnieces, Caroline Tarbell Tupper and Ella Tarbell Price, who gave me much guidance, information, and personal joy, and Lawrence J. Brady, my brother, who read the manuscript in its early stages and provided invaluable help and encouragement.

I sincerely thank my agent, Berenice Hoffman, and my editor, Nancy J. Perlman, who cared about every word of the manuscript, and special thanks to everyone at the University of Pittsburgh Press. The words are very small on the page but my thanks are very great. These are the sorts of people one hopes to encounter in publishing.

I would also like to acknowledge a great spiritual debt to Ida Tarbell and all her friends and relatives, most of whom have gone from the world but who, through their papers, were wonderful company to me over the last several years.

Finally, I honor the New York Public Library, not just the great institution itself, which is truly open to all, but the people there—the librarians who helped me so much, the guards, the people in the cafeteria, and Walter Zervas who "manages," to the extent that such is possible, the Allen Room, where this book was written.

Notes

Some last words are in order. Ray Stannard Baker said that anyone who attempted to write Ida Tarbell's life would have the problem of writing about goodness. This proved to be true, but the real challenge was trying to explain an enigma. "I have often found it difficult to explain myself to myself, and I do not often try," she told her best friend. She was seldom more forthcoming with anyone else, and those who knew her best have long been dead.

Adding to the task of unraveling Tarbell's personality is the difficulty of organizing her papers, which are scattered nationwide in various degrees of disarray. I searched through every folder at Allegheny College, the Drake Well Museum, and the Little Chapel of All Nations. This was daunting, but provided the thrill of a treasure hunt and the opportunity to work with material no one else had ever seen. To aid future researchers, I have given titles of cited manuscripts, memoranda, and so on.

Incredibly, Tarbell did not date the clippings she pasted into her scrapbook. I searched for the dates and page numbers; those I failed to find are indicated simply by their inclusion in her scrapbook at the Drake Well Museum. There is also some duplication of materials. In these notes, I have cited the institution which possesses the original. The private Tarbell family papers are in the collection of Ella Tarbell Price.

Most frequently cited libraries are the Pelletier Library of Allegheny College, Meadville, Pennsylvania; Drake Well Museum, Titusville, Pennsylvania; the Sophia Smith Library, Smith College, Northampton, Massachusetts; the Lilly Library, Indiana University, Bloomington; the Huntington Library, San Marino, California; the Petroleum History and Research Center, the University of Wyoming, Laramie; and the Little Chapel of All Nations, Tucson, Arizona. I have abbreviated the citations, but the locations should be clear.

Other libraries with important documents are the Milton S. Eisenhower Library, The Johns Hopkins University, Baltimore; University of Pennsylvania, Philadelphia; State Historical Society of Wisconsin, Madison; Olin Library, Cornell University, Ithaca, New York; the New York Public Library; the Library of Congress, Washington, D.C.; Swarthmore College Peace Library, Swarthmore, Pennsylvania; Columbia University Libraries, New York City; Rockefeller Family Archives, New York City; University of Illinois at Urbana-Champaign; Bentley Historical Library, University of Michigan, Ann Arbor; Kentucky Library, Western Kentucky University, Bowling Green; Sterling and Beinecke Libraries, Yale University, New Haven, Connecticut; and the Newberry Library, Chicago.

Tarbell's letters are usually indicated by the initials of the most frequent correspondents, such as:

> RSB—Ray Stannard Baker
> AB—Albert Boyden
> CDH—Charles Downer Hazen
> HDL—Henry Demarest Lloyd
> SSM—Samuel S. McClure
> APM—Ada Peirce McCormick
> JSP—John S. Phillips
> VR—Viola Roseboro
> JMS—John McAlpin Siddall
> EMT—Esther M. Tarbell
> FST—Franklin S. Tarbell
> IMT—Ida M. Tarbell
> SAT—Sarah A. Tarbell
> WWT—William W. Tarbell
> WAW—William Allen White

1. AN UNACCOMMODATING CHILD

All of Ida Tarbell's quotes are taken from Chapters 1 and 2 of her autobiography, *All in the Day's Work* (New York: Macmillan Co., 1939), unless otherwise noted.

1. "Petrolia," *The Leisure Hour*, May 12, 1866, pp. 295–301.
2. EMT to IMT, July 1896, Allegheny College.
3. Tucson Dialogues, Little Chapel.
4. IMT to VR, December 9, 1935, Allegheny.
5. Tarbell, *All Day's*, p. 14. Tarbell said here that her friend's name was Ida Hess, but everywhere else in her papers she indicates it was a Laura Seaver, sometimes spelled Seaber.
6. "Notes and Comments in Old Age," Allegheny.
7. Matthew Josephson, *The Robber Barons* (New York: Harcourt, Brace & Co., 1934), pp. 9–11.
8. Esther Tarbell Aldrich, "Grandpa," Allegheny.
9. *All Day's*, pp. 65–66.
10. Tarbell, "The Uneasy Woman," *The American Magazine*, January 1912, pp. 259–62.

2. PANTHEISTIC EVOLUTIONIST

All of Ida Tarbell's quotes are taken from Chapter 3 of her autobiography, *All in the Day's Work* (New York: Macmillan Co., 1939), unless otherwise noted.

1. IMT to John Reynolds, October 25, 1939, Allegheny College.

2. *Allegheny Literary Quarterly* manuscript, Allegheny.

3. Frederick Tisden interview, Allegheny.

4. Iris Barr interview, March 30, 1944, Drake Well Museum.

5. Comments of Robert Walker, Allegheny.

6. *The Youngstown Vindicator*, April 30, 1939.

7. Tarbell, "Woman Suffrage as I See It," Allegheny.

8. WWT to William Bayliss, March 30, 1882, Western American Collections, Beinecke Rare Book and Manuscript Library, Yale University.

3. A YOUNG LADY OF FINE LITERARY MIND

1. *The Chautauqua Assembly Herald* IX, no. 4, p. 1.

2. Mary Mullett, "A Famous Writer Who Never Intended to Write," *The American Magazine*, January 1925, p. 64.

3. Tarbell, "Women in Journalism," *The Chautauquan*, April 1887, pp. 393, 395.

4. Tarbell, *All in the Day's Work* (New York: Macmillan Co., 1939), p. 89.

5. IMT to Ada Vincent, September 18, 1892, Huntington Library.

6. Interview with Iris Barr, March 30, 1944, Drake Well Museum.

7. Harriet Carter, "A Cooperative Experiment," *The Chautauquan*, November 1890, pp. 224–26.

8. IMT to Mrs. George Warnsing, August 31, 1928, Allegheny.

9. Early writing in the Chautauqua Period, Allegheny.

10. "Bee" to IMT, January 25, 1942, Ella Tarbell Price collection.

11. Jesse Hurlbut, *The Story of Chautauqua* (New York: G. P. Putnam's Sons, 1921), p. 239.

12. IMT to her family, February 16, 1893, and August 8, 1892, Little Chapel.

13. Rudyard Kipling, *Abaft the Funnell* (New York: B. W. Dodge & Co., 1909), pp. 180–203; William James, *Talks to Teachers* (New York: Henry Holt and Co., 1900).

14. IMT to Herbert Baxter Adams, March 28, 1893, Herbert B. Adams Collection, the Milton S. Eisenhower Library, The Johns Hopkins University.

15. Tarbell, *All Day's*, pp. 75–76; Tarbell, "Women as Inventors," *The Chautauquan*, March 1887, pp. 355–57.

16. Tarbell, "The Queen of the Gironde," *The Chautauquan*, March 1891, pp. 756–61.

17. Tarbell, *All Day's*, p. 85.

18. Ibid., p. 78.

19. Ibid., p. 88.

20. T. L. Flood to IMT, Allegheny; IMT to her family, n.d., and October 26, 1891, January 25, 1892, February 2, 1893, Little Chapel.

21. IMT to family, January 9, 1892, Little Chapel.

22. Mullet, "Famous Writer," p. 64.

23. Tarbell, *All Day's*, p. 88.

4. UNE FEMME TRAVAILLEUSE

Tarbell's correspondence to her family written from France is in the collection of the Little Chapel of All Nations in Tucson.

1. Tarbell, "The Compatriot," *New England Magazine,* September 1894.
2. IMT to family, September 9, 1891.
3. Ibid.
4. IMT to family, January 19, 1892.
5. Ibid.
6. IMT to family, December 27, 1891.
7. Tarbell, *All in the Day's Work* (New York: Macmillan Co., 1939), pp. 93–94.
8. *Meadville Morning Star,* June 27, 1895.
9. Tarbell, *All Day's,* p. 92.
10. IMT to family, March 1, 1892.
11. IMT to family, November 13, 1891.
12. IMT to family, May 24, 1892.
13. IMT to family, December 27, 1891.
14. IMT to family, July 1893.
15. EMT to IMT, June 29, 1893.
16. SAT to IMT, October 15, 1892.
17. Tarbell, *Madame Roland* (New York: Charles Scribner's Sons, 1896), pp. 232–33.
18. CDH to IMT, March 30, 1896, Allegheny College.
19. Peter Lyon, *Success Story: The Life and Times of S. S. McClure* (New York: Charles Scribner's Sons, 1963), p. 14.
20. Ibid., p. 117.
21. IMT to family, July 1892.
22. IMT to family, December 1893.

5. THE FRENCH SALON

Tarbell's correspondence to her family written from France is in the collection of the Little Chapel of All Nations in Tucson.

1. IMT to family, July 13, 1893.
2. IMT to APM, December 27, 1930, Allegheny College.
3. IMT to APM, September 18, 1936, Allegheny.
4. IMT to family, January 12, 1894.
5. Tucson Dialogues, Little Chapel.
6. Henry Wickham Steed, *Through Thirty Years, 1892–1922,* vol. I (Garden City, N.Y.: Doubleday, Page & Co., 1924), p. 47.
7. IMT to family, June 2, 1893.
8. IMT to family, early March 1893.
9. IMT to family, February 18, 1893.
10. Tarbell, "Pasteur at Home," *McClure's Magazine,* September 1899, p. 333.
11. *McClure's,* July 1894, pp. 177–85.
12. IMT to family, Summer 1893.
13. IMT to family, November 22, 1893.
14. Tarbell, *All in the Day's Work* (New York: Macmillan Co., 1939), p. 143.
15. Madame Roland, *Mémoires de Madame Roland,* with Notes by C. A. Dauban (Paris: Henri Plon, 1864), p. 24.

16. Tarbell, *Madame Roland* (New York: Charles Scribner's Sons, 1896), pp. 288–89.

17. Ibid., p. 173.

18. IMT to Alice French, January 18, 1906, Newberry Library.

19. Tarbell, *Madame Roland*, p. 233.

20. Tarbell, "The Compatriot," *New England Magazine*, September 1894, pp. 83–91.

21. IMT to family, February 1894.

22. "The Edge of the Future," *McClure's*, January 1894, pp. 199–216. All mottoes are cited in this feature.

23. IMT to family, December 1, 1894. All her descriptions of the writers are in this letter.

24. IMT to family, March 16, 1894.

25. Tarbell, *All Day's*, p. 145.

6. THE AMERICANIZATION OF IDA TARBELL

1. Harold Odum, ed., *Masters of American Social Science* (New York: H. Holt and Co., 1927).

2. Gardiner Green Hubbard to IMT, October 31, 1894, Allegheny College.

3. Tarbell, "Napoleon Bonaparte," *McClure's Magazine*, April 1895, p. 436.

4. Tarbell, *All in the Day's Work* (New York: Macmillan Co., 1939), p. 152.

5. *Profitable Advertising*, October 15, 1897.

6. Tarbell, *All Day's*, p. 153.

7. Ibid., p. 191.

8. Ibid., p. 180.

9. VR to APM, 1929 or 1930, Little Chapel.

10. Benjamin Thomas, *Portrait for Posterity* (New Brunswick, N.J.: Rutgers University Press, 1947), p. 110.

11. *McClure's*, November 1895, p. 501.

12. Thomas, *Portrait*, pp. 173, 188–90; Tarbell-Hitchcock correspondence, Smith College.

13. November 6, 1897, memorandum at Allegheny; *Ladies' Home Journal*, February and March 1928. Later biographers, possibly at the suggestion of Tarbell, cited this incident. See Carl Sandburg and Paul Angle, *Mary Lincoln: Wife and Mother* (New York: Harcourt, Brace & Co., 1932).

14. Thomas, *Portrait*, p. 187.

15. *The Nation*, March 1, 1900, p. 164; Scrapbook, Drake Well Museum.

16. IMT to Herbert Baxter Adams, February 21, 1896, Herbert B. Adams Collection, the Milton S. Eisenhower Library, The Johns Hopkins University.

17. SSM to IMT, May 2, 1938, Allegheny.

18. Samuel S. McClure, *My Autobiography* (New York: Frederick A. Stokes Co., 1914), p. 222.

19. IMT to APM, December 16, 1928, Allegheny.

20. CDH to IMT, n.d., but probably 1896, Allegheny.

21. *Leslie's Weekly*, August 27, 1896.

22. William Allen White, *The Autobiography of William Allen White* (New York: Macmillan Co., 1946), pp. 300–301.

23. Ray Stannard Baker, *American Chronicle* (New York: Charles Scribner's Sons, 1945), p. 80.

24. Peter Lyon, *Success Story: The Life and Times of S. S. McClure* (New York: Charles Scribner's Sons, 1963), p. 135.

25. Tarbell, *All Day's*, p. 178.

26. IMT to WWT, 1908, Allegheny.

27. An 1897 memorandum, IMT to Candace Stone, February 24, 1938, Allegheny; SSM to JSP, June 30, 1933, Lilly Library; *The Dial*, March 1, 1899, and *American Historical Review*, April 1899.

28. Tarbell, *All Day's*, p. 184. Langley may well have regarded Rock Creek as his own preserve. He convinced Congress to fund it because the Smithsonian Institution needed live animals as models for its taxidermists. However, Langley's days ended in disappointment. In 1903, shortly before the Wrights flew at Kitty Hawk, North Carolina, he attempted to launch a manned aerodome and failed. Eight years later it was discovered that Langley's machine had merely been launched incorrectly. Had it been fitted with pontoons, it would have flown and Langley would have gotten the credit that went to the Wrights.

29. *National Geographic Magazine*, 1900; IMT to JSP, April 17 and 24, 1900, Lilly Library.

30. Tarbell, *All Day's*, pp. 189–90.

31. Ibid., p. 195.

32. IMT to Herbert B. Adams, February 21, 1896, Herbert B. Adams Collection, the Milton S. Eisenhower Library, The Johns Hopkins University.

33. FST to IMT, April 8, 1899, Collection of Ella Tarbell Price.

34. IMT to Gertrude Hubbard, n.d., Library of Congress.

35. EMT to IMT, July 1896, Allegheny.

36. WWT to IMT, June 9, 1896, Allegheny.

37. Lewis Emery to HDL, March 10, 1903, State Historical Society of Wisconsin.

38. *Profitable Advertising*, October 15, 1897.

39. The obituary of the first Mrs. John S. Phillips appeared in *The New York Times*, May 1, 1888; the description of Jennie is found in VR to APM, "Miss Tarbell," Little Chapel.

40. IMT to JSP, August 18, 1936, Smith College.

41. IMT to Herbert B. Adams, May 24, 1899, the Milton S. Eisenhower Library, The Johns Hopkins University.

42. IMT to SSM, December 13, 1899, Lilly Library.

43. IMT to VR, February 21, 1934, Allegheny.

44. Clara Tarbell Tupper, "My Aunt, Ida Tarbell," *The Villager*, December 31, 1935, Allegheny.

45. IMT to Theodore Dreiser, October 11, 1899, University of Pennsylvania.

46. VR to APM, n.d., Little Chapel. The "masculine" female was probably Mary Bisland who went on to head the London office.

47. IMT Dialogues, Allegheny.

48. White, *Autobiography*, p. 386.

49. *Princeton University Library Chronicle*, Winter 1955, pp. 54–57.

50. IMT to APM, Tucson Dialogues, Little Chapel.

51. John S. Phillips, ed., *Albert A. Boyden: Reminiscences*, privately printed.

52. Cale Young Rice, *Bridging the Years* (New York: D. Appleton-Century Co., 1939), p. 182; Baker Notebook LIV, p. 121, Library of Congress.

53. Phillips, *Reminiscences.*

54. CHD to IMT, August 14, 1899, Allegheny.

55. CDH to IMT, December 4, 1900, Allegheny.

56. Witter Bynner to APM, March 1, 1944, Allegheny.

7. LADY OF THE MUCKRAKE

Most reviews, especially from smaller publications, can be found in the scrapbook in the collection of the Drake Well Museum, often without dates. Tarbell-Siddall correspondence, unless otherwise noted, is from the Petroleum History and Research Center, University of Wyoming. The Henry Demarest Lloyd letters are from the H. D. Lloyd Collection, the State Historical Society of Wisconsin, unless otherwise noted.

1. Ray Stannard Baker, *The American Chronicle* (New York: Charles Scribner's Sons, 1945), p. 117.

2. SSM to JSP, September 14, 1899, Lilly Library.

3. IMT to RSB, April 29, 1901, Library of Congress.

4. Memo in the Standard Oil file, Allegheny College.

5. Tarbell, *All in the Day's Work* (New York: Macmillan Co., 1939), p. 204.

6. Ibid., p. 206.

7. JMS to IMT, September 9, 1901; IMT to JMS, September 11, 1901.

8. IMT to JMS, September 11, 1901.

9. IMT to JMS, January 22, 1902.

10. *Rochester Herald,* 1904.

11. Tarbell, *All Day's,* p. 213, and *All Day's* notes, Allegheny.

12. Ibid., p. 219.

13. IMT to JMS, February 26, 1902.

14. Martin Knapp to IMT, March 3, 1902, Drake Well Museum.

15. IMT to JMS, June 24, 1902.

16. IMT to AB, August 17, 1902, Lilly Library.

17. IMT to Andrew White, August 8 and August 24, 1902, Cornell University Library.

18. IMT to HDL, September 29, 1902.

19. HDL to IMT, April 11, 1903, Lilly Library.

20. IMT to JMS, February 6, 1902.

21. VR to APM, March 2, 1930, Allegheny.

22. Elmer Ellis, *Mr. Dooley: A Life of Finley Peter Dunne* (New York: Alfred A. Knopf, 1941), pp. 146–47.

23. Ellery Sedgwick, *The Happy Profession* (Boston: Little, Brown & Co., 1946), p. 142.

24. Lincoln Steffens to APM, 1930s, Allegheny.

25. M. J. Boutelle to IMT, February 21, 1903, Drake Well Museum.

26. IMT to JMS, February 21, 1903.

27. Lewis Emery to HDL, March 10, 1903.

28. Ibid.

29. IMT to Alice Hegan Rice, January 21, 1933, Allegheny.

30. SSM to Richard Gilder, December 31, 1902, Richard Watson Gilder

Papers, Rare Book and Manuscript Division, the New York Public Library.

31. Mark Sullivan, *The Education of an American* (New York: Doubleday, Doran & Co., 1938) pp. 202–3.

32. James D. Richardson, ed., *Messages and Papers of the Presidents of the United States* (Washington: Bureau of National Literature and Art, 1910), pp. 6645–46.

33. *New York World,* December 17, 1902.

34. Tarbell, *All Day's,* p. 211.

35. VR to APM, 1929, Little Chapel.

36. Cale Young Rice, *Bridging the Years* (New York: D. Appleton-Century Co., 1939), p. 186.

37. Tarbell, *All Day's,* p. 242.

38. *New York Evening Journal,* February 16, 1903.

39. IMT to JMS, March 25, 1903.

40. IMT to JMS, June 4, 1903.

41. JMS to IMT, September 22, 1903, Drake Well Museum.

42. Tarbell, "John D. Rockefeller, a Character Study," *McClure's Magazine,* July 1905; *All Day's,* p. 235.

43. Talk to Rachel Crother's Group, Allegheny.

44. *All Day's,* pp. 227–28.

45. *All Day's,* p. 104; FST to IMT, May 8, 1900, family letters.

46. Notes in the Little Chapel; Clara Tarbell Tupper, "My Aunt, Ida Tarbell," Allegheny; Scrapbook, Drake Well Museum.

47. CDH to IMT, April 24, 1903, and December 23, 1903; SSM to IMT, April 6, 1903, and March 29, 1905, Allegheny.

48. Peter Lyon, *Success Story: The Life and Times of S. S. McClure* (New York: Charles Scribner's Sons, 1963), p. 259.

49. SSM to IMT, n.d. [1905?], Allegheny.

50. SSM to IMT, March 1903; Allegheny.

51. IMT to JSP, December 23, 1903, Lilly Library.

52. *The Reader,* July and December 1904.

53. A. G. Robinson to IMT, December 23 [1903 or 1904], family letters.

54. VR to APM, March 2, 1930, Allegheny.

55. Henry S. Pritchett to IMT, 1900, family letters.

56. Tucson Dialogues, Allegheny.

57. AB to JMS, March 16, 1904, Wyoming; Tarbell's memo is at the Drake Well Museum.

58. WWT to IMT, May 7, 1904, Allegheny.

59. *The Nation,* January 5, 1905, p. 15.

60. *McClure's Magazine,* August 1905, pp. 397–98.

61. *Chicago Record Herald,* July 14, 1905.

62. IMT to AB, March 20, 1905, Smith College.

63. *All Day's,* p. 250.

64. Ibid., p. 247; quotes are from a clipping in the Drake Well Museum Scrapbook.

65. Lincoln Steffens, *Autobiography of Lincoln Steffens* (New York: Harcourt, Brace & Co., 1931), vol. I, pp. 391–93; Arthur and Lily Weinberg, *The Muckrakers* (New York: Simon & Schuster, 1961), p. 432; *Collier's,* December 16, 1905, p. 12.

66. W. G. Joerns, "John D. Rockefeller: A Study in Character, Motive and Duty," *The Arena,* August 1905, p. 156.

67. James R. Garfield to IMT, June 11, 1906, Allegheny.
68. Theodore Roosevelt, *Presidential Addresses and State Papers* (New York: Review of Reviews Company, 1910), p. 741.
69. IMT to Washington Gladden, November 17, 1906, Allegheny.
70. IMT to William Kent, December 13, 1911, Sterling Library, Yale University.
71. Dr. Paul Giddens to author, October 1980.

8. UNEXPLORED LAND

1. Peter Lyon, *Success Story: The Life and Times of S. S. McClure* (New York: Charles Scribner's Sons, 1963), p. 260.
2. IMT to JSP, n.d. [1904], Allegheny College.
3. Lincoln Steffens, *The Autobiography of Lincoln Steffens* (New York: Harcourt, Brace & Co., 1931), vol. I, p. 535.
4. SSM to Hattie McClure, 1904; Peter Lyon, *Success Story: The Life and Times of S. S. McClure* (New York: Charles Scribner's Sons, 1963).
5. SSM to IMT, n.d., Allegheny.
6. SSM to IMT, June 29, 1904, Allegheny.
7. IMT to Hattie McClure, July 12, 1904, Allegheny.
8. IMT to SSM, October 18, 1904, Allegheny.
9. Tarbell's diary is in the Collection of Allegheny College.
10. IMT to Annie Fields, November 9, 1900, Huntington Library; IMT to John Burroughs, July 7, 1905, Collection of Elizabeth Kelley.
11. IMT to APM, undated correspondence, Allegheny; Tarbell's diary, as noted in the text, is the source for all quotes on James's visit.
12. Tarbell's diary, Allegheny.
13. Henry James to IMT, August 14, 1905, Allegheny.
14. IMT to AB, July 20, 1905, Lilly Library.
15. AB to IMT, "the 19th," Allegheny.
16. Esther Tarbell Aldrich, "My Aunt," Little Chapel.
17. Ibid.
18. IMT to JSP, June 1905, Drake Well Museum.
19. Ella Winter and Granville Hicks, eds., *The Letters of Lincoln Steffens* (New York, Harcourt, Brace & Co., 1938), vol. I, p. 173.
20. Elmer Ellis, *Mr. Dooley's America* (New York: Alfred A. Knopf, 1941), p. 225.
21. Drake Museum Scrapbook.
22. IMT to AB, February 11, 1906, Lilly Library.
23. Draft in McClure business file, Allegheny.
24. Curtis F. Brady, "The High Cost of Impatience" (manuscript in the collection of the Lilly Library).
25. TR to SSM, October 4, 1905, Library of Congress.
26. Theodore Roosevelt, *Presidential Addresses and State Papers* (New York: Review of Reviews Company, 1910), p. 716.
27. *Selections from the Correspondence of Theodore Roosevelt and Henry Cabot Lodge, 1884–1918* (New York: Charles Scribner's Sons, 1925), vol. II, p. 248.
28. *Collier's*, May 26, 1905; *Atlantic Monthly*, May 1906.
29. SSM to JSP, April 5, 1906, Lilly Library.
30. McClure business file, April 27, 1906, Allegheny.
31. Ibid.

9. A SECOND CRUSADE

1. JMS to RSB, May 29, 1906, Library of Congress.
2. Ray Stannard Baker, *The American Chronicle*, p. 228.
3. JMS to RSB, May 29, 1906, Library of Congress.
4. William Allen White, *The Autobiography of William Allen White* (New York: Macmillan Co., 1946), p. 387.
5. Esther Tarbell Aldrich, "My Aunt," Little Chapel.
6. AB to RSB, July 24, 1906, Library of Congress.
7. IMT to AB, August 23, 1906, Smith College.
8. Max Eastman, *The Enjoyment of Living* (New York: Harper & Brothers, 1948), p. 406.
9. IMT to AB, July 1, 1907, Lilly Library.
10. William James, "The Powers of Men," *The American Magazine*, November 1907.
11. Lincoln Steffens, *The Autobiography of Lincoln Steffens*. (New York: Harcourt, Brace & Co., 1931), vol. II, p. 541.
12. August Jaccaci to IMT, family papers, Collection of Ella Tarbell Price.
13. Steffens, *Autobiography*, p. 576.
14. JSP to Max Eastman, June 9, 1945, Lilly Library.
15. WWT to IMT, February 27, 1908, Allegheny; IMT to APM, February 1928, Little Chapel.
16. McCormick notes, Little Chapel.
17. IMT to Jane Addams, October 17, 1908, Swarthmore College Peace Collection.
18. Tucson Dialogue, Little Chapel.
19. SSM to IMT, July 1, 1907, Allegheny.
20. Tarbell, *All in the Day's Work* (New York: Macmillan Co., 1939), p. 268.
21. Ida M. Tarbell, "Juggling the Tariff," *The American*, April 1909, p. 578.
22. *All Day's*, pp. 270–71; Tarbell, "In the Hands of the Democrats," *The American*, June 1907, pp. 180–82.
23. *The American*, March 1909, 437–49.
24. Tarbell, "A Tariff-Made City," *The American*, April 1909, p. 578.
25. *The American*, February 1910, p. 570.
26. *The New York Times*, January 16, 1910, p. 1.
27. IMT to VR, October 2, 1909, Little Chapel.
28. *American Economist*, December 9, 1910.
29. Tarbell, "Mr. Aldrich and the Tariff," *The American*, December 1910. This was not the first time that Senator Aldrich and his state had been the targets of muckraking. Lincoln Steffens had "exposed" the state in the February 1905 *McClure's*.
30. Tarbell, "A Tariff-Made State," *The American*, January 1911, p. 354.
31. Ibid., p. 361.
32. IMT to Lillian Wald, January 11, 1911, Columbia University Libraries.
33. *All Day's*, p. 278.
34. Ibid., p. 281; Upton Sinclair in *The Brass Check* and Louis Filler in *Crusaders for American Liberalism*, p. 364, claimed that *The American* relieved author John Kenneth Turner from the series as a concession to business interests. Turner was fired, according to letters from Tarbell and Phillips, for

inaccuracies. The several authors of subsequent installments continued to indict conditions south of the border and America's role there.

35. H. M. Biggs, "An Intimate View of JDR," *The American*, December 1910, p. 106.
36. IMT to RSB, November 2, 1910, Smith College.
37. *All Day's*, p. 306.
38. IMT to RSB, May 3, 1911, Library of Congress.
39. IMT to RSB, February 29, 1912, Library of Congress.
40. Baker Notebook N, Library of Congress.
41. VR to APM, Correspondence, n.d., Allegheny.
42. Arnold Bennett, *The Journal* (New York: Viking Co., 1932–33), November 8, 1912.
43. IMT to WAW, December 1, 1909, Library of Congress.
44. IMT dialogues, Allegheny College.
45. Clara Tarbell Tupper, "My Aunt," Little Chapel.
46. VR to APM, n.d., Little Chapel.
47. John S. and Robin M. Haller, *The Physician and Sexuality in Victorian America* (Urbana: University of Illinois Press, 1974), pp. 34 and 35.
48. Elizabeth Marbury, *My Crystal Ball* (New York: Boni and Liveright, 1923), p. 36.

10. A BAD WOMAN

1. *The American Magazine*, February 1912, p. 430.
2. *The Woman Voter*, June 1912, pp. 7–12.
3. IMT to Florence Kelley, January 9, 1912, Allegheny College.
4. IMT to APM, n.d., and Jane Addams notes, Allegheny.
5. RSB Notebook L, p. 43, Library of Congress.
6. Janet Straner to IMT, n.d., Allegheny.
7. Letters to Scott Tarbell, Allegheny.
8. WWT to IMT, September 9, 1912, Allegheny.
9. "Theory and Practice" manuscript, Allegheny.
10. Ida M. Tarbell, *All in the Day's Work* (New York: Macmillan Co., 1939), p. 260.
11. IMT to Jane Addams, October 17, 1908, Swarthmore College Peace Collection.
12. IMT to VR, September 14, 1938, Allegheny.
13. Ray Stannard Baker, "Our Next President," *The American*, June 1912, p. 140.
14. Tarbell, "Woman Suffrage as I See It," Allegheny.
15. *The Titusville Herald*, August 27, 1977, p. 8.
16. Tarbell, "Disillusion," Allegheny.
17. Tarbell, "Flying—A Dream Come True," *The American*, November 1913, pp. 65–66.
18. *The New York Times*, February 8, 1914.
19. *All Day's*, p. 280.
20. Lincoln Steffens, *The Autobiography of Lincoln Steffens* (New York: Harcourt, Brace & Co., 1931), vol. II, pp. 851–53.
21. IMT to John Fitch, October 6, 1914, Allegheny.
22. IMT to RSB, March 24, 1912, Library of Congress.

23. *New York Herald;* also *The New York Times, New York Tribune,* January 20, 1915.

24. IMT to JSP, October 22, 1919, Industrial Conference notes and reports, Allegheny.

11. WORKHORSE

1. IMT to APM, February 1929, Allegheny College; IMT to John and Ada Vincent, May 21, 1927, Huntington Library.

2. Tarbell, *All in the Day's Work* (New York: Macmillan Co., 1939), p. 309.

3. VR to APM, February 24, 1944, Allegheny.

4. *All Day's,* p. 305.

5. Ibid., p. 356.

6. IMT to RSB, February 29, 1912, Library of Congress.

7. Mary G. Newell to IMT, February 4, 1934, Allegheny.

8. Ibid., and IMT to Anna Shaw, Allegheny.

9. IMT to E. I. Hubbard, Allegheny.

10. Tarbell, "Disillusionment of Women," Allegheny; Tarbell, "IMT Talking," Little Chapel.

11. *Red Cross Magazine,* September 1919.

12. "Jane Addams Talk to Pen & Brush," Allegheny.

13. Tarbell, "IMT Talking," Little Chapel.

14. Tucson Dialogues, Little Chapel; William Allen White, *My Autobiography* (New York: Macmillan Co., 1946), pp. 564–65.

15. Notes for *All Day's,* Allegheny.

16. Nathaniel Peffer, "Pollyanna at the Washington Conference," *The New Republic,* July 26, 1922, p. 262; *The American Review of Reviews,* June 1922, p. 670.

17. Tarbell-Reynolds/Ober correspondence, 1924, Columbia University Libraries.

18. Reynolds-Tarbell correspondence, Columbia.

19. *All Day's,* pp. 388–89.

20. Clara Tarbell Tupper, "My Aunt, Ida Tarbell," Allegheny.

21. Teapot Dome memo, June 6, 1922, Drake Well Museum.

22. *The New York Times,* February 16, 1924, p. 3.

23. Francis Russell, *The Shadow of Blooming Grove* (New York: McGraw-Hill Book Co., 1968), p. 350.

24. Teapot Dome memo, June 6, 1922, Drake Well Museum.

25. Ibid.

26. Ibid.

27. Committee on U.S. Public Lands and Surveys, *Leases Upon Naval Oil Reserves* (Washington: The Government Printing Office, 1924), pp. 220 and 406.

28. Teapot Dome memo, June 6, 1922, Drake Well Museum.

29. Carl Solberg, *Oil Power* (New York: The New American Library, 1976), p. 99.

30. John D. Rockefeller, Jr., to W. O. Inglis, February 19, 1918, Rockefeller Family Archives.

31. John D. Rockefeller, Jr., to George E. Vincent, May 9, 1924, and letters in the Rockefeller Family Archives.

32. IMT to Rutger Bleeker Jewett, January 31, 1924, Allegheny.
33. IMT to JSP, October 20, 1919, Allegheny.
34. Benjamin Stolberg, "St. Elbert of the Heavenly Trust," *The Nation,* April 14, 1926, p. 414.
35. W. O. Inglis to Nestor W. Davis, November 16, 1925, Rockefeller Family Archives.
36. Benjamin Thomas, *Portrait for Posterity* (New Brunswick, N.J.: Rutgers University Press, 1947), p. 187; IMT to Carl Sandburg, November 7, 1925, University of Illinois at Urbana-Champaign.
37. Thomas, *Portrait,* p. 284.
38. IMT to R. C. Sturgis, December 19, 1939, Allegheny; VR to APM, 1929 or 1934, Little Chapel.
39. IMT to APM, January 13, 1929, Allegheny.
40. VR to APM, n.d., Little Chapel.
41. Ada McCormick manuscript, Little Chapel.
42. IMT to JSP, April 26, 1926, Smith College.
43. *All Day's,* p. 163.
44. Draft of the Mussolini manuscript, Allegheny.
45. Peter Lyon, *Success Story: The Life and Times of S. S. McClure* (New York: Charles Scribner's Sons, 1963), p. 401.
46. Lincoln Steffens, *The Autobiography of Lincoln Steffens* (New York: Harcourt, Brace & Co., 1931), vol. II, p. 813.
47. VR to APM, March 2, 1930, Allegheny.
48. Ibid.
49. IMT to John B. Andrews, March 9, 1938; VR to APM, undated, Allegheny.
50. Tarbell, "Why Smith Gets My Vote," *Collier's,* September 15, 1928, p. 8.
51. IMT to William C. Chenery, November 12, 1928, Allegheny.

12. AT REST

1. IMT to APM, September 14, 1928, Allegheny College.
2. IMT to APM, January 9, 1929, Allegheny.
3. IMT to SAT, October 23, 1929, Allegheny.
4. Tucson Dialogues, March 20, 1931, Little Chapel.
5. Patricia Paylore to author, March 1980.
6. Tucson Dialogues, February 20, 1921, Little Chapel.
7. Ibid.
8. McCormick notes, Allegheny.
9. McCormick ledgers, Little Chapel.
10. Dialogue with IMT, 1936, Allegheny.
11. IMT to VR, October 1935, Allegheny.
12. IMT to VR, December 9, 1935, Allegheny.
13. APM to Dorothy Canfield, October 24, 1936, Allegheny.
14. *Atlantic Monthly* correspondence, Allegheny.
15. IMT to VR, November 6, 1937, Allegheny.
16. *Titusville Herald,* January 26, 1939.
17. VR to APM, December 24 [no year], Little Chapel.
18. IMT to APM, Little Chapel.

19. IMT to John H. Kellogg, October 28, 1939, Michigan Historical Collection, Bentley Historical Library, University of Michigan; IMT to VR, January 8, 1940, Allegheny.

20. IMT to JSP, August [no year], Smith College.

21. IMT to Alice Hegan Rice, December 11, 1940, Rice Collection, Kentucky Library, Western Kentucky University.

22. IMT to JSP, August [no year], Smith College.

23. IMT to Mollie Best, December 17, 1941, family letters, collection of Ella Tarbell Price.

24. The draft of *Life After Eighty*, Collection of Ella Tarbell Price.

Bibliography

Selected Works of
Ida Tarbell

BOOKS

Madame Roland. New York: Charles Scribner's Sons, 1895.
The History of the Standard Oil Company. 2 vols. New York: Macmillan Co., 1904.
He Knew Lincoln. New York: Doubleday, Page and Co., 1909.
The Tariff in Our Times. New York: Macmillan Co., 1911.
The Business of Being a Woman. New York: Macmillan Co., 1914.
Peacemakers—Blessed and Otherwise. New York: Macmillan Co., 1919.
The Rising of the Tide. New York: Macmillan Co., 1919.
In the Footsteps of the Lincolns. New York: Macmillan Co., 1924.
The Life of Elbert H. Gary. New York: D. Appleton and Co., 1925.
Owen D. Young: A New Type of Industrial Leader. New York: Macmillan Co., 1932.
The Nationalizing of Business, 1878-1898. New York: Macmillan Co., 1936.
All in the Day's Work. New York: Macmillan Co., 1939.

ARTICLES

"Arts and Industries of Cincinnati," *The Chautauquan,* November 1886, pp. 160–62.
"Women as Inventors," *The Chautauquan,* March 1887, pp. 355–57.
"Women in Journalism," *The Chautauquan,* April 1887, pp. 393–95.
"The Queen of the Gironde," *The Chautauquan,* March 1891, pp. 756–61.
"France Adorée," *Scribner's,* May 1892, p. 643.
"Pasteur at Home," *McClure's Magazine,* September 1893, pp. 327–40.
"In the Streets of Paris," *New England Magazine,* November 1893, pp. 259–64.

"Madame Roland," *Scribner's,* November 1893, pp. 561–78.

"A Paris Press Woman," *Boston Transcript,* December 16, 1893.

"The Principles and Pastimes of the French Salon," *The Chautauquan,* February 1894.

"The Compatriot," *New England Magazine,* September 1894, p. 83.

"Napoleon Bonaparte," *McClure's Magazine,* November 1894 to April 1895.

"Abraham Lincoln," *McClure's Magazine,* November 1895 to November 1896.

"Charm of Paris," *Scribner's,* April 1900, pp. 387–404.

"The History of the Standard Oil Company," *McClure's Magazine,* November 1902 to July 1903; December 1903 to October 1904.

"John D. Rockefeller," *McClure's Magazine,* July and August 1905.

"Kansas and the Standard Oil Company," *McClure's Magazine,* September and October 1905.

"Commercial Machiavellianism," *McClure's Magazine,* March 1906, pp. 453–63.

"Tariff in Our Times," *The American Magazine,* December 1906, January 1907, March 1907 to June 1907.

"He Knew Lincoln," *The American Magazine,* February 1907, pp. 2–13.

"Roosevelt vs. Rockefeller," *The American Magazine,* December 1907 to February 1908.

"Where Every Penny Counts," *The American Magazine,* March 1909, pp. 437–49.

"Juggling with the Tariff," *The American Magazine,* April 1909, pp. 578–86.

"Where the Shoe Is Pinched," *The American Magazine,* June 1909, pp. 155–59.

"American Woman," *The American Magazine,* November 1909 to May 1910.

"The Mysteries and Cruelties of the Tariff," *The American Magazine,* October 1910 to January 1911; May 1911.

"Testing the Tariff by Moral Effects," *The American Magazine,* June 1911, pp. 186–93.

"Uneasy Woman," *The American Magazine,* January 1912, pp. 259–62.

"Making a Man of Herself," *The American Magazine,* February 1912, pp. 427–30.

"Business of Being a Woman," *The American Magazine,* March 1912, pp. 563–68.

"Homeless Daughters," *The American Magazine,* April 1912, pp. 563–68.

"Irresponsible Woman and the Friendless Child," *The American Magazine,* May 1912, pp. 49–53.

"Woman and Democracy," *The American Magazine,* June 1912, pp. 217–87.

"The Hunt for a Money Trust," *The American Magazine,* May 1913 to July 1913.

"Flying—A Dream Come True," *The American Magazine,* November 1913, pp. 65–66.

"The Golden Rule in Business," *The American Magazine,* October 1914 to September 1915.

"Twenty-Cent Dinner," *Woman's Home Companion,* May 1915, p. 9.

"Talk with the President of the United States," *Collier's,* October 18, 1916, pp. 5–6.

"What Shall We Do for Maids?" *Good Housekeeping*, November 1917, pp. 22–23.
"The French Woman and Her New World," *Red Cross Magazine*, June 1919 to August 1919.
"The Homing Instinct of Woman," *Red Cross Magazine*, September 1919.
"That Brave Northwest," *Red Cross Magazine*, December 1919.
"Old Times at Allegheny," *The Allegheny Literary Monthly*, October 1922, pp. 4–7.
"Is the Standard Oil Crumbling?" *The New Republic*, November 14, 1923, pp. 300–301.
"Florida—And Then What?" *McCall's*, May to August, 1926.
"The Greatest Story in the World Today," *McCall's*, November 1926 to February 1927.
"Why Smith Gets My Vote," *Collier's*, September 13, 1928, pp. 8–9.
"Women as Honest Grafters," *Century*, July 1929, pp. 302–10.
"As Ida Tarbell Looks at Prohibition," *Delineator*, October 1930, p. 17.
"Arizona Trails," *Delineator*, March 1932, p. 12.
"Old Sewing Room," *North American Review*, March 1938, pp. 154–58.

Selected Works for Further Reference

BOOKS

Abbott, John S. C. *Marie Jeanne Roland de la Platière*. New York: Harper & Brothers, 1850.
Addams, Jane. *Twenty Years at Hull House*. New York: New American Library, 1961.
Allen, Frederick Lewis. *Only Yesterday*. New York: Harper & Brothers, 1931.
———. *Paul Revere Reynolds*. Privately printed, 1944.
Atkinson, John. *The Class Leader*. New York: Nelson & Phillips, 1875.
Ayer, N. W., & Son's. *American Newspaper Annual*. Philadelphia: N. W. Ayer & Son, 1894–1908.
Baker, Osman C. *A Guide-book in the Administration of the Discipline of the Methodist Episcopal Church*. New York: Carlton & Phillips, 1855.
Baker, Ray Stannard. *American Chronicle*. New York: Charles Scribner's Sons, 1945.
Barrus, Clara. *The Life and Letters of John Burroughs*. New York: Russell & Russell, 1968.
Bates, J. Leonard. *The Origins of Teapot Dome*. Urbana: University of Illinois Press, 1963.
Bates, Samuel P. *Our Country and Its People*. Crawford County, Pennsylvania: W. A. Fergusson & Co., 1899.
Bennett, Arnold. *The Journal*. New York: Viking Co. Vol. II, 1932–1933.
Bertaut, Jules. *Paris 1870–1935*. London: Eyre and Spottiswoode, 1936.

Bishop, John Bucklin. *Theodore Roosevelt and His Times.* 2 vols. New York: Charles Scribner's Sons, 1920.

Blind, Mathilde. *Madame Roland.* Boston: Roberts Brothers, 1886.

Brady, Curtis F. "The High Cost of Impatience." Manuscript in the Lilly Library, Indiana University.

Bruce, Robert V. *Alexander Graham Bell and the Conquest of Solitude.* Boston: Little, Brown & Co., 1973.

Burgess, Gelett, ed. *My Maiden Effort.* New York: Doubleday, Page & Co., 1921.

Burke's Royal Families of the World. Vol. II. London: Burke's Peerage Ltd., 1980.

Chamberlain, John. *Farewell to Reform.* New York: Liveright, 1932.

Clark, John D. *Federal Trust Policy.* Baltimore: Johns Hopkins Press, 1931.

Colton, Joseph H. *Common School Geography.* New York: Shelton & Co., 1874.

Committee on U.S. Public Lands and Surveys, United States Senate. *Leases Upon Naval Oil Reserves.* Washington: Government Printing Office, 1923, 1924.

Cowles, Anna Roosevelt. *Letters from Theodore Roosevelt to Anna Roosevelt Cowles.* New York: Charles Scribner's Sons, 1924.

Croly, Herbert David. *Mark Alonzo Hanna.* New York: Macmillan Co., 1912.

De Roux, Paul, ed. *Mémoires de Madame Roland.* Paris: Mercure de France, 1966.

The Derrick's Handbook of Petroleum. 2 vols. Oil City, Pa: Derrick Publishing Co., 1898.

Dunn, Andrew Wallace. *Gridiron Nights.* New York: Frederick A. Stokes Co., 1915.

Eastman, Max. *Enjoyment of Living.* New York: Harper & Brothers, 1948.

Edel, Leon. *Henry James: The Master 1901–1916.* New York: Harper & Row, 1974.

Ellis, Elmer. *Mr. Dooley's America: A Life of Finley Peter Dunne.* New York: Alfred A. Knopf, 1941.

Ely, Richard T. *Ground Under Our Feet.* New York: Macmillan Co., 1938.

Executive Committee of the Petroleum Producers Union. *A History of the Rise and Fall of the South Improvement Company.* Oil City, Pa., n.d.

The Federal Antitrust Laws, with Summary of Cases Instituted 1890–1951, 1957.

Filler, Louis. *Crusaders for American Liberalism.* New York: Harcourt, Brace & Co., 1939.

Flexner, Eleanor. *Century of Struggle.* New York: Atheneum, 1973.

Flower, Dean. *Henry James in Northampton.* Northampton, Mass.: Smith College, 1971.

Flynn, John T. *God's Gold.* New York: Harcourt, Brace & Co., 1932.

Fosdick, Raymond B. *John D. Rockefeller, Jr.: A Portrait.* New York: Harper & Bros., 1956.

Fuess, Claude Moore. *Carl Schurz, Reformer.* New York: Dodd, Mead & Co, 1932.

Giddens, Paul. *The Early Days of Oil.* Princeton, N.J.: Princeton University Press, 1948.

Goldman, Eric F. *Rendezvous with Destiny.* New York: Alfred A. Knopf, 1952.

Graham, Jane Kirkland. *Viola, The Duchess of New Dorp.* Danville, Illinois Printing Co., 1955.

Green, Constance McLaughlin. *Washington: Capital City.* 2 vols. Princeton, N.J.: Princeton University Press, 1963.

Greene, Theodore P. *America's Heroes.* New York: Oxford University Press, 1970.

Haller, John S., Jr., and Haller, Robin M. *The Physician and Sexuality in Victorian America.* Urbana: University of Illinois Press, 1974.

Hapgood, Hutchins. *Victorian in the Modern World.* New York: Harcourt, Brace & Co., 1939.

Hawke, David Freeman. *John D.: The Founding Father of the Rockefellers.* New York: Harper & Row, 1980.

Hays, Samuel P. *The Response to Industrialism, 1885–1914.* Chicago: The University of Chicago Press, 1957.

Henry, J. T. *The Early and Later History of Petroleum.* Philadelphia: Jas. B. Rodgers, Printers, 1873.

Hofstadter, Richard. *The Age of Reform.* New York: Alfred A. Knopf, 1955.

Hoover, Herbert. *The Memoirs of Herbert Hoover.* New York: Macmillan Co., 1952.

Howe, Frederic Clemson. *The Confessions of a Reformer.* New York: Charles Scribner's Sons, 1925.

Huisman, Phillippe. *Lautrec by Lautrec.* New York: Viking Press, 1964.

Hurlbut, Jesse. *The Story of Chautauqua.* New York: G. P. Putnam's Sons, 1921.

Inglis, William O. "The Inglis Papers." Manuscript in the Rockefeller Family Collections, 1918–1919.

Israel, Fred L., ed. *The State of the Union Messages of the Presidents, 1790–1966.* New York: Crown Publishers, 1965.

James, Henry. *The American Scene.* Bloomington and London: Indiana University Press, 1968.

Johnson, Charles Albert. *The Frontier Camp Meeting.* Dallas: Southern Methodist University Press, 1955.

Jordan, David Starr. *The Days of a Man.* Yonkers-on-Hudson, N.Y.: World Book Co., 1922.

Josephson, Matthew. *The Robber Barons.* New York: Harcourt, Brace & Co., 1934.

Kaplan, Justin. *Lincoln Steffens.* New York: Simon and Schuster, 1974.

King's Handbook of New York City. Boston: Moses King, 1892.

Lasch, Christopher. *The New Radicalism in America, 1889–1963.* New York: Alfred A. Knopf, 1965.

Leary, Lewis, ed. *Mark Twain's Correspondence with Henry Huttleston Rogers.* Berkeley and Los Angeles: University of California Press, 1969.

Lodge, Henry Cabot, ed. *Selections from the Correspondence of Theodore Roosevelt and Henry Cabot Lodge, 1884–1918.* 2 vols. New York: Charles Scribner's Sons, 1925.

Lundberg, Ferdinand. *The Rockefeller Syndrome.* Secaucus, N.J.: Lyle Stuart, 1975.

Lyon, Peter. *Success Story: The Life and Times of S. S. McClure.* New York: Charles Scribner's Sons, 1963.

Mack, Gerstle. *Toulouse-Lautrec.* New York: Alfred A. Knopf, 1938.

McClure, Samuel S. *My Autobiography.* New York: Frederick A. Stokes Co., 1914.

McCullough, George Grant. *Fragmentary Records of the McCullough and Connected Families.* Privately printed, 1918.

MacLauren, Gary. *Morally We Roll Along.* Boston: Little, Brown & Co., 1938.

MacLaurin, John J. *Sketches in Crude Oil.* Harrisburg, Pa.: Published by the Author, 1896.

Marbury, Elizabeth. *My Crystal Ball.* New York: Boni and Liveright, 1923.

Montague, Gilbert. *The Rise and Progress of the Standard Oil Company.* New York: Harper & Bros., 1903.

Morris, Edmund. *The Rise of Theodore Roosevelt.* New York: Coward, McCann and Geoghegan, 1979.

Morrison, Theodore. *Chautauqua.* Chicago: The University of Chicago Press, 1974.

Mott, Frank Luther. *A History of American Magazines.* 5 vols. Cambridge, Mass.: Harvard University Press, 1938–1968.

Nevins, Allan. *Study in Power: John D. Rockefeller.* 2 vols. New York: Charles Scribner's Sons, 1953.

Noggle, Burl. *Teapot Dome Oil and Politics in the 1920s.* Baton Rouge: Louisiana State University Press, 1962.

Noyes, Alexander D. *Forty Years of American Finance.* New York: G. P. Putnam's Sons, 1909.

Odum, Howard, ed. *Masters of American Social Science.* New York: H. Holt and Co., 1927.

O'Neill, William L. *Everyone Was Brave.* Chicago: Quadrangle Books, 1969.

Phillips, John S., ed. *Albert A. Boyden: Reminiscences and Tributes by His Friends.* New York: Privately printed.

———. "A Legacy to Youth." Manuscript, 1929.

Rader, Benjamin G. *The Academic Mind and Reform.* Lexington: University of Kentucky, 1966.

Rice, Alice Hegan. *The Inky Way.* New York: D. Appleton-Century Co., 1941.

Rice, Cale Young. *Bridging the Years.* New York: D. Appleton-Century Co., 1939.

Richardson, James D., ed. *Messages and Papers of the Presidents of the United States.* Washington: Bureau of National Literature and Arts, 1910.

Robbins, Philip Porter. "The Tarbell Papers and the History of the Standard Oil Company." Ph.D. dissertation, Graduate Faculty, Division of Social Sciences, University of Pittsburgh, 1966.

Rockefeller, John D. *Random Reminiscences of Men and Events.* London: William Heinemann, 1909.

Roland, Marie Jeanne. *Mémoires de Madame Roland,* with Notes by C. A. Dauban. Paris: Henri Plon, 1864.

Roosevelt, Theodore. *Presidential Addresses and State Papers.* New York: Review of Reviews Co., 1910.

Schurz, Carl. *The Reminiscences of Carl Schurz.* New York: The McClure Company, 1907–1908.

Scudder, Moses Lewis. *American Methodism.* Hartford, Conn.: S. S. Scranton & Co., 1867.

Sedgwick, Ellery. *The Happy Profession*. Boston: Little, Brown & Co., 1946.

Shotwell, James T. *At the Paris Peace Conference*. New York: Macmillan Co., 1937.

Sinclair, Upton. *The Brass Check*. Pasadena, Calif.: Privately published by the author, 1919.

Slayden, Ellen Maury. *Washington Wife*. New York: Harper & Row, 1962.

Smith, Ernest. *Allegheny: A Century of Education*. Meadville, Pa.: The Allegheny College History Co., 1916.

Smith, Jane. *Elsie de Wolfe: A Life in High Style*. New York: Atheneum, 1982.

Solberg, Carl. *Oil Power*. New York: New American Library, 1976.

Steed, Henry Wickham. *Through Thirty Years, 1892–1922*. Garden City, N.Y.: Doubleday, Page & Co., 1924.

Steffens, Lincoln. *The Autobiography of Lincoln Steffens*. 2 vols. New York: Harcourt, Brace & Co., 1931.

Sullivan, Mark. *The Education of an American*. New York: Doubleday, Doran & Co., 1938.

Thomas, Benjamin. *Portrait for Posterity*. New Brunswick, N.J.: Rutgers University Press, 1947.

Tomkins, Mary E. *Ida M. Tarbell*. New York: Twayne Publishers, 1974.

Tuchman, Barbara W. *The Proud Tower*. New York: Macmillan Co., 1966.

Twain, Mark. *The Autobiography of Mark Twain*. New York: Harper & Bros., 1959.

Van Vleck, George W. *The Panic of 1857*. New York: Columbia University Press, 1943.

Weinberg, Arthur, and Weinberg, Lila. *The Muckrakers*. New York: Simon & Schuster, 1961.

Werner, M. R. *Privileged Characters*. New York: Robert M. McBride & Co., 1935.

White, William Allen. *The Autobiography of William Allen White*. New York: Macmillan Co., 1946.

Wiebe, Robert H. *The Search for Order, 1877–1920*. New York: Hill and Wang, 1967.

Wight, Charles Henry. *Thomas Tarbell and Some of His Descendants*. Boston: Northeast Historical Genealogical Society, 1907.

Wilson, Harold S. *McClure's Magazine and the Muckrakers*. Princeton, N.J.: Princeton University Press, 1970.

Winter, Ella, and Granville Hicks, eds. *The Letters of Lincoln Steffens*. Vol. I. New York: Harcourt, Brace & Co., 1938.

ARTICLES

Chalmers, David M. "The Muckrakers and the Growth of Corporate Power: A Study in Constructive Journalism." *American Journal of Economics and Sociology*, April 1959, pp. 295–311.

Coats, A. W. "The First Two Decades of the American Economic Association." *The American Economic Review*, September 1960, pp. 555–74.

Conway, Jill. "Women Reformers and American Culture, 1870–1930." *Journal of Social History*, Winter 1971–1972, pp. 164–77.

French, J. L. "The Story of McClure's." *Profitable Advertising*, October 15, 1897, pp. 139–45.

Hocking, Elton. "Ferdinand Brunetière: The Evolution of a Critic." *University of Wisconsin Studies in Language and Literature*, no. 36, 1936.

Joerns, W. G. "John D. Rockefeller: A Study in Character, Motive and Duty." *The Arena*, August 1905, p. 156.

McDonald, M. Irwin. "Ida M. Tarbell: The Woman Who Has Made People Comprehend the Meaning of the Trusts." *The Craftsman*, April 1908.

Miller, Ernest C. "Ida Tarbell's Second Look at Standard Oil." *The Western Pennsylvania Historical Magazine*, Winter 1956, pp. 223–41.

Montague, Gilbert H. "Ida M. Tarbell: How She Has Written the Story of the Standard Oil Co." *Boston Evening Transcript*, January 6, 1904.

Mullet, Mary. "A Famous Writer Who Never Intended to Write." *The American Magazine*, January 1925, pp. 34, 64, 66, 68.

"Petrolia," *The Leisure Hour*, May 12, 1866, pp. 295–301.

Trambell, Caroline T. "Ida Tarbell and Her Farm." *Country Life in America*, November 1915, pp. 19–22.

Index